The Origins
of the
Second World War

The Origins
of the
Second World War

American Foreign Policy and World
Politics, 1917–1941

ARNOLD A. OFFNER

PRAEGER PUBLISHERS

New York

Published in the United States of America in 1975
by Praeger Publishers, Inc.
111 Fourth Avenue, New York, N.Y. 10003

© 1975 by Praeger Publishers, Inc.

Library of Congress Cataloging in Publication Data

Offner, Arnold A
  The origins of the Second World War.

  Bibliography: p.
  Includes index.
  1. United States—Foreign relations—20th century.
2. World War, 1939–1945—Causes. I. Title.
E744.043   327.73   72–82775
ISBN 0-275-50270-8
ISBN 0-275-84750-0 pbk.

Printed in the United States of America

For Deborah and Michael

Contents

Preface

The involvement of the United States in the Second World War in 1941 has evoked more than thirty years of debate and brought forth at least three or four schools of historical writing. The eminent historian Charles A. Beard began collecting materials for his two-volume study (published in 1946–48) of the foreign policy of Franklin D. Roosevelt's administration from the moment the Japanese attacked Pearl Harbor. There soon followed numerous other "revisionist" works that argued that the Roosevelt administration made a deceptive turn from nonintervention, or "isolation," toward intervention after 1937 and assumed an almost belligerent policy toward Germany during 1939–41, as evidenced by the material aid afforded first to Great Britain and then to the Soviet Union through such devices as the exchange of destroyers for naval bases in 1940, Lend-Lease in 1941, revision of the neutrality laws, and increasing naval warfare in the Atlantic. Ultimately, however, the revisionists claimed, the administration was able to lead the United States into the European war only through the Pacific "back door," that is, by taking an increasingly rigid diplomatic stance toward Japan on the issue of China and then challenging or tempting the Japanese into a first strike at Pearl Harbor—and perhaps even manipulating or withholding intelligence information vital to the security of the forces stationed there.

More traditional analysts, who viewed themselves as "realists," but who were occasionally dubbed "court historians," usually argued that Roosevelt really was an internationalist in the mold of Woodrow Wilson, that he was constrained by the disillusioning legacies of the First World War, political isolationists, and the effect of the Great Depression to follow a cautious foreign policy during 1933–38, and that the "hard line" against Germany thereafter resulted from his responsible reading of the necessities of history and a wise change in public opinion. His administration's position in the Pacific, meanwhile, accorded with America's traditional Open Door policy—friendship for China and equal commercial opportunity for all nations—while Germany, Japan, and Italy, or the Axis Alliance, chose aggression because of Western policies of appeasement.

In the last decade, a third school of historians—known as "neorevisionist" or "New Left"— has argued that American foreign policy has always been an extension of a liberal corporate society that desired to secure Open Doors for American capital to dominate markets and materials on a global scale. The result has been that American governments from at least 1898 to the present era have opted for war when their domestic economic policies were in bad straits and corporate capitalists felt that another nation threatened American political and economic hegemony in a crucial region.

There has also appeared a fourth group of historians, more difficult to categorize than the others, which has tried to examine American foreign policy in a multinational or world political context, assessing the interaction of each nation's policies with those of other nations. These historians have frequently made use of foreign, not just American, sources and have sought to stress the complexity of international affairs and the frequency of misunderstanding and miscalculation. These writers have often found that diverse political, economic, and historical influences have shaped the extremely complex processes of policy-making and decision-making, that a nation's movement from one point to another along the diplomatic or historical spectrum rarely has been as direct or straightforward as appeared upon first analysis, and that the results of policies have often been entirely different from what their makers intended. Hence, while some statesmen or nations have been more guilty than others of iniquitous or irrational behavior in certain circumstances, they have also been caught up in the forces and norms of their era and have failed to master their diplomatic destiny, with events frequently outrunning negotiations and causing ironic as well as tragic consequences.

No school of thought is monolithic, and none has a monopoly on truth. Most writers have made critical points that were timely, in that they helped their own era to see the significance of actions taken by people of an earlier day that withstood the test of historical verification. Most early revisionists were men of conservative political instinct who disliked the domestic impact of the New Deal and believed that the Roosevelt administration not only maneuvered the United States into the Second World War but surrendered the fruits of victory in Eastern Europe and the Far East to the Soviet Union. (Charles Beard, an exception, was a domestic liberal who believed as early as 1935 that the New Deal would succumb to the temptation of war mobilization to solve domestic economic problems.)

Traditional historians were usually content with, or adjusted to, New Deal domestic policies; their primary concern was with foreign policy, and especially that the United States assume responsible leadership in world affairs after 1945. These writers deplored the political and economic aspects of Republican foreign policy, which kept the United States out of the League of Nations after the First World War and contributed to the "isolationist" mood of the 1920's and early 1930's, and they defended the Roosevelt administration's increasing opposition to German and Japanese expansionism during 1938–41. Indeed, in seeking to explain the lessons of history for both the past and present eras, traditionalist historians often drew implicit analogies between Roosevelt's efforts to stem the tide of lawlessness and aggression in the later 1930's and the necessity for the United States to do so in the later 1940's. In short, the failure to contain Nazi Germany and Imperial Japan before the Second World War demonstrated the need to contain the Soviet Union thereafter, or, conversely, the need to be resolute with the Soviet Union in the 1940's demonstrated the folly of those men who had wished to appease Germany and Japan in the 1930's.

The neorevisionist, or New Left, historians, more the intellectual heirs of Charles Beard than of the conservative revisionists, have been inspired by at least two broad considerations. They point out that since the middle of the nineteenth century the United States has been involved in more extensive wars than any other nation in the world, and that, for all of this nation's alleged commitment to democracy and social justice, there has always existed the "other America" (as Michael Harrington wrote in 1962). This other America comprises at least one-fourth of the population—white and black, urban and rural—and has been condemned to perpetual poverty. The neorevisionists have argued that America's fundamental problems have not resulted from an unintended or unbridgeable gap between idealistic rhetoric and hard reality; rather, the nation's liberal-capitalist institutions have been designed to exploit whole classes of people at home and abroad. In short, the United States is committed to perpetual war in order to maintain perpetual prosperity for a privileged few who have presided over their nation's corporate society and the "informal" global empire that stretches from the Caribbean to Camranh Bay.

Those who have sought to explain American foreign policy in a multinational context have been no less committed to finding the root causes of American expansion, or imperialism, and have deplored the tragedy of their nation's irrational behavior, wasted resources, and institutionalized forms of domestic and foreign repression. But they have probably been influenced by a more skeptical or fatalistic, if not tragic, view of human and national behavior than their neorevisionist colleagues and are convinced that just as no group of historians has a monopoly on truth, so no nation has a monopoly on virtue. Or put another way, no nation has a monopoly on racism, exploitation, and violence, as the myriad civil and global international wars of this century have demonstrated.

The multinational approach has also benefited from the passage of time, which allows historians to place events within a long-term context, and from the continual opening of new resources and increased multi-archival research, which frequently affords new insights into how or why events occurred. Indeed, the full record of the U.S. Department of State, along with the personal papers of many significant diplomatic and political figures, bearing on events through 1941, were not available to scholars until the mid-1950's, while the copious records of the British Cabinet and Foreign Office, covering the entire interwar period, were not open to researchers until the late 1960's. Only a small portion of the German and Japanese diplomatic records have been published, and scholars must painstakingly work their way through vast archival collections or pore over thousands of reels of microfilmed documents. The diplomatic archives of France and the Kuomintang regime of Chiang Kai-shek, which formerly governed China, remain virtually closed. The Soviet Union's archives are closed. In short, scholars have really just begun to comb some of the enormously valuable materials that have become available recently, and that must be studied before anyone might hazard definitive judgments about the long, complex, and interrelated train of events that led from one world war to the other.

The period I have chosen to analyze in this book is 1917–41; for, while historians tend to divide American history by presidential administrations, the events leading to the Second World War clearly seem to be rooted in both the general and specific questions and problems posed at the time of the First World War. From the Wilson administration on, American statesmen had to deal as never before with the general issues of European security and the balance of power, as well as with such specific matters as German revisionism and the Treaty of Versailles, disarmament negotiations, trade, tariff, and monetary problems, and so forth. The problems in the Far East revolved chiefly around Japan's increasing great-power status and its expanding political and economic hegemony in Manchuria and North China. For American and European statesmen, there were also the crucial, and related, questions of how to deal bilaterally with China as well as with one another over China, which had undergone a governmental and near-revolutionary transformation and was seeking stability at home and respect abroad. Both European and Asian diplomatic and political questions were further complicated, of course, by the Russian Revolution and Soviet diplomacy. Thus, the principles and problems of the Roosevelt administration were rooted in the Wilson era, and in many ways the Second World War was the outgrowth of the junction of European and Asian developments in a fashion that was not entirely foreseen, and to a surprising extent not entirely controlled, by those who brought about the apocalyptic confrontation.

My purpose is to explore how the United States envisioned and conducted itself in international affairs and what the foreign as well as domestic forces were that moved policy in one direction or another. And conversely, how did American policy influence that of other powers? Some of my conclusions, I suspect, will differ from traditional views. For example, President Wilson was deeply concerned about reintegrating Germany into the political and economic mainstream. The Republicans made this a cardinal point of their policy in the 1920's, and much of this policy persisted in the Roosevelt administration throughout the 1930's and even until the spring of 1940. And just as Germany became a large factor in American policy, so throughout 1919–33 German statesmen sought to use American influence to alter the political and economic balance in Europe; and after 1933 German diplomats continued to argue with Nazi officials over whether America held the fateful balance of power, and what, accordingly, German policy toward the United States would be.

To take another example, it is customary to acknowledge the "special" —that is, unusually good—relationship between the United States and Great Britain stemming from political and cultural affinities. Consequently, historians have ignored the almost shockingly bad relations between the two countries during the interwar years. The United States and Great Britain disagreed not only over the more publicized war debts–reparations tangle and naval ratios, but also on how fast and on what terms Germany should be rehabilitated and reintegrated, and how to deal with Japan bilaterally as well as multilaterally over the China question. Also, Anglo-American battles over international markets, resources, and finance virtually precluded political cooperation to stem the tide of aggression. Indeed, analysis of the many forms of Anglo-American imperial rivalries in the 1920's and 1930's afford insight into both the structure of international politics in the interwar era and the origins of the Second World War.

The shape of this volume has not been determined exclusively by the influence of any single school of thought. My approach, however, probably most closely resembles that of historians who, without shrinking from criticism of the individual and institutionalized failings of their own and other nations' foreign policies, have tried to place American foreign policy within a multinational or world political context. My purpose in this book is neither to search for heroes or villains nor to impose a conspiracy thesis on the ultimate outcome. Rather, I wish to offer a multinational perspective on American involvement in interwar problems and to explain the intentions, purposes, and responsibilities, as well as the limits or possibilities, of American foreign policy in the events leading up to the Second World War.

Acknowledgments

It is my pleasure to acknowledge the institutions and the people who have provided me with assistance and encouragement to research and write this book. The American Council of Learned Societies awarded me a grant-in-aid that made possible several months of research in the British Cabinet and Foreign Office records at the Public Record Office in London. The National Endowment for the Humanities provided a Summer Stipend that allowed me to read without interruption and to draft my ideas. The Graduate School of Arts and Sciences at Boston University provided additional research and typing funds, and Boston University afforded me a sabbatical leave in the autumn of 1972, which allowed me to do further research in London and to write half the book.

I should like to express my thanks to Maldwyn A. Jones, Commonwealth Professor of History at the University of London, and to D. C. Watt, Professor of International Relations at the London School of Economics, for allowing me to put forward in their seminars some of my ideas about Anglo-American relations, and for their apt criticisms. My friend and colleague at Boston University, Professor William J. Newman, has been unfailingly thoughtful and generous in reading and criticizing numerous chapters, lending me countless books, and listening and responding patiently to my ideas. Professor James P. Shenton of Columbia University deserves my acknowledgment not only because he suggested I write this book, but because he has been a masterful teacher of so many students, and because at a formative stage in my academic education he strengthened my resolve to make my profession the study of history. And, once again, Professor Robert H. Ferrell of Indiana University has afforded my work an extraordinarily knowledgeable substantive critique and editorial review. Along with scores of his friends, colleagues, and former students, I never cease to be amazed at how much he knows, how devoted he is to helping others, and how much we are all indebted to him.

xv

Finally, I must acknowledge my wife, Ellen, who as usual has been a perceptive editorial critic and my constant source of inspiration.

Any errors of fact or interpretation in this book are, of course, my responsibility.

AAO

Boston University
Boston, Massachusetts
January, 1975

The Origins
of the
Second World War

1

Waging Peace

In late May 1921, George Harvey, the American Ambassador to Great Britain, created a minor diplomatic and public uproar when he told the Pilgrim's Club in London, whose audience included Prime Minister David Lloyd George and Foreign Secretary Lord Curzon, that the United States had not sent its troops to Europe in 1917 to save the world for democracy, but, rather, "we sent them solely to save the United States of America." Harvey's words jarred the sensibilities of his audience, accustomed on these occasions to after-dinner speeches extolling the virtue and highmindedness of Anglo-American traditions and friendship, and drew sharp criticism in the press on both sides of the Atlantic. The speech also upset the new administration in Washington (although evidently President Warren G. Harding had approved the text in advance) and prompted Secretary of State Charles Evans Hughes, who shortly thereafter delivered the commencement address at Brown University, to reassure everyone that the United States had gone to war because "we found our fate linked with that of the free peoples who were struggling for the preservation of the essentials of freedom."

Harvey's statement was probably less a diplomatic indiscretion than a blunt, if overstated and crass, assessment of American foreign policy in the age of Woodrow Wilson and, as the ambassador undoubtedly hoped, a verbal portent of future American policy. Harvey was a conservative, a former Democrat, who had made a fortune speculating in electrical traction lines, gained ownership and editorship of the *North American Review,* and then, through an arrangement with J. P. Morgan, became president of Harper & Brothers and the editor of *Harper's Weekly.* He had come to know Wilson when the latter was president of Princeton University, and in 1910, in an effort to blunt genuine reform in New Jersey politics, he promoted him for Governor and then helped him to achieve the Democratic nomination for President in 1912. By 1916, however, Harvey had broken with Wilson, especially angered over what

3

he considered timorous neutrality policies, and he supported the more conservative and seemingly more interventionist-inclined Hughes for President. In 1919, Harvey vehemently opposed, whether with or without reservations, American entry into the League of Nations, and in 1920 he was among the coterie of men who secured the Republican nomination for Harding. Harvey might have been named Secretary of State but for his short tenure as a Republican and the fear that his well-known, caustic anti-League sentiments might become the object of too much controversy. So he accepted America's most prestigious ambassadorship, to the Court of St. James's.

Harvey had chosen the occasion of his first public address at the Pilgrim's Club primarily to declare that it was "utterly absurd" to believe any hope remained that the United States might join the League of Nations. But by insisting as well that national self-interest had been at the root of American intervention in the First World War, he was suggesting to his listeners in England, and to Americans who might read his words, that the idealism that had come to be associated with that venture and with the name of Woodrow Wilson had never been genuine. Or if it had, it was now dead. Hereafter the United States would revert to its traditional policy. There would be no more great crusades, no more efforts at setting other people's houses in order. The return to normalcy, Harvey would have had his audience believe, meant that the United States would pursue national self-interest only: What was good for America would have to be good for the rest of the world.

Considered from their point of view, Wilsonians were right to dispute Harvey's contentions, the more so perhaps because it was the likes of Harvey who had done so much in the past few years to defeat Wilsonian policies at every turn and prevent the triumph of whatever shred of idealism there remained in a bitter and battle-weary world. But in certain respects Harvey's contentions had more merit, or reality, than Wilsonians then or later might have cared to admit. To be sure, Wilson had not led America to war in 1917 "solely" to save the United States. But it is also unmistakably clear that Wilson identified America's national interest so closely with the interest of the rest of the world, and *vice versa,* that he came to conclude that the two were far more in harmony than in conflict, and that where he was acting for the good of the United States he was also acting for the good of the rest of the world. Consequently, Wilson's decision to go to war in 1917 can best be understood in terms of his view of the conjunction of American and world interests and his conclusion that it was necessary first to wage war in order to be able to save the world for peace and democracy.

Wilson was pre-eminently a man of Victorian heritage, nurtured in the South by his Presbyterian minister father to adulate things English and disposed to assuming the superiority of the political, economic, legal, and social systems of white Anglo-Saxon society. His ethical system was fiercely Calvinist and his stern morality easily overflowed into self-righteousness that allowed little or no room for other men's transgressions. The liability of such a disposition, of course, was the proclivity to irremediable conflict not only with opponents, such as Dean Andrew F. West of the Graduate School at Princeton University and Senator Henry Cabot Lodge, but with supporters as well, as was the case with his closest political adviser, Colonel Edward M. House, and two of his Secretaries of State, William Jennings Bryan and Robert Lansing. Economically, Wilson was a combination of traditional Southerner and British Manchesterian who favored the lowest of all possible tariffs and the least possible government intervention in the business or social-justice side of the economy. He idealized the beneficent results of a nineteenth-century liberal capitalist order and insisted that if there were special privileges for none and equal opportunity for all (and the price of Southern staples remained high), the industrious and the godfearing would inherit the earth. Private property was sacrosanct, and the idea of viewing society in terms of class or socio-economic structure was anathema, as was the idea of using anything other than constitutional or electoral means to bring about change. But he was disposed to change, albeit in a Burkean fashion of gradualism, and the pressure of politics and the presidency, and his conceptions of leadership, would move him from being a spokesman for conservative states-rights democracy, to the economic reform concepts of the New Freedom, to the social-justice emphasis of the New Nationalism.

Socially, Wilson was a genteel white supremacist: His attitude toward blacks was at best paternalistic, if not indifferent. This was reflected not only in his domestic politics, but in his statement to House in January 1917 that the United States was the "only one of the great white nations that is free from war today, and it would be a crime against civilization for us to go in." Similarly, at the Paris Peace Conference he subscribed to the views of General Jan Smuts of South Africa (Smuts argued with foresight and enlightenment on most issues) that the mandate system be adopted because the inhabitants of the former colonial realms were, in Smuts's words, "barbarians." War, in Wilson's world, was not something civilized nations waged, except for remedial purposes on nonwhite or "backward" societies.

Wilson also shared with his contemporaries an unyielding conviction that America the bountiful was truly the exceptional society. America had been spared feudalism, reaction, and violent revolution (the American Revolution was an exceptional one, being essentially a propertied, bourgeois, and legal revolt against a King's usurpation of established liberties), and the growth and development of the American City-upon-the-Hill was to serve as the model for mankind. In the realm of foreign affairs, there was no escaping the fact that the United States was a great power, and that it required the material trappings of that status—markets, mineral resources, opportunity for overseas capital investment, coaling stations, and a great navy second to none, as Wilson's 1916 appropriations bill indicated. But in Wilson's mind, America was not in the mold of traditional imperialist powers. The nearly divine right of the Monroe Doctrine had justified President Grover Cleveland and Secretary of State Richard Olney's interposing themselves into the argument in 1895 between the sovereign states of Great Britain and Venezuela over the boundary of British Guiana. The war against Spain in 1898 was a historical and geopolitical inevitability that would move Cuba and the Philippines toward self-government even while nationalistic or revolutionary movements were suppressed. And as President, of course, Wilson would extend his conception of American order—and armed forces—into Mexico, the Dominican Republic, Haiti, and Nicaragua on a scale sufficient to boggle the minds of imperialists on the order of Henry Cabot Lodge and Theodore Roosevelt.

But if Wilson could be scored easily for the many contradictions in his thought and action, it is clear that he often acted courageously and with consistency, and that his original motives were highminded. A case in point is Mexico, where in 1911 a revolution led by Francisco Madero had ended more than three decades of Porfirio Diaz's dictatorial rule. In February 1913, however, General Victoriano Huerta overthrew, and then murdered, Madero. In the United States, the administration of President William Howard Taft had been hostile to the goals of the Mexican Revolution, and Ambassador Henry Lane Wilson even had abetted Huerta's coup. In an effort to preserve long-standing American commercial and mineral advantages in Mexico, Taft's administration refused to recognize Huerta's regime, whereas the European powers, in accord with standard diplomatic practice, recognized Huerta. Recognition coincided with European hopes of winning Huerta's favor to preserve or expand their concessions, especially in oil.

When Wilson became President in March 1913, he continued Taft's nonrecognition of Huerta's regime, not to bargain for commercial concessions, but because, as he said privately, he would not recognize a "government of butchers." Moreover, Wilson was sympathetic to the Mexicans' need to establish a new social order. He became tragically embroiled in Mexican affairs in the fall of 1913, however, when he decided to use American economic and military power to oust Huerta. Wilson ultimately found himself opposing not only Huerta, who abdicated in July 1914, but various contending revolutionary forces. By 1917 the United States had reached the brink of war with Mexico. Wilson then withdrew American troops, if only because of his intent to intervene in Europe.

Wilson in 1913 publicly rebuked American bankers for seeking government guarantees for a prospective $125 million they proposed to muster for a Six-Power Consortium that would lend money to China for railroad construction. He might have believed American bankers would do better working independently of the Consortium, in which they would have a minority voice, but he also sincerely believed that the controls the bankers wished to place upon China's administrative apparatus in order to guarantee loan repayment meant too much interference in Chinese domestic affairs. He also would not sanction the use of American forces to guarantee repayment. That same year Wilson became the first head of state of a great power to recognize the Republic of China, established in 1912, and in 1915 he moderated the Twenty-One Demands that Japan sought to impose upon China. Again, he did so not merely because America and Japan were constant commercial rivals for Chinese markets and materials, but because he believed Japan intended to establish a protectorate over Manchuria and the Shantung Peninsula. Wilson also successfully battled with a nationalistic Congress in 1914 to repeal the Panama tolls legislation of 1912, which, in violation of the spirit of the 1901 Hay-Pauncefote Treaty, discriminated in favor of American shipping and thereby, he believed, impaired American honor.

Thus, in the world of foreign policy, which is dominated by political and power relationships, Wilson as often as not worked with the intensity of his conviction to do what was honorable, rational, and most fruitful in the long run. When, in the summer of 1914, war broke out between the Entente, or Allied Powers of England, France, and Russia, on the one hand, and the Central Powers of Germany and Austria-Hungary, on the other, he was as surprised and appalled as everyone else and shared the typical *New York Times* editorial sentiment that the Europeans had lapsed into the condition of "savage tribes," with statesmen behaving like "chieftains clad in skin and drunk with mead." He also believed with the people of the time, and as the generals on both sides had predicted, that the war would be short, and he sincerely meant his appeal of August 19, 1914, for Americans to remain "neutral in fact" and "impartial in thought as well as in action."

The contemporary political and later historical debates over whether Wilson and the United States pursued strict neutrality during the ensuing three years have somewhat obscured the fundamental purpose underlying the decision to go to war in April 1917. To be sure, the President's appeal for absolute neutrality—drafted by Lansing, then Counselor of the State Department and always regarded as a man of strong practical and legalistic bent—perhaps was unrealizable if only because of the diversity of Americans' national backgrounds, which gave them reason to identify with the powers embroiled in the war, and because, in certain instances, whatever policy Wilson opted for was bound to favor one side or the other. If Americans lent money to the British and French, they were favoring them; but to deny them the funds they could normally borrow, or the goods they could purchase, especially since there were no laws that forbade this, was to discriminate against them. The result, by 1917, was more than $2 billion in bankers' loans to the British and French and an annual foreign trade that had grown from $824 million in 1914 to over $3.2 billion in 1916.

Wilson's insistence on holding the Germans to strict accountability for the loss of American lives on the high seas, and his insistence that the submarines behave like surface vessels (give warnings before attacking and take on passengers from torpedoed ships), collided almost irreconcilably with the physical limitations of the submarines and the nature of the warfare that made them effective. His insistence that Americans had the right to travel on belligerent ships was a doubtful principle, the more so since the British (to his ire) constantly armed their merchant ships, which carried contraband as well as passengers.

In dealing with Congress over the problem of travel and trade, Wilson also obscured issues and exhibited a penchant for vilifying his opposition. After Germany, for the third time in three years, had announced unrestricted submarine warfare at the end of January 1917, Wilson on February 26 asked Congress for authority to arm merchant ships and "to employ any other instrumentalities or methods that may be necessary and adequate to protect our ships and people in their legitimate and peaceful pursuits on the high seas." The House of Representatives passed the measure overwhelmingly, but without the broad authority allowing the President "to employ any other instrumentalities." In the Senate, Republican leaders sought to restore this clause, but about a dozen senators, led by progressives Robert La Follette and George Norris, filibustered the bill. Wilson publicly assailed them as "a little group of willful men," representing only themselves, who "have rendered the great Government of the United States helpless and contemptible." In fact, the senators would have agreed to arm the ships but refused to give a blank check to the President "to employ any other instrumentalities." Wilson's attack on his opponents in the Senate was unnecessary, because on March 9 he used executive authority to arm the merchant ships and put naval gun crews on board.

Assumptions about the "rules" of civilized warfare notwithstanding, Wilson was unrealistic to insist that the United States could carry on normal commerce and passenger travel (especially greatly expanded commerce with the British and French who were dependent on credits and imports to remain in the war) while Europe's Great Powers were locked in a struggle to the finish. The only way to avoid constant incidents and dilemmas, if the belligerents jeopardized life or property, was to give up virtually all trade and travel, even with neutral powers. But no one seriously advocated trying the kinds of measures that had failed miserably in the agricultural age of Thomas Jefferson and during the Napoleonic Wars and now were even more likely to cause severe economic dislocations—as well as achieve the major objective of Germany's submarine warfare.

Within the Wilson administration, key individuals clearly held views that favored the Entente. The President was an Anglophile who was convinced that no matter what differences arose between the United States and Great Britain over neutral rights, there were "no very important questions of principle" that could not be resolved by postwar arbitration or adjudication, as had been the case after the American Civil War. He also approved Colonel House's letter to Foreign Secretary Sir Edward Grey in mid-October 1915, which stated that if the Germans rejected an American appeal for peace terms to restore the *status quo ante* (which the British would secretly help to outline), "it would probably be necessary for us to join the Allies and force the issue."

Prior to 1914, House had favored an Anglo-German *rapprochement* to rationalize international competition—that is, to work out a division of world resources and markets in order to avoid old-fashioned wars of imperial rivalry. But after the outbreak of the World War, he, too, inclined to the British and French side and insisted, as he wrote to Wilson from Europe on February 3, 1916, that a German victory would mean that "the war lords will reign supreme and democratic governments will be imperilled throughout the world." Four days later, according to his diary, House told the French that if they and the British were successful during the next months, the United States would stay out of the war, but "in the event they were losing ground, I promised the President would intervene." This sweeping assertion was not likely to encourage the French to seek a compromise or negotiated settlement, and in reporting to Wilson on his mission House glossed over his "commitment." On February 14, 1916, he also told Prime Minister Herbert Asquith that if the Germans put forward unjust negotiating terms, Wilson would "throw the weight of the United States on the side of the Allies." Three days later, House initialed the famous memorandum, drawn up after conversations with Grey, declaring that if Wilson, after hearing from the British and French, called a conference to negotiate the end of the war and the Germans refused to attend, "the United States would probably enter the war against Germany."

Similarly, Secretary Lansing, who at first had advocated firmness toward both sides, was convinced by July 1915 that Germany was the real enemy, whose "success would mean the overthrow of democracy in the world, the suppression of individual liberty, the setting up of evil ambitions . . . and the turning back of the hands of human progress two centuries." He was constantly prepared to have the United States intervene in the event of a German victory or a stalemate.

German diplomacy and attitudes did not help the German cause. Chancellor Theobald von Bethmann-Hollweg's alleged assertion in 1914 that the treaty that guaranteed Belgium's neutrality was only so many "scraps of paper," Kaiser Wilhelm's dictum that he would dictate the peace at the point of his soldiers' bayonets, and Foreign Minister Arthur Zimmermann's intercepted telegram of January 1917 promising Mexico a return of the territorial losses sustained during 1846–48 if it joined the German side in the event of a German conflict with the United States, reinforced the stereotype of the "Hun" and the alleged fate of the world at German hands. More important, by December 1916 Germany's terms for peace had escalated to the point where they could be neither revealed nor achieved at the conference table. German claims included territorial gains and economic concessions in the East at Poland's expense and the establishment of a Kingdom of Poland to ensure against Russian influence; annexation of Courland (in present-day Latvia), Lithuania, Luxembourg, the industrial sectors of eastern Belgium, the Belgian Congo, and the French mineral-producing regions of Briey and Longwy; further boundary readjustment of the provinces of Alsace and Lorraine; the return of most of Germany's African and Asian colonies; and heavy indemnities or reparations. Thereafter, the Germans would become even more expansive politically and economically with regard to Russia, the Balkans, and the eastern Mediterranean. When Wilson, unaware of the full scope of German aims, sought on December 18, 1916, to get all the belligerents to define their objectives, the Germans insisted that only the belligerents could take part in the peace negotiations, with the United States being admitted to the councils of the powers afterward to ensure adherence to the peace-treaty terms. Negotiations between House and the German Ambassador to the United States, Count Johann von Bernstorff, broke down in January 1917 over this point, and Germany's resumption of unrestricted submarine warfare at the end of the month seemed to confirm the worst suspicions about German intentions.

Wilson distrusted the British, too. Referring to British violation of American neutral rights in 1916, he said that if Germany was not the "scourge of the world," he would be "ready then and there to have it out with Great Britain on that point." The British were just as capable of "commercial savagery" as the Germans, and he always reassured his

advisers of his intention to build a navy and merchant marine big enough
to ensure against British encroachments. "Militarism is no different on
sea than it is on land," he said to his aides in 1918, and he rejected the
idea of joint Anglo-American sea patrols as "militaristic propaganda."
Wilson's administration would also support vigorously the protests of
American oil companies that the British were preventing them from
developing claims in the Middle East—notwithstanding the British
charge that the United States already controlled 80 per cent of the
world's known oil reserves. Wilson determined in November 1916 that
the war must be ended even if this ran counter to British interests. When
House argued that the time might be inopportune for the Allies, and that
if Germany appeared more reasonable, and the United States drifted
into a sympathetic alliance with the Central Powers, the British and
French might declare war on America, Wilson purportedly "went so far
as to say that if the Allies wanted war with us he would not shrink from
it." The Wilson administration was dismayed the next month when the
coalition government of Prime Minister Lloyd George and Foreign
Secretary Arthur Balfour replaced the Liberal government of Asquith
and Grey. British policy, House worriedly wrote on December 3, now
might well be based on a "knock-out blow" and preclude an early peace.
In July 1917, Wilson told House that British and French views with
regard to peace were not "by any means" the same as American views,
but he hoped to force the Allies to his way of thinking after the war
"because by that time they will, among other things, be financially in our
hands."

Wilson's belief that the British were as commercially rapacious as the
Germans and intended likewise to seek a harsh peace accounted in good
part for the tenor of his December 18, 1916, appeal to the belligerents
to state their terms for ending the war. He said that both sides had indicated common objectives on general terms, and he affirmed America's
willingness to share in the "ultimate arrangements" for maintaining
permanent peace. Lloyd George was outraged, feeling that Wilson's approach relegated the British cause to the same level as the German, and
when the Entente replied to Wilson on January 10, 1917, they made
clear their intention to secure just reparations, restitutions, and guarantees against future German aggression. Foreign Secretary Balfour also
sent a supplementary note insisting that only an Entente victory could
ensure a just peace.

Disagreement with the British was plainly evident in Wilson's famous
address of January 22, 1917. He deplored the old-time balance of power
and similar organized rivalries and insisted that these would have to give
way to a new community of power and organized common peace, and
that only a peace without victory, a peace between equals, could endure.

Thus, peace would have to rest on the principle of equality among nations, the right of all peoples to national self-determination, freedom of the seas, and limitation of armaments. These were, he added characteristically, American principles, but he believed he spoke as well for "the silent mass of mankind everywhere" who had no chance "to speak their real hearts out concerning the death and ruin they see to have come already upon persons and homes they hold most dear." British Liberal and Labour radicals applauded these sentiments, but the British Government was not pleased. Lloyd George later wrote that the speech was an offense to the Allies and a jest to the Germans, and others asked why the President intended not to punish Germany for violating the laws he hoped to make the basis of his new world order. Just after the United States entered the war as an "associated" power, Sir William Wiseman, a Britisher loosely attached to the embassy in Washington and on intimate terms with House, concluded in a report for his superiors in London that Americans opposed any formal treaty arrangements because "subconsciously they feel themselves to be arbitrators rather than allies." Wilson very consciously labeled Wiseman's judgment accurate.

In this context, the underlying motives for Wilson's war decision are clear and take on their full significance. He would not have accepted the Marxist view of history that war represented the final stages of capitalism and imperialism, and that all the great powers were equally responsible and guilty in bringing on the present conflict, but he did believe that war was an anachronistic legacy from an old imperial order that was either dying or in need of being put to a merciful death. The war was monstrously wasteful, irrational in every political and economic sense, and entirely disruptive of the orderly processes and development of civilization. Wars of the current variety were no longer acceptable in the modern world or the world that had to be called into being.

For three years Wilson had remained, in his view, as neutral as was humanly and politically possible. Surely, as critics then and later would charge, the United States had a strong political and psychological predilection for the Allies and growing financial and commercial ties with them. But Wilson's restraint in the face of those mundane matters, and in the cases of his copious note-writing and extraction of "pledges" from the Germans over the sinking, with loss of American lives, of the *Lusitania* in May 1915, the *Arabic* in August 1915, and the French Channel steamer *Sussex* in March 1916, demonstrated his determination to keep America out of the war. Even after the Germans resumed unrestricted warfare for the third year in a row at the start of February 1917, Wilson resisted vilifying them, as Lansing would have liked him to do, and only broke diplomatic relations. When the President asked Congress to arm merchant ships, he purposely avoided mentioning the provocative Zimmermann telegram, and he maintained almost discreet silence when the Germans, in their last desperate gamble for victory, intensified their war upon the seas and sank, with loss of American lives, the British liner *Laconia* on February 25 and the American merchantmen *Memphis, Illinois,* and *Vigilancia* in mid-March, the latter two vessels without warning. What these factors meant, however, was not that the United States necessarily would go to war against Germany, but that in the event the United States had to choose one side or the other, war in behalf of Germany, or on the German side, was unthinkable, while war on the Allied side could be made to serve useful purposes.

By April 1917 the time to choose had come. Wilson's efforts over the past three years to use his good offices had brought no results. Neither side showed any disposition to end the war on terms that the other side might accept. Both sides, especially the German side, seemed committed to a struggle to the finish and to imposing a victor's peace that would create an overwhelming preponderance of power on one side, which would only serve as the starting point for some future conflict.

Wilson's views of the Allies show that he was nearly as suspicious of their war aims as he was of those of the Central Powers, and he never wholly subscribed to the theory that the war was, in pure terms, a contest between democracy and autocracy. He did believe that in prosecuting the war the Germans had committed crimes against civilization for which they would have to atone, but as his position from the time he asked for a declaration of war until the Armistice talks and the Peace Conference would show, he believed that whereas the German Government was irredeemable, the German people were not. His April 2, 1917, war message insisted that Americans had no quarrel with the German people, who had been victimized as in past ages when peoples were not consulted by their rulers and wars were waged for the benefit of dynasties or of little groups of men who used their fellow men as pawns and tools. What the Germans needed was to be purged of their leaders and their sins and reintegrated into the political and economic mainstream of Western civilization.

The presence of Czarist Russia on the British and French side further gave the lie to the democracy-versus-autocracy argument and posed a dilemma for Wilson, but that issue was temporarily resolved by the revolution of March 1917. The "conversion" of Russia was not reason enough to join the Allied cause, but it was, Wilson told his Cabinet, a "glorious act" that had "changed things." The March Revolution, Wilson believed, was the ultimate expression of the "true" Russia, or as he put it in his April 2 address, the autocracy that had crowned Russia's political structure "was not in fact Russian in origin, character, or purpose; and now it had been shaken off and the great, generous Russian people have been added in all their naive majesty and might to the forces that are fighting in the world, for justice, and for peace. Here is a fit partner for a League of Honor."

Here, too, was that convergence of circumstances that at once impelled Wilson to ask for war and seemed to hold out such a unique opportunity to serve America's interest and that of the rest of the world. The Great Power struggle evidently had disrupted every form of normal international behavior. Incidents upon the high seas and diplomatic dilemmas were likely only to worsen, and American prestige would inevitably suffer, especially in Wilson's view, since he had a penchant for equating "national honor" with upholding every alleged principle of international law. In addition, dissent between ethnic and partisan groups was likely to intensify whether the issue was German brutality in the war, British brutality in repressing the Irish Easter Rebellion of 1916, self-determination for nationalities within the Austro-Hungarian or Ottoman Empire, or opposition to, or advocacy of, American preparedness, with all the attendant congressional rancor and civil violence. But, Wilson believed, the introduction of a half million fresh American troops, and a liberal supply of money and war matériel for the Allies would bring the war to a swift end. The United States, he said, sought neither conquest, nor dominion, nor indemnities, and he believed that by participating as a belligerent he would be able to control the Allies, limit their demands upon the Germans (who would need to be rehabilitated and reintegrated into Western society), and take a decisive role in establishing the laws by which nations would be governed in the international arena. He would also be able to bring into being that League of Honor that would enforce a just and lasting peace.

This is what Wilson meant when he said that the world must be made safe for democracy. He was not describing the present, nor the condition of the Allies, nor envisioning a revolutionary transformation of societies around the world that at one blow would eradicate social and political injustice. He was envisioning a future in which the major autocratic governments, such as the deposed Czarist regime or later the Kaiser's Germany, would be eliminated, and the impulses of the major imperial powers, and every other nation, would be curbed and governed by the rule of law. Only under such circumstances was it possible to eradicate war and its causes and create the conditions of peace and prosperity in which other societies could move by stages toward democratic polities resembling most closely, of course, the American model.

This invocation has often been criticized, and with good reason. Wilson's entire approach to waging war and peace frequently reflected his missionary zeal, moral self-righteousness, and occasional hypocrisy. The fact that America denied itself the fruits of imperial victory owed as much to its position as a satisfied power—a commercial and industrial giant that had now outstripped its commercial competitors—as it did to any exceptional virtue, as its own past imperial transgressions in the Pacific and Latin America attested. Similarly, Wilson's emphasis on championing the rights of mankind not only overlooked American political and social injustice at home and abroad, but tended to obscure the extent to which national self-interest was either confused with, or concealed in the guise of, national honor and universal principles. Nevertheless, statesmen leading their nations to war always choose the rhetorical high road. What proved to be Wilson's undoing was less the gap between rhetoric and reality, or the extent to which he raised expectations beyond conceivable realizations, than the way in which events overtook his diplomacy and misjudgment compounded misjudgment. In the end Wilson and his entire program for peace were fatally vulnerable to assault from all sides and overwhelmed by political and diplomatic crossfire.

There were a number of difficulties. First, the time required to mobilize and equip American forces, and to achieve complementary war-matériel production, was much greater than anticipated. The war, rather than being brought to a swift end, took a year and a half of harsh struggle and high casualty rates. The outcome at times seemed to sway in the balance. The rout of the Italian Army at Caporetto in northern Italy in late October 1917 was one such critical development. Italy, originally bound to Germany and Austria-Hungary in the Triple Alliance, had opted for neutrality in 1914 on the technical ground that Germany's decision to strike first against Russia and France negated Italy's obligations to enter a defensive war only. In 1915, the Allies, through the secret Treaty of London, which promised imperial gains in North Africa, enticed Italy into the war, first against Austria-Hungary in May 1915 and then against Germany in August 1916. Viewed as a counterforce to the Central Powers, Italy turned into a liability when its army, which had suffered enormous casualties, collapsed and huddled in its defenses on the Piave outside Venice, awaiting British and French reinforcements.

Italy's collapse pointed up an American dilemma. Wilson had always entertained the notion, vain though it proved, that Austria-Hungary might be induced into a separate peace or might influence the Germans to a negotiated settlement. He had tried especially hard, but unsuccessfully, to achieve this goal between January and April 1917, and he continued the effort even into 1918. For these reasons, Wilson studiously avoided declaring war on Austria-Hungary in April 1917, although his public statement merely said that Americans had no quarrel with the Austro-Hungarians, who were not threatening American lives or principles on the seas. But with the movement of German and

Austro-Hungarian forces into Italy and the need to reinforce the Italians and bolster their spirits, he and Lansing concluded that a declaration of war was inescapable, no matter how much it countered their original diplomatic intentions or contradicted Wilson's insistence in his April 1917 speech that "we enter this war only where we are clearly forced into it because there are no other means of defending our rights." Wilson asked for a declaration of war against Austria-Hungary on December 4, 1917, and Congress assented three days later. His policy had moved from preserving peace with Austria-Hungary to waging war against it, and shortly thereafter, owing doubtless as well to factors long in the making, to dismemberment of the Dual Monarchy and creation of a host of new problems, none of which he had been anticipating six months before.

Far worse were the almost simultaneous developments in Russia. In the spring of 1917, Wilson was sure the provisional government under Premier Alexander Kerensky was even more committed than the Czarist regime had been to staying in the war. The Kerensky regime did want to remain in the war, but the Allies and Wilson made a disastrous misjudgment by insisting upon that commitment. By the spring of 1917, the political and economic structure of Russia was a shambles. Only by withdrawing from the war and concentrating upon the problems of bread, land, and peace could it avoid a complete breakdown. It was inevitable, as George F. Kennan has written, that Russia should leave the war in 1917, but it was not inevitable that it leave under the regime it did or under the terms the Germans would impose in 1918. But the British and French feared relaxing the pressure on Germany's eastern flank, and an American mission to Russia in June 1917, under the Republican elder statesman Elihu Root, drew a wholly unrealistic picture of the provisional government's capacity not only to maintain the war effort but to maintain itself in power. Lansing at once said that he was astounded at the committee's optimism ("I cannot see upon what it is founded"), but no serious review of the situation or policy alternatives were then considered. Russia's effort at mounting an offensive in late June 1917 quickly culminated in military disaster, with many war-weary and retreating troops mutinying against their officers (the soldiers had voted with their feet, Lenin remarked). This precipitated the final downhill slide that brought the dissolution of the army, government, and order in Russia, and the Bolshevik "seizure" of power in early November 1917.

From the Allies' standpoint, neither the Bolsheviks nor Bolshevism posed any threat except insofar as they feared that Russia's withdrawal from the war, coming after the Italian disaster, would give the Germans additional resources, incentive, and control in the East and provide opportunity for an offensive in the West that might succeed before, or in spite of, the introduction of a large number of American troops. Lenin's Decree of Peace, issued as soon as he came to power, revealed his intentions. The Decree repudiated the secret diplomacy and treaties between the British and French, on the one hand, and the Czarist governments, on the other (these secret treaties were published in the *Manchester Guardian* on December 13, 1917); it called for a just peace, with no annexations and no indemnities, and an immediate general armistice. At the same time, Russian emissaries crossed German lines to seek a separate peace, if need be—which the Germans were only too glad to grant. For Lenin, the highest priority was breathing room in which the Bolsheviks could deal with domestic chaos, even if this meant peace with Imperial Germany instead of revolutionary war to encourage the German proletariat to rise against its oppressors.

By mid-December 1917, the Russians and Germans had negotiated and signed an armistice and then began to discuss peace terms at Brest-Litovsk, the site of the eastern-front headquarters of the German High Command. Talks were soon broken off as the Germans pressed seemingly impossible demands, which included control of the Baltic states and Russian Poland. Then, in February 1918, Germany resolved the diplomatic impasse by renewing its offensive, which cut through the Russian lines and forced removal of the capital from Petrograd to Moscow. Lenin at this time showed some slight disposition, as he said, to accept "potatoes and ammunition from the Anglo-French imperialist robbers," but as no such aid was forthcoming, he determined on peace at any price. On March 3, 1918, the Russians signed the Treaty of Brest-Litovsk. Under its terms, Russia renounced all rights to Finland, Estonia, Latvia, and Lithuania and the whole of Poland, leaving their fate to Germany and Austria-Hungary. A German police force would occupy Estonia and Lithuania until their national institutions were restored, and Russia was to conclude a peace with the Ukraine that recognized its independence and allowed Germany to exploit that area economically, a development that would not have occurred if the Kerensky regime had left the war in 1917. Russia had to recognize Turkey's claim to the districts of Ardahan, Kars, and Batum, and Russo-German economic relations were to be structured according to German determination. The draconian terms of the Treaty of Brest-Litovsk sliced off approximately a third of Russia's population, land mass, and natural resources, and placed this enormous area stretching from the Baltic to the Black Sea under German political and economic hegemony. Then, in August 1918, the Germans forced the Russians to sign a supplementary treaty recognizing the independence of the Russian province of Georgia and pledging enormous indemnities in gold and goods to Germany, Austria-Hungary, and Turkey.

However much it might be argued that the Bolsheviks were not themselves forced to surrender much—for at the time they did not control these regions and people—the fact remains that the Germans had imposed a *Diktat* upon Russia that fed the anxiety of those elsewhere who feared peace at the hands of the Kaiser and his army. It also reinforced the views of those who insisted on military victory before discussing peace aims or terms. As Theodore Roosevelt would say, "Let us dictate peace by hammering guns and not chat about peace to the accompaniment of clicking typewriters." Germany's *Diktat* not only smashed Wilson's all but vanished hopes of achieving an end to the war without first imposing military defeat on Germany but strengthened the hands of those Allies who sought to impose a *Diktat* on Germany and undercut Germany's moral justification for its later claim that it was entitled to peace terms more generous than those provided by the Treaty of Versailles.

In the midst of these monumental war and revolutionary developments came Wilson's speech of January 8, 1918, which set forth his Fourteen Points. This speech should not be seen, as it has frequently been in critical hindsight, as an Olympian or prophetic pronouncement but as a shrewd effort to reorder or re-establish control over events that unfolded between the autumn of 1917 and the spring of 1918. In some ways, as will be seen, the most significant aspect of Wilson's speech was not the Fourteen Points but his opening and closing statements about Russia and Germany.

Like the Allies, Wilson feared that from a military standpoint Russian withdrawal from the war, combined with the rout of the Italians, would provide enormous impetus to the German war effort. He was as furious with the Bolshevik leaders in the autumn of 1917 for their evident intention of leaving the war as he was with the Imperial German Government, whose "peace" terms were already generally known by late December 1917, for the brutal conditions they imposed on Russia at Brest-Litovsk. Wilson detested Bolshevik ideology, which he called "poison," but in the same breath he added that it had enormous appeal because "it is a protest against the way in which the world has worked." In November 1917, he had tried to act prudently in the aftermath of the Bolshevik Revolution. Although he rejected the proposal by General Ferdinand Foch, the French representative to the newly established Supreme War Council, for military intervention in Russia to restore a pro-Allied, anti-Bolshevik regime, he agreed a month later to Lansing's more modest proposal to afford financial aid to pro-Allied, anti-Bolshevik forces and not to recognize the Bolshevik claim to the railroads in Manchuria that had been built by Russia's former Czarist regime. Generally, however, Wilson and Colonel House, though not the more militantly anti-Bolshevik Lansing, tended to hope that Bolshevik excesses would be moderated in time, and that perhaps they themselves could even aid in the transformation.

Thus, Wilson delivered his Fourteen Points message. As House recollected, the purpose of the speech was, first, to attempt to persuade the Russians to end peace talks with the Germans and resume the war in behalf of the democratic, liberal Allied cause; second, to appeal to German Socialists in the Reichstag who had gone on record in July 1917 as favoring a peace without annexation or indemnities; and third, to serve notice on the Allies that their war aims, about which they had been so evasive but about which so much was now known as a consequence of the exposed secret treaties, needed to be more liberal.

Wilson actually devoted the entire first half of his speech to the problem of Russian-German peace talks, depicting sincere and earnest Russian delegates being confronted by Teutonic statesmen who, behind closed doors, pressed proposals of conquest and domination. In an open appeal to Russian nationalism, he expressed hope that the thrilling and more compelling voice of the Russian people would be heard, that their soul, which is "not subservient," would sustain them, and that they "will not yield either in principle or in action." Whether or not the Russian leaders believed him, he said, "it is our heartfelt desire and hope that some way may be opened whereby we may be privileged to assist the people of Russia to attain their utmost hope of liberty and ordered peace."

Only then, after pledging open negotiations and a peace with neither conquest nor aggrandizement, did Wilson elaborate his Fourteen Points. The first five were essentially long-held liberal sentiments: open covenants of peace openly arrived at; freedom of the seas; removal "so far as possible" of international trade barriers and equality of trade; reduction of armaments to the lowest point consistent with domestic safety; and an impartial adjustment of colonial claims, taking into account the welfare of the colonial peoples as well as the ruling government. The next eight were territorial proposals, and not very controversial: German evacuation of Russian territory, assistance by all nations to help Russia achieve "an unhampered and unembarrassed opportunity for independent determination of its own political development and national policy," and a welcome for Russia into the society of free nations; German evacuation of Belgium; the return of the provinces of Alsace and Lorraine to France; readjustment of Italian frontiers along the lines of nationality; "autonomous development" for the peoples of Austria-Hungary; evacuation of Rumania, Serbia, and Montenegro, access to the sea for Serbia, and guarantees of political and economic independence for the Balkan states; autonomy for the people of the Ottoman Empire under Turkish rule and the opening of the Dardanelles to ships of all nations; an independent Poland, inhabited by "indisputably Polish populations," with free and secure access to the sea. The fourteenth point was a "general association of nations" to guarantee political independence and integrity to great and small states alike.

Wilson's closing paragraphs implied a fifteenth point. He held out the lure of lenient peace terms for Germany, an obvious contrast to the demands the Germans were then making on the Russians. "We have no jealousy of German greatness," he said, and in no way wished to impair it or legitimate German influence or power. He wanted an end to conflict by arms or hostile trade arrangements; he wanted Germany to accept a place of equality among the nations of the world. He demanded only to know whether those who would speak for Germany represented "the military party and the men whose creed is imperial domination" or the Reichstag majority that in July 1917 had demanded domestic reform and a peace without annexation or indemnities.

The geographical, ethnic, and economic structure of the newly independent political units that would emerge out of the Austro-Hungarian and Ottoman empires would hazard many problems. But here again, as in Wilson's first five points, his view about national self-determination and ethnographic divisions was in harmony with the long-held liberal and nationalistic currents of the nineteenth and twentieth centuries, and the solutions arrived at, however imperfect, were insufficient by themselves to bring about a second World War.

Wilson recognized the central problem of his time and of twentieth-century European politics: namely, that no peace structure could endure that did not encompass both German *and* Russian ambitions and energies. The solution to the problem, however, was not to establish, in the old imperial sense, a balance of power (or terror) between these two great nations but to integrate them fully into the diplomatic, political, and economic mainstream of Western civilization. It was to this enormous task, still awaiting resolution more than a half-century later, that the President was addressing himself and the world in January 1918. In the meantime, war between the Great Powers continued to rage, along with revolutionary and civil wars of increasingly international effect. Yet there was still hope in Wilson's mind at the start of the New Year in 1918 that he might be able to impose his rational order on these events or at least, in general, shape their outcome, and it was to this ambition that he devoted nearly his entire energies during the next two years.

2

War, Revolution, and Treaties

For a considerable time in the spring of 1918, Russian withdrawal from the war seemed about to fulfill the worst fears of the British and the French. The Germans, freed from most of their eastern obligations, now had an additional forty divisions, almost a million men, which they could move to the western front. Late in March 1918, they opened an offensive that by June carried close enough to Paris so that they could bombard the city with heavy, long-range guns while the French prepared to evacuate. At this point, however, the Allied forces held, and heartened by the free flow of American supplies and more than a million new American troops, they gradually mounted their own broad offensive, which by the summer's end had driven the Germans back through eastern France. On October 4, 1918, the German Chancellor, Prince Max of Baden, appealed through the Swiss Government to President Wilson for an armistice and peace negotiations on the basis of the Fourteen Points. Within five weeks, armistice terms were agreed upon, but in many ways the events of the previous six months had moved further and faster than most of the participants in the great struggle understood. These events revealed the extent to which the tragedy already inherent in the war years would be carried over into the years of peace by men who were too frequently unable or unwilling to alter their thinking or courses of action.

The German decision to ask Wilson for an armistice in October 1918 was highly logical. The High Command had concluded that militarily they could not win the war, but neither, in their view, had they been defeated. The war in the West had been waged and the damages had been wrought chiefly on French and Belgian soil. Germany suffered some damages from air raids, but no Allied troops crossed into Germany proper until after the formal Armistice. Hence, in October 1918, the

21

Germans thought that, in dealing directly with Wilson and bypassing the British and French and the Supreme War Council, they could achieve advantageous, or liberal, terms commensurate with their military position.

Politically, German intentions were then more subtle. The Germans hoped to exploit the differences in both war and peace aims between the United States, on the one hand, and the British and French, on the other, and to use the United States as a buffer against Anglo-French retribution. Equally significant, German strategy envisioned moving beyond using the United States as a shield against England and France to incorporating all three powers into a Western bloc that would oppose Bolshevism and Bolshevik Russia at home and abroad.

As elucidated to his Cabinet colleagues in January 1919 by the conservative Count Ulrich von Brockdorff-Rantzau, who had become Foreign Minister in December 1918, Germany had to cultivate American good will in order to secure the capital that would be necessary for postwar reconstruction. The Americans, he reasoned, would welcome the opportunity to invest in Germany as a means of maintaining their own prosperity, which was heavily dependent on overseas investment and expanded world trade. Also, by accepting American capital, Germany would begin to bring the United States "in her own interest, over to our side." Further, Germany and the character of the German people were the best barrier against Bolshevism in Europe, and until German power was wholly restored American and British troops would have to co-operate with German troops in defense of eastern borders against this "Socialismus Asiaticus." In brief, Brockdorff-Rantzau's vision of world politics and the mutual benefits to be derived from a German-American coalition was not limited in time to 1918 or 1919 but remained a key tenet of German foreign policy throughout the era of the Weimar Republic; it would persist among traditional diplomats during the age of Adolf Hitler right up until December 1941 and would re-emerge at the end of the Second World War and the ensuing two decades of the cold war.

Within the Wilson administration, key officials harbored sentiments similar to those of Brockdorff-Rantzau. The President loathed Bolshevism and never wavered in his refusal from November 1917 onward to accord diplomatic recognition to Lenin's regime; in February 1918, he vetoed a French proposal to afford the Bolsheviks war matériel, even if they chose to continue the fight against Germany. Secretary Lansing was even more militantly anti-Bolshevik and reinforced Wilson's views and decisions in these matters. In November 1918, Lansing, who in 1915 had labeled Germany the world's menace, now insisted that the British and French were thinking too much about indemnities and not enough about the fact that "Bolshevism is worse than any autocracy, a greater enemy to individual liberty," and by March 1919 he was arguing that Germany had to be made strong enough to resist "the hideous despotism of the Red Terror." Almost everyone in the Wilson administration favored food relief for Germany as fast as possible to calm Bolshevist uprisings ("the madness of famished men," Lansing called the outbreaks) and was delighted when the government of President Friedrich Ebert and the Reichswehr crushed the Spartacist uprisings in Berlin of January 1919. The Communist leaders Rosa Luxemburg and Karl Liebknecht, who in 1918 had opposed Lenin's use of terror in both Germany and Russia, were killed during this struggle. In the spring of 1920, the United States and Great Britain responded favorably to Germany's request to send its own troops, in violation of the Treaty of Versailles, into the demilitarized Rhineland to suppress a left-wing revolt. When the French objected to this movement of troops, and in turn sent their own occupation forces into Darmstadt and Frankfurt, the United States, through the militantly anti-Bolshevik Secretary of State, Bainbridge Colby, insisted that any further French occupation moves would only serve to coalesce militaristic forces in Germany with those elements "striving for revolution and the overthrow of political and economic order." The French promised not to act again without prior consultation.

Wilson's purposes, however, encompassed much more than merely an alliance of conservative German (as well as British and French) and liberal American ambitions joined in a mindless anti-Bolshevik or anti-Soviet crusade. Nor should his opposition to Bolshevism in Germany, or even in Russia, be allowed to obscure the larger foreign-policy objectives he set for himself in his effort to achieve what he considered to be a beneficent new world order. Closer analysis of his objectives also explains the extent to which his goals differed from those of conservative Germans, and why the Germans, who probably never really understood Wilson, always felt he had betrayed or misled them.

Wilson despised German imperialism no less than Bolshevism, and the Treaty of Brest-Litovsk and the following German offensive probably hardened his attitude toward the German people and made him steadfast in his determination to reform German institutions. In January 1918, Wilson offered the Fourteen Points as a basis for peace; in a subsequent address on February 9, he said that he favored a peace without annexations or indemnities. Thereafter his declarations concerning Germany were much more harsh. In Baltimore on April 6, he denounced the Treaty of Brest-Litovsk and said that the only possible response to Germany now was "force, force to the utmost, force without stint or limit." In a ringing July Fourth speech at Mount Vernon, he depicted the current struggle as a deadly one between the Past and the Present. He insisted that the settlement must be final, with no compromise, and he inveighed against the "blinded rulers of Prussia," warning them that they had unleashed forces they did not understand, forces that would never be crushed, forces that were "the very stuff of triumph." Again on September 27 he said that there could be no compromise with the Central Powers. In the message to Congress on November 11 in which he acknowledged the Armistice agreement, he rejoiced in the defeat of the armed imperialism and "arbitrary power of the military caste of Germany."

Wilson's words, of course, were bound to stir passions in favor of imposing some sort of retributive peace on Germany, despite the fact that in all his speeches he pleaded for an equitable peace, impartial justice, and an organization of peace to act as a tribunal for disputes and a check upon "every invasion of right." Wilson's expressions, however, were not necessarily contradictory. If he had entered the war convinced that the United States had no quarrel with the German people, he now believed that the corrupting influence of the ruling imperial or military caste went so deep that German society needed to be reformed. In that regard, the peace treaty would have to be punitive, or therapeutic. As he would write to General Smuts in May 1919 amidst the debate over the final form of the Treaty of Versailles, he thought its terms were harsh but not unjust in the circumstances. Then, he added, "invariably my thought goes back to the very great offense against civilization which the German state committed and the necessity for making it evidence once and for all that such things can lead only to the most severe punishment." The central issue, Wilson also said shortly thereafter, was not whether the terms were hard, "for they are hard—but the Germans earned that," but whether the terms were just. In fact, in some ways for Wilson the specific terms of the Treaty of Versailles would be less crucial than the way in which Germany would respond to his and Allied demands, not merely at the Peace Conference but in the years after. As he said in his September 27, 1918, address, "Germany will have to redeem her character, not by what happens at the peace table, but by what follows." Implicit in this approach was not only the demand that Germany reform itself before being fully reintegrated into the international community, or League of Nations, but the belief that Germany had lost the war and would have to suffer certain consequences. But the Germans were unwilling to acknowledge their defeat.

Wilson's reformist and gradual integrationist approach to the problem of Germany accounts in large measure for the procedures he adopted at the time Germany appealed for an armistice, for his increasing disagreement with the British and the French, who were determined to treat defeated Germany more harshly, and for one crucial aspect of his domestic partisan political problems as they were revealed in both the congressional elections of November 1918 and the composition of his Peace Commission. These problems spilled over into the problem of intervention in the civil war in Russia and, ultimately, into the final struggle over ratification of the Treaty of Versailles, with its covenant of the League of Nations.

When Prince Max of Baden made his original approach for an armistice on October 4, 1918, Wilson responded quickly and bypassed the French, the British, and the Supreme War Council because he feared that their peace terms would be too punitive and their ultimate aims too imperial. On October 8, he told the Germans that they could have an armistice and peace talks if they fully accepted his Fourteen Points and the principles he had laid down in subsequent addresses, if they could assure him that the Chancellor spoke for the German people as well as the war leaders, and if they would evacuate all Allied territory prior to the formal Armistice. The British and French, apprised of these diplomatic exchanges through French intelligence, were furious. They argued that mere German evacuation of Allied territory would afford the Germans a chance to refix and fortify their lines farther to the East and resume hostilities if the talks broke down. Only the military experts, or the Supreme War Council, could determine the military requirements for an armistice.

More important were the political considerations. Both the British and the French felt, with some justification, that Wilson had usurped their diplomatic authority. Then, as one of Lloyd George's associates noted in his diary at the time, the Prime Minister worried that, if too much emphasis were put on the Fourteen Points as an "indispensable" condition of an armistice, "the Huns will try to assume that it is the only condition, and, when we insist on other conditions, will say that we intervened and upset a promising negotiation for peace." Further, Wilson's emphasis on the Fourteen Points seemed to imply that the British and French had accepted them, which they had not. The British adamantly opposed Wilson's concept of freedom of the seas; they were unwilling to allow any multinational organization to impinge on what they considered their unilateral right or obligation to deal however they saw fit with problems relating to blockade and shipping on the high seas in time of war. The British also had no intention of concluding a peace without indemnities.

As for the French, at the time of Wilson's Fourteen Points address Premier Georges Clemenceau, in a calculated omission, did not even bother to send the customary cable of congratulations. Later, he would remark, with classic Gallic cynicism, "God has given us the Ten Commandments, and we broke them. Wilson gives us the Fourteen Points. We shall see." For Clemenceau, the central fact of international life was the destruction and humiliation Germany had inflicted upon France in 1870–71 and now in 1914–18. His major, if not sole, objective was to see that Germany would never be strong enough to do this again. All tactics and principles were subordinate to that end.

The upshot of British and French objections was twofold. At the Allies' suggestion, Wilson sent Colonel House to Europe to discuss the Fourteen Points, which they accepted, with two major reservations. The British agreed, in principle, to freedom of the seas and to a full discussion of the matter at the forthcoming peace conference, although not before House threatened that Wilson would resume bilateral negotiations with the Germans if the British did not acquiesce, and Lloyd George swore that Britain would spend "her last guinea to keep a navy superior to that of the United States or any other power." On the matter of indemnities, or restoration of invaded territories, the definition was expanded to encompass "all damage done to the civilian populations of the Allies and their property by the aggression of Germany by land, by sea, and from the air." Clearly, Germany would have to pay reparations, and implicit in the phrase "aggression of Germany" was the concept of "war guilt."

In the meantime, on October 14, 1918, Wilson told the Germans that they had to allow the Allies to fix armistice terms that would guarantee Allied military supremacy, and that the Germans had to end their wartime activities on land and sea. A week later, the Germans agreed, giving verbal assurance, too, that the Chancellor represented the German people and the Reichstag. Wilson was relatively satisfied, although he had to submit the correspondence for British and French approval; but he also continued to express to the Germans his skepticism about the representative—or legitimate—nature of their government. Finally, on November 5, Secretary Lansing told the Germans that the United States would make peace on the basis of the Fourteen Points and the two British and French reservations concerning freedom of the seas and compensation for war damages.

By this time, however, Germany's domestic political and economic structure had virtually collapsed. There were mutinies and revolutionary outbreaks in Kiel, Hamburg, and, later, Berlin. On November 9, Kaiser Wilhelm abdicated the throne, while in the Reichstag the Socialist leader Phillip Scheidemann "proclaimed" Germany a Republic. In Marshal Foch's railway car in the Forest at Compiègne, the Great Powers formally signed the Armistice on the morning of November 11, 1918. From the German point of view, the Armistice had come not a moment too soon, given the increasingly chaotic and revolutionary situation within the country. From a long-run political point of view, however, the Armistice came too late. It had been delayed both by Wilson's reluctance to deal with the representatives of Imperial (as opposed to republican) Germany and by the Allies' need, and insistence on, working out their own differences and the long list of Armistice terms pertaining to the disposition of war and industrial equipment, military personnel, prisoners of war, transportation and communication facilities, and countless other matters. Hence, as it was technically not the Kaiser's government that had agreed to the Armistice and subsequent peace terms, many Germans would later place the "onus" for this mythical "stab in the back" on the newly proclaimed Weimar Republic.

Wilson, too, was having political difficulties in 1918 that had serious future implications. In the course of a congressional debate in May over an administration proposal to raise revenue for wartime expenditures by increasing taxes on high incomes and excess profits, Wilson successfully appealed to Congress that, in the name of national unity, "politics be adjourned." He seemingly reversed himself when, on October 24, he publicly declared that, if the electorate did not return a Democratic majority to Congress in the November 5 elections, this would be interpreted in Europe "as a repudiation of my leadership." The election results gave the Republicans a majority of 2 in the Senate and 45 in the House (net gains of 8 and 50 seats, respectively) and elevated Henry Cabot Lodge to the chairmanship of the Senate Foreign Relations Committee, with a Republican voting majority.

Ever since, Wilson has been criticized even by admirers for having fatally introduced partisan politics into the election through his October 24 pronouncement, and, indeed, at the time even Wilson's wife had opposed his making the appeal. Colonel House, then involved in the peace preparations and not privy to Wilson's decision, also remarked, not long afterward, that it was "politically unwise" and cost Wilson a Democratic majority in Congress. Compounding Wilson's problems, and doubtless shading men's perspective on this issue, was the fact that early in December 1918 Lloyd George's coalition, in the famous "khaki" election, ran a campaign that clearly suggested a harsh peace and won a resounding majority of 526 out of 707 seats in the House of Commons. And at the end of that month, Clemenceau turned a debate on the budget in the Chamber of Deputies into a vote of confidence and won a smashing 414 to 6 victory. Thus, men have judged that precisely when he could least afford a domestic political defeat (the British and French being no longer dependent on American supplies and troops to defeat the Germans, and Lloyd George and Clemenceau being about to reinforce their political positions and arouse their nations' "jingoist" instincts), Wilson, with his appeal for a Democratic Congress, risked and lost much political prestige and power that he needed for diplomatic purposes.

The fact is that Wilson took the risk he did precisely because he recognized his political difficulties at home and abroad. First, politics in the United States had not been adjourned in 1918, certainly not insofar as the Armistice and peace terms were concerned. The Republicans had long been trying to make political capital out of both of these matters. In the Senate on August 23, 1918, Lodge insisted that there "cannot be a negotiated peace" but only "unconditional surrender," and that "no peace that satisfies Germany in any degree can ever satisfy us." Peace had to be won "finally and thoroughly in German territory" and the ultimate terms "dictated." In October, Lodge opposed Wilson's negotiations with Prince Max of Baden, insisting again on unconditional surrender. Similarly, in October and November 1918, George Harvey, through his influential *North American Review,* campaigned for "justice without discussion or debate, as inexorable as the wrath of God," and insisted that the Allies would have to minister to the Germans until "the blond beast was tamed and humanized." Other Republicans challenged the President's right to negotiate an armistice without resort to the Senate Foreign Relations Committee, while still others attacked the (Democratic) free-trade aspects of his Fourteen Points. Wilson rose to the bait and appealed for a Democratic Congress, which now allowed the Republicans to mount their carefully planned attack, insisting, as did their national chairman, Will Hays, that the Republican party was pledged to uphold the Allies in whatever demands they made upon the Germans. Then Theodore Roosevelt declared open war on Wilson's Fourteen Points on October 27, when he called them a sellout of American principles and said that they had been welcomed by Germans, by pro-Germans in America, and "especially by Germanized Socialists and by Bolshevists of every grade."

Perhaps Wilson committed a tactical error in October 1918. Possibly he recalled that President McKinley had made a similar, and successful, plea for the return of a Republican Congress at the end of the Spanish-American War in 1898. More important, Wilson's appeal revealed the nature of his dilemma and his strategy. He was under attack on both foreign and domestic issues by the Republicans, and he was having great difficulties with the Allies but could say nothing publicly about it. He hoped, therefore, to strengthen his hand and forestall his Republican opposition from linking up with the conservative British and French forces that sought to impose a *Diktat* on Germany and threatened to destroy the League of Nations and the reign of law that he envisioned. These same forces, incidentally, as will be seen, sought to enmesh the United States even further in the already deepening problem of the civil war in Russia.

Within this immediate context, it is also important to note the strategy underlying Wilson's choice of a delegation to negotiate the peace. He chose himself, as head of the delegation, and Lansing, House, General

Tasker Bliss (the American representative on the Supreme War Council), and Henry White, a career diplomat and nominal Republican. Wilson has been criticized primarily for not appointing at least one politically influential Republican member and making the peace an effort in bipartisan foreign policy. However, political affiliations aside, the crucial fact that emerges about the commissioners is that they all favored mild peace terms for Germany and reintegration of Germany into a liberal, capitalist world order. In making his choices Wilson overrode Clemenceau's objection that the President was a head of state who should not negotiate with him and Lloyd George (who were heads of government). This was really a mask for Clemenceau's harsh peace objectives and his fear that Wilson would become the rallying point for a liberal and left-wing popular assault on French (and British or Italian) imperial designs. Similarly, Wilson felt that he could not find an appropriate Republican political figure who favored a mild peace for Germany and was progressive on domestic matters, and who would have been satisfactory both to him and to Lodge and the Republican leadership.

Indefensible on virtually every political or military ground in 1918 was the American decision to intervene in Russia. Here, Wilson revealed his most tragic and fatal flaws, and his administration pursued a policy that led into a political quagmire, isolating it from friend as well as foe and creating long- and short-range foreign and domestic political problems with serious consequences. From November 1917 to March 1918 the British and French had proposed a joint intervention with the United States in European Russia, with the Japanese being invited to intervene in Siberia, ostensibly to restore a pro-Allied regime that would resume the war against Germany. After Brest-Litovsk and the German spring offensive, the Allies insisted that it was imperative to reopen an eastern front and to protect their large quantities of war matériel stored in the northern Russian ports of Archangel and Murmansk and the Siberian port of Vladivostok. The Allies pointed to Germany's intervention in behalf of the Whites in the civil war in Finland, which often spilled into the Murmansk region, and the threat to Siberia and Vladivostok posed by German troops and the approximately 1.5 million former Austro-Hungarian and German prisoners of war in Russia and Siberia. The French also hoped to "restore" Russia as their traditional ally and to recover the fortune they had invested in Czarist government enterprises, bonded debts that the Bolsheviks had repudiated. The British, always fearing Imperial Russia's penetration of the eastern Mediterranean and North Pacific, were concerned about the effect of revolutionary Russia on the nationalist, or home-rule, movements within the empire, especially in India.

By March 1918, British and French staff planners had devised a scheme to achieve their governments' military and political objectives. Within Russia, there was a Czech legion, composed of some 40,000 to 50,000 men, some of whom were former Czech nationals in Russia and others Austro-Hungarian army defectors, which had been made part of the provisional government's army in 1917. This group, which had remained intact after the collapse of 1917 and Brest-Litovsk, now subordinated itself to the French Supreme Command. Allied military planners proposed to evacuate the legion eastward across Siberia to Vladivostok and then to France, ostensibly to fight on the western front. But the planners also envisioned using the troops to garrison Murmansk and Archangel, later sending them into the Russian interior via the Urals, where they would link up with a Japanese army moving west across Siberia and destroy Bolshevism in Russia. The British and French governments had not accepted the latter proposal when, in the spring of 1918, they negotiated permission from the Soviet regime to evacuate the Czech legion to the western front. By mid-May, 15,000 Czechs had reached Vladivostok, with the remainder spread across three thousand miles of the Trans-Siberian Railroad from the Volga River to Irkutsk.

Wilson opposed Anglo-French entreaties from November 1917 to March 1918 for either cooperative military intervention in Russia or unilateral Japanese intervention in Siberia, and he continued to resist them throughout the spring. He and his military advisers doubted the practicality of the undertaking and suspected that Anglo-French claims about wartime exigencies cloaked traditional imperial goals. Above all, Wilson believed that Bolshevism's appeal, as he would later tell Lloyd George and Clemenceau in January 1919, stemmed from the world-wide "revolt against the large vested interests which influenced the world in the economic and in the political sphere," and that foreign military intervention only rallied the Russian people to the Bolshevik side. Similarly, in March 1919 Wilson would oppose military intervention against a Communist regime in Hungary (but not a food blockade) with the argument that "to try and stop a revolution with field armies is like using a vast broom to stop a vast flood. The only way to act against Bolshevism is to destroy its causes." Most Wilsonians agreed, including Herbert Hoover, who as Wilson's Director of Relief would argue against military intervention in Hungary, insisting that Bolshevism was a condition to be cured rather than a conspiracy to be crushed, that Bolshevism had a certain spiritual appeal, and that military intervention would have reactionary consequences.

Running counter to these attitudes in the spring of 1918, however, were those of State Department personnel who argued that the Germans were playing a deadly double game with Russia: They had promoted revolution there, in the form of aid to Lenin, to cripple Russia and deprive the Allies of support, but in the future they would combine with White counterrevolutionaries—as they were already doing in Finland, the Baltic states, and the Ukraine—to suppress the revolution and gain political and economic hegemony over Russia. State Department officials also insisted that Lenin was an agent of German imperialism and world-wide revolution, or, as Ambassador David R. Francis wired Washington amidst the Brest-Litovsk talks, Lenin and Trotsky "may possibly not have been Germany's agents continuously but if [they] had been [they] could not have played more successfully into Germany's hands." Wilson was not wholly convinced, but his own anti-imperial and anti-Bolshevik attitudes inclined him toward aiding liberal or conservative Russians who opposed the reaction of the old regime or the extremism of the new one, which by no means governed all of Russia. Ironically, the same liberal nationalist, reformist, and messianic instincts that allowed Wilson to recognize the "genuine grievances" upon which Bolshevism rested also drew him toward intervention. By April 1918, he was talking to intimates of his desire to support "the most nearly representative" self-governing units in Russia that opposed the Bolsheviks, and by late May he was pondering the advantages that might have accrued had an Anglo-American force been landed in Siberia to rally the people against the Germans and away from the Bolsheviks. For Wilson, the real purpose of intervention, then, was not to satisfy Anglo-French demands for military assistance but to rally a coalition of Russians against the Bolsheviks and to restore Kerensky's provisional government or its equivalent.

The ultimate temptation came with word in late May 1918 that Czech forces moving across Siberia toward Vladivostok had become embroiled in a conflict with Soviet forces and had rallied anti-Bolsheviks to their side and gained control of several cities in Siberia. Wilson's highly favorable view of the Czechs and their (anti-Hapsburg) nationalism bolstered his interventionist sentiments. By mid-June, he told the Allies he was reconsidering the entire situation. On June 29, the Czechs in Vladivostok seized the city from Bolshevik authorities and appealed for help as they battled westward to reopen the Trans-Siberian Railroad. Within a week, on July 6, Wilson authorized sending 7,000 American troops to Vladivostok to cooperate with an equal number of Japanese troops in guarding reopened sections of the railway. At Lansing's instruction, the public pronouncement insisted that railway duty was the only purpose of such intervention and emphasized that there was no intention of interfering in Russian internal affairs or of infringing Russian sovereignty. At the same time, Wilson also agreed to dispatch three battalions of American troops to assist the Allies in guarding their military supplies at Murmansk.

The ambiguity of the intervention was quickly revealed on July 8, when Lansing suggested to the Japanese Ambassador, Viscount Ishii, that perhaps the Czechs would become "a nucleus about which the Russians might rally, even to the extent of becoming a military factor in the war." This could happen only under a non-Bolshevik regime, given Lenin's refusal to fight for the Allies and Wilson's stated refusal to aid him even if he would. Then came Wilson's even more suggestive aide-mémoire of July 17, circulated among the Allies and American diplomats. Here, the President reiterated that military action in Russia was permissible only to aid the Czechs and guard military stores, but he also said that Allied forces in Siberia would be allowed to "steady any efforts at self-government or self-defense in which the Russians may be willing to accept assistance," and in northern Russia they could "render such aid as may be acceptable to the Russians in the organization of their own self-defense" and could "make it safe for Russian forces to come together in organized bodies."

Thus, while the size of the American and Allied forces that Wilson agreed to send was large enough only to guard military supplies or a railway, he hoped his so-called modest and experimental undertakings would encourage anti-Bolshevik forces in northern Russia and Siberia to become the nucleus for a politically and economically moderate challenge to the Bolsheviks. Further, his "cooperation" with the Japanese was intended not only to forestall their acting unilaterally, and perhaps seizing the Soviet Maritime province but also to exercise control over the Anglo-Japanese relationship. Here, Wilson was expressing his opposition—which would be carried to a successful conclusion by his Republican successors and maintained by the Democrats of the 1930's —to the Anglo-Japanese Alliance (negotiated in 1902 and renewed in 1911), and asserting that these two imperial powers would never be permitted to strike a sphere-of-influence bargain that might negate the Open Door Policy and exclude American political and commercial influence from the North Pacific.

Wilson's subtle, sophisticated intervention scheme bogged down in contradictions and tragic developments. First, the bulk of the Allied supplies were not in Murmansk but Archangel and had been taken by the Bolsheviks. Without a word to Wilson, however, the Allied command rerouted American troops slated for Murmansk to Archangel, and there they were used to battle not German but Soviet forces contesting for control of the city. By the time the American troops reached Vladivostok, the Czechs had reopened the Trans-Siberian Railroad and linked up with their countrymen in western Siberia. The Japanese, meanwhile, refused to be bound by Wilson's 7,000-man limit on their forces—on July 24, they informed the American Government that their initial detachment would be 12,000 troops—and proceeded to occupy all of northern Manchuria and seize the Russian-owned and -operated Chinese Eastern Railroad. The British and French, meanwhile, encouraged the Czechs in the Urals to align with White forces and battle the Bolsheviks, and in December 1918 the French began to land forces at Odessa that soon reached a total of 12,000, including 3,500 Poles and 2,000 Greeks.

Wilson could have ended American intervention in Russia when the November 1918 Armistice eliminated its justification as a war effort, but he ignored Secretary of War Newton D. Baker's advice for immediate withdrawal. This led not only to more complex problems in Russia but to erosion of Wilson's political credibility at home. Progressive Republicans such as Hiram Johnson of California, William E. Borah of Idaho, and Robert La Follette of Wisconsin now challenged the policy they had tacitly accepted during the war and called not for total but gradual withdrawal and more frank public discussion of American and Allied purposes. As Borah said in December 1918, intervention in Russia appeared to be only a prelude to "war against revolution in all countries, whether enemy or ally," and a sure sign that the prospective League of Nations was bound to degenerate into another Holy Alliance. On the conservative side, Lodge, who denounced the Bolsheviks as "anthropoid apes," did not attack Wilson's policies but insisted that he had erred only by not intervening with even more troops. In short, Wilson's Russian policy was already bringing together that curious political coalition that would defeat his peace program of 1919–20.

Despite the foreign and domestic storm signals of 1918, Wilson and his advisers went to Europe in December confident that the preponderance of American power—credits, manufactures, and food supplies— would enable them to coerce the Allies into accepting peace terms and a League of Nations of liberal persuasion. Early in the proceedings, Wilson told the Council of Ten that they should reject the analogy of the Congress of Vienna of 1814–15. That, he said, had been an ignoble restoration of "monarchical and arbitrary government," designed to maintain the status quo in foreign and domestic affairs.

The revolutionary civil war in Russia, however, complicated Wilson's peacemaking efforts. In January 1919, Clemenceau opposed receiving Bolshevik representatives at the Paris Peace Conference; Lloyd George thought that, because they were probably "the prevalent opinion in Russia," they were as likely representatives of Russia as anyone. Wilson's silence in the discussion tipped the balance in favor of not receiving formally any Russian representatives. Next, the French, especially Marshal Foch, pushed for a vast military intervention to destroy the Bolsheviks, and the idea gained support from Winston Churchill, newly appointed Secretary of State for War.

Neither Lloyd George nor Wilson would countenance this. The Prime Minister said that it was ridiculous to believe Bolshevism posed the threat German militarism had posed, or that anyone would send a million troops to fight in Russia, and he insisted that a *cordon sanitaire,* or food blockade, would starve only the Russian people. The solution to the conflict was to get the Russian factions to agree to a truce and to negotiate a coalition. Wilson supported this policy, and drafted an Allied proposal, which went out on January 22, 1919, calling for a truce and conference of all Russian factions in mid-February on Prinkipo Island in the Sea of Marmora. Wilson hoped thereby, he told his colleagues, that the conference proposal would negate the charge that the Allies wished "to enslave" the Russian people by restoring a reactionary regime. He also hoped to weaken the Bolshevik hold on the Russian people. Lenin was not keen on the conference but acceded. But Wilson's hopes for undermining the Bolsheviks, or negotiating them out of power, collapsed when the White regimes rejected the conference invitation, convinced they were winning the civil war, or that the Bolsheviks were disintegrating.

Here again Wilson might have extricated himself from the military debacle, for on the basis of the Prinkipo proposals the Senate, on February 7 and February 14, 1919, voted on resolutions sponsored by Hiram Johnson calling for withdrawal of all American troops from Russia. The first measure failed by five votes, and the second was defeated by Vice-President Thomas R. Marshall's tie-breaking vote. Had Wilson wished, he might have used his influence among Democratic senators (as he had in securing passage of the New Freedom legislation and as he would on the League of Nations issues) who opposed Johnson to secure passage of a resolution favoring withdrawal if the Whites remained intransigent.

Instead, Wilson grew more stubborn, as evidenced by his response to William C. Bullitt's undertaking. Bullitt, then a young diplomat attached to the American delegation in Paris, secured permission from Lansing and House in late February 1919 to go to Russia to find out under what circumstances the Bolsheviks would agree to a cease-fire. Lansing viewed the mission as unofficial and noted cynically that he was "sending Bullitt to Russia to cure him of his Bolshevism." Nonetheless, unknown to either Wilson (who had briefly returned to America) or Lansing, Bullitt took along a set of proposals, which had been discussed earlier in both British and Bolshevik circles, that called for a stationary armistice, withdrawal of all foreign troops, the establishment of trade relations, and a Soviet pledge to moderate its foreign policy. On this basis, Lenin agreed to a two-week renewable armistice and even suggested resurrecting the Prinkipo Conference idea if the agenda could be agreed upon in advance.

Under these circumstances, the Whites would have been left in *de facto* control of large portions of the Baltic states and northern Russia, the Ukraine, Bessarabia, Transcaucasia, and Siberia, while the Bolsheviks would have consolidated their revolution within a Russia much smaller than that of 1917. But when Bullitt returned from Moscow in late March 1919, Wilson refused to see him. Lansing and other members of the delegation opposed the proposal, and Lloyd George insisted that the British press and public opinion were too hostile toward Bolshevism to permit any approach to the Soviets.

Wilson's refusal to receive Bullitt has been explained away by circumstances: The President had neither authorized the mission nor seen the original proposals; he may well have been ill at the time, as he claimed; and Bullitt was a low-ranking diplomat. Further, negotiations over the Treaty of Versailles had reached a crucial stage. But more important is the fact that Wilson had no interest in a new Prinkipo Conference with an agenda because this implied what he would never grant —*de facto* recognition of the Soviet regime. The Lenin-Bullitt proposals thus remained unexplored.

From this time on to the end of 1919, Wilson and the Allies made a final effort to bolster the Siberian White regime of Admiral Alexander Kolchak by providing military and economic aid in return for his pledging political and economic reforms. But Kolchak remained vague on the reforms, and his regime proved to be so oppressive that the American commander in Siberia, General William S. Graves, refused to allow his troops to participate in any of Kolchak's efforts to rid the country of "Bolsheviks" or their supporters. In fact, Kolchak's suppression of the non-Communist Social Revolutionaries was so brutal that he lost all standing among the peasantry and so alienated the Czechs who had originally made common cause with him that they, too, abandoned him at the end of 1919 and turned him over to the Bolsheviks for trial and execution. No other White regime or leader elsewhere proved any better, and between June 1919 and early 1920 they all suffered military and political defeat. Meanwhile, American troops withdrew from northern Russia in June 1919. In December, all American troops finally began to withdraw from Siberia, the last leaving by April 1920.

Diplomatically, the Wilson government remained intransigent and on August 10, 1920, formally articulated its policy of nonrecognition. The occasion was a request from the Italian Government for a policy statement to help settle the war then raging between Poland and Russia, which had been unwisely initiated early in 1920 by the invasion of Russian territory by newly reconstituted Poland in an effort to grab what it could of the formerly White-held territories. The then Secretary of State, Bainbridge Colby, replied to the Italian request by stating that, while the United States favored a Polish-Russian armistice, the Soviet regime was "based upon the negation of every principle of honor and good faith, and every usage and convention underlying the whole structure of international law," that Communist practice and ideology meant "no compact or agreement made with a non-Bolshevist government can have any moral force for them," and that, insofar as diplomatic relations were concerned, the Soviets would merely use their diplomatic corps for intrigues and inciting revolts. In October 1920, the Russians and Poles agreed to an armistice, and by the Treaty of Riga in 1921 established a boundary line, in Poland's favor, some 150–200 miles to the east of the so-called Curzon line suggested in 1919 by Lord Curzon and the Paris Peace Conference.

America's Russian policy was a failure. As even the sharpest critics of the Soviet regime have admitted, American and, even more, European intervention only prolonged the Civil War and in the process brutalized society to the point where force and terror became a way of political life, wiped out whatever humanitarian and democratic traits the Bolsheviks once possessed, and opened the way for the later and worse totalitarianism in Russia. It also excluded Russia from a responsible role in international affairs. All these factors only made dealing with Germany (as Wilson had recognized in 1917), and later Japan, all that much more difficult, if not impossible. Nonrecognition served no useful diplomatic purpose and could not be justified (as was attempted) by arguing that the Bolsheviks had repudiated Russia's debts when none of the Allies was prepared to make reparations for the damages their intervention in the Civil War had caused. The policy estranged the United States and Russia and in 1919 intensified the Red Scare at home, which was led nationally by Attorney General A. Mitchell Palmer. This intolerance rebounded against the administration in the 1920 election and opened the way for the Republicans of the 1920's and later to oppose nationalist liberation movements by discrediting them as Communist-inspired.

The business of the Paris Peace Conference frustrated Wilson no less than the Russian situation, although the brutal realities of power politics were more responsible for the alleged failure of the resulting settlements than was Wilson's personality or policies. He acceded to Italy's incorporating the South Tyrol, and thereby 200,000 Austrians, but felt the Italians were "obsessed" over expansion into the eastern Adriatic. He adamantly opposed Italy's claim to the port of Fiume, which he insisted should either belong to Yugoslavia or perhaps become a Free City. In fact, the secret Treaty of London of 1915 under which Italy had entered the war indicated that Fiume would go to Serbia (now Yugoslavia), and on the basis of nationality and necessity (Fiume was the major Adriatic outlet for Yugoslavia, Hungary, Rumania, and Czechoslovakia, while Italy already had Trieste), Wilson was clearly right. The Italians remained obstinate. Foreign Minister Baron Sidney Sonino accused America of "trying to recover her virginity at Italy's expense by invoking the purity of principles," and on April 23, 1919, Wilson publicly refuted Italian claims to Fiume. This caused Italian Premier Vittorio Orlando to leave the conference in a huff, and it set off violent jingoist demonstrations in Italy. The Allies, too, were infuriated with Wilson, especially Lloyd George, who believed that, while Wilson was right on Fiume, it was more important to appease Italy. Eventually, Wilson prevailed to the extent that negotiations between Italy and Yugoslavia established Fiume as a Free City in 1920, only to have Italy seize it in 1922. The issue served to strain Anglo-American as well as Italo-American relations, and in April 1919 it provided Senator Lodge with a chance to stir Italian Americans against Wilson by insisting that Fiume was vital to Italy's security.

In the Pacific, the principles of a liberal peace ran smack against Japan's determination to take the former German colonies of the Mariana, Caroline, and Marshall islands, as well as Germany's former railroad and mining concessions, and Kiaochow Bay on Shantung Peninsula. The Paris conferees, with some misgivings, granted the Japanese mandates over the islands, but Wilson's own principles, his delegation, the American Minister to China, Paul Reinsch, and an American public aroused by missionary propaganda urged that Shantung be returned to China. The Chinese, however, had compromised their own position in 1918 when the government in Peking accepted $20 million in loans from the Japanese, who were allowed to take over police functions in Shantung. The British (and French) were bound to support Japan's claims both by the general obligation of the Anglo-Japanese Alliance and by the specific terms of a secret agreement concluded in February 1917. The Japanese threatened not to sign the Treaty of Versailles unless their demands were met.

When this issue arose during the difficulties with Italy, the President had to give in, securing only a verbal pledge from the Japanese that they would return political sovereignty over Shantung to China. Wilson said privately that it was "the best that could be had out of a dirty past," but in China announcement of the compromise touched off virulent nationalist protests, which became the starting point for the May Fourth Movement aimed at restoring full sovereignty in all China. It also caused the Chinese delegation in Paris, which was not allowed to register a formal reservation over the Shantung settlement, to refuse to sign the Treaty of Versailles. In the United States the Wilson administration was accused of betraying China and the Fourteen Points. Minister Reinsch resigned his post, and anti-Japanese politicians in the Western states, abetted by Senator Lodge's denunciation of Japan as the "Prussia of the East," again raised the specter of a "yellow peril" while agitating for Oriental exclusion laws.

While the Fiume and Shantung issues aroused passions disproportionate to their political significance, the statesmen at Paris proceeded with drafting a peace treaty for Germany. The opinion which prevailed afterward was that Clemenceau and Lloyd George "bamboozled" Wilson (as John Maynard Keynes put it in his influential *The Economic Consequences of the Peace* in late 1919) into imposing a *Diktat* on Germany, which was disarmed, shorn of territory, population, and colonies, made to accept a "war guilt" clause, and burdened with impossible reparations. Certainly, the peace was not one between equals, nor was it without indemnities, but there is little likelihood that this could or should have been so in 1919. As noted earlier, Wilson had taken a "punitive" turn toward Germany in 1918, which was reinforced by Germany's harsh dealings with the Russians over the Treaty of Brest-Litovsk. Nonetheless, the Treaty of Versailles was intended primarily not to keep Germany in political or economic shackles but to prevent future German aggression and to respond to the demands of the predominant political nationalism (especially national self-determination) and the economic views of the era. Limiting Germany's Army to 100,000 men—half of what might have been allowed—stemmed chiefly from French fears regarding security. French occupation of the western Rhineland and German demilitarization of the eastern area were also a security measure and less punitive than the original French demand for detachment of the western area from Germany. Most important, Germany remained intact at the war's end, and the Allies remained committed to Germany's unity and to its full sovereignty and administration of its own affairs. Territory or population lost by making Danzig a Free City and establishing a corridor across East Prussia was inevitable once Poland was reconstituted, especially in view of the universal belief (as in the Fiume case) that independent nations should have access to the sea. Similarly, the minority German population in the Sudetenland was subordinated to the military and economic necessities of making Czechoslovakia a state with defensible frontiers by incorporating all of Bohemia, a fact that Adolf Hitler would understand only too well, and which became painfully and embarrassingly obvious in 1938–39. The ban on German-Austrian unity affected the Austrians, not the Germans, and no one questioned returning Alsace-Lorraine to France. The Saar's rich coal mines were given to France for fifteen years as an economic indemnity, after which time the region was returned by plebiscite to Germany.

The famous Article 231, or "war guilt" clause, of the Treaty of Versailles was less a judgment than a political compromise. Wilson would not allow the Allies to include the total cost of the war in the calculation of German reparations but agreed that the Allies might appease their public by establishing Germany's theoretical responsibility for war costs, an idea divined by John Foster Dulles, then a financial adviser to the American delegation. Hence, Article 231 made "the aggression of Germany and her allies" responsible for war costs, but Article 232 immediately acknowledged that German resources were inadequate to make complete reparation. As for the reparations, the Americans favored setting a fixed sum based on Germany's capacity to pay, insisting, as did their financial adviser, Norman Davis, that Europe's social and economic problems were directly related to a practical reparations solution that allowed Germany to prosper.

Any fixed sum that pleased the Germans was bound to infuriate the French, who insisted that German reparations be set for the first few years only while a Reparations Commission determined a final bill based on costs rather than capacity to pay. Lloyd George at first favored the moderate American approach but then acceded to French pressure and his own public opinion, thus tipping the balance against Wilson. He insisted on including military separation allowances and pensions as part of the civil damages, which virtually doubled Germany's obligations. Wilson gave in partly from fatigue and partly because he thought this would only increase England's percentage share of a fixed, modest reparations bill. He insisted that the Allies pay to the United States their almost $10 billion in debts incurred during and after the war. He refused to allow these to be linked to reparations, fearing both adverse public opinion and that the procedure would, in effect, make the United States the guarantor of German reparations and load the American money market with tax-free German bonds, while depreciating Liberty Bonds and reducing U.S. Government revenue. Wilson worked hard to moderate reparations, but by not really considering war-debts cancellation (even though cancellation of such huge and unprecedented debts would have brought sharp Republican, even some Democratic, criticism), he missed a chance to kill at once the reparations issue—the most politically poisonous issue of the succeeding decades.

German Foreign Minister Brockdorff-Rantzau summarily rejected the preliminary peace terms on May 7, 1919, and in the next six weeks the United States and the Allies made four more compromises. They agreed to a plebiscite in Upper Silesia, despite fears that German industrialists would defeat a legitimate Polish majority and its interests; Germany was promised admission to the League of Nations "in the early future"; the French said they would evacuate the Rhineland sooner than the stipulated fifteen years if the Germans met their obligations; and Germany was allowed to offer a reparations plan. The Germans still did not want to sign, but no party would form a government and accept the political (or military) consequences of rejection. Therefore, on June 28, 1919, the Germans signed the Treaty of Versailles, while insisting that the terms had been "imposed."

The Treaty of Versailles, emerging from a welter of conflicting interests and passions, was neither written by nor drawn up for angels. Perhaps its worst feature, as the French ultranationalist Jacques Bainville said at the time, was that it was "too soft for being so hard." It depended essentially on German willingness to fulfill its obligations rather than on either the weak Control Commission that scarcely supervised disarmament or the few remaining occupation forces. Within less than a decade, Germany had the highest standard of living in Europe, and in a few years, in the 1930's, it spent more on armaments than it ever paid in reparations. For Wilson, the most important achievement was that he, more than anyone else, had established the League of Nations and had had its Covenant written into the Treaty of Versailles. Accordingly, he believed, all change and growth in international affairs, as well as the revision of outworn treaties and resolution of conflicts, would be achieved under the rule of law. Wilson believed that Article X of the Covenant, by which the League members agreed "to protect and preserve as against external aggression the territorial integrity and existing political independence of all members of the League," was neither an unconstitutional advance commitment of the United States to any League action nor a commitment of the League to maintain the *status quo*. Rather, this guarantee—which, he told the Senate Foreign Relations Committee, was more moral, and therefore "higher," than legal—was an effort to take the nations of the world out of their Hobbesian state of warfare and move them toward a system that provided for both rational solution of conflicts and genuine collective security for all, as opposed to imperial balances of power.

To achieve these transcendent goals, Wilson had made numerous concessions to the British, French, and Italians, while at the same time seeking to satisfy conservative American demands by getting the Allies to accede to reservations to the Covenant that allowed members to withdraw from the League, exempted domestic questions from League jurisdiction, and stated that the Covenant did not contravene "regional understandings like the Monroe Doctrine." When Wilson left the Paris Peace Conference, he had to know from the public silence in Europe that contrasted with the nearly hysterical welcome he had received on arrival, from the disaffections in his own ranks, and from the protracted, bitter bargaining sessions over a period of six months, that the emerging peace settlement was far from being his alone or all to his liking. But to the extent that one national leader might impose his will upon others, Wilson had gone as far as was politically possible in achieving a peace and creating a system under the League of Nations whereby both liberal America's and the world's best interests (inseparable in Wilson's mind) would be realized.

Wilson's greatest failure proved to be not the positions he took in Paris but his unyielding stance at home. Two major groups opposed the peace terms and the League of Nations. The first was the so-called Irreconcilables, approximately sixteen senators who would not consent to the Treaty of Versailles under any circumstances. This group, which was not monolithic, was composed of six men of advanced progressive standing, eight who were highly conservative, and two (Senators James Reed of Missouri and Charles Thomas of Colorado) whose opposition was extraordinarily personal. In varying degrees, Senators Borah, Johnson, Joseph I. France of Maryland, Robert La Follette of Wisconsin, Asle Gronna of North Dakota, and George Norris of Nebraska believed that Wilson had abandoned domestic progressivism, that he accepted too punitive a peace for Germany, and that he linked the United States to a new dollar diplomacy and an imperial British and French League of Nations that aimed at maintaining the *status quo*. Also, Borah and Senator France were enraged at Wilson's intervention in Russia and his nonrecognition of the Bolsheviks. Basically, these men believed that America could best serve mankind by putting its own house in order. Their opposition to a collective security system through the League of Nations derived less from an isolationist or "fortress America" attitude than from anxiety over the use of force as an instrument of policy and a fear that force would be used far less to curb aggression than to thwart change. The eight conservatives (Frank Brandegee of Connecticut, Albert Fall of New Mexico, Bert Fernald of Maine, Philander Knox of Pennsylvania, Joseph M. McCormick of Illinois, George Moses of New Hampshire, Miles Poindexter of Washington, and Lawrence Sherman of Illinois) were essentially opponents of Wilson's New Freedom legislation and of progressive or liberal reforms abroad and preferred the unilateral use of American power in the international arena to any form of international cooperation. The Irreconcilables were a powerful group, but by themselves could not have blocked the Treaty of Versailles.

The Republican majority, led by Senator Lodge, presented the strongest opposition to Wilson. It was nearly inevitable that the Republicans should try to make political capital out of the peace settlement. Domestically, Wilson's first administration had been the most successful in American history, and in his second term he had made war and won the peace. The Republicans were determined to do something that would enhance their position—or diminish that of the Democrats—before battling Wilson, or his successor, in the 1920 elections. The Republicans had benefited from their principled and expedient partisanship in the 1918 congressional elections and in the Fiume and Shantung disputes. Additionally, not only did Lodge's conservative, imperialist outlook clash with Wilson's world views, but these two "scholars in politics" disliked one another intensely. For personal and political reasons, a fight loomed.

What was not necessary was Wilson's playing into Lodge's hands. In March 1919, Lodge announced a pledge from thirty-nine Republican senators and senators-elect that they would not accept the League in its current form. Wilson replied that the Treaty of Versailles and League Covenant were indivisible, implying an unalterable package. During the spring and summer of 1919, Lodge and the Senate Foreign Relations Committee drew up a series of reservations providing for America's unilateral determination whether it had met its obligations in the event it decided to leave the League, the sanctity of the Monroe Doctrine, the nonrestriction by reparations of German-American trade, and congressional assent to membership in the International Labor Organization. None of the reservations was serious enough to alter the substance of commitment to the League, even if Wilson felt they reflected less than full American support of League responsibilities. Article X came under attack, chiefly as a threat to American sovereignty and congressional war-making authority, but these "dangers" were largely imaginary. No guarantees had been made under it; external aggression was hard to define (especially in border disputes); only Congress could declare war; and presidential authority to act without congressional sanction was already well established in cases of intervention in Latin America.

Wilson would not accept any reservations, and with the poor advice of Democratic Minority Leader Gilbert Hitchcock of Nebraska, decided against any Democratic-Republican compromises in the Senate. On September 3, 1919, he set off on his projected nationwide tour to rouse public sentiment. Following twenty days and 8,000 miles of travel, including thirty-two major speeches and eight minor ones, he collapsed after speaking in Pueblo, Colorado. After returning to Washington, he suffered a stroke and paralysis on the left side of his face and body. Although he was out of danger fairly soon, he remained incapacitated for the next six months, during which time he nonetheless continued to maintain his grip over the voting loyalties of the Democratic senators.

The Senate voted three times on the Treaty of Versailles. Two votes were taken on November 19, 1919: The treaty, with fourteen Lodge reservations, was defeated 55–39, Wilson Democrats joining the Irreconcilables in a majority; the treaty, without the Lodge reservations, was defeated 53–38, Republicans joining the Irreconcilables to form this majority. In the third and final vote, on March 19, 1920, the treaty, with the Lodge reservations, gained a 49–35 simple majority, failing by 7 votes to gain the two-thirds majority needed for ratification. Twenty-one Democrats had defied Wilson's appeal for a negative vote, but twenty-three Southern Democrats, loyal to President, party, and section —and probably not enamored of the League—joined with the Irreconcilables to defeat the treaty and virtually end any hope that the United States might join the League of Nations.

Wilson was as responsible for this development as anyone, and it is likely, as his biographer Arthur Link has suggested, that in the end "disease had dethroned his reason." Certainly his attitude was uncompromising, and his dealings with the Senate, especially in the face of powerful opposition, were high-handed and politically unreal. Having gone so far to establish his "parliament of man," and having made so many compromises, Wilson, by not being able to compromise at the end, added that much more, and needless, tragedy to his most ambitious undertaking. As for Lodge, his motives may never be fathomed, but it is clear from his imperial views and political opportunism throughout 1918–19 (and his adamant opposition thereafter to joining the League on any terms) that he would be relentless in squeezing political advantage out of every international issue, and that he knew only too well how to exploit Wilson's personal failings. His reservations were as much a tactical maneuver as a substantive proposal. In 1920, Wilson and the Democrats were left with the vain hope that the November elections would provide them with a "solemn referendum" on the League of Nations, while the Republicans, increasingly confident that the Democratic party was discredited and in disarray, insisted that the only way in which the United States might join the League of Nations would be under a Republican administration.

3

Politics and the Diplomacy of the Dollar

War generally catalyzes, or revolutionizes, transformations long in process, and the results are seen not only in new domestic political structures but in world political or diplomatic ones as well. Certainly this was the case with the First World War. In Europe, the Austro-Hungarian Empire, long in process of dissolution and long allied to Germany, was now broken into its successor states, several of which—Poland, Czechoslovakia, and Yugoslavia—came to ally themselves with France against Germany. Similarly, Czarist Russia, long in domestic political trouble and allied to France, underwent the Bolshevik Revolution and saw the Baltic states of Estonia, Latvia, and Lithuania, together with Finland, achieve independence. Then the new Soviet Union, partly by its own choice and partly by American, British, and French design, was largely excluded from the European diplomatic scene. The United States, meanwhile, moved from a small part in pre-1914 European Continental diplomacy to a major one during and after the war, even without political alliances. The United States sought to rehabilitate defeated Germany, restrain victorious Great Britain and France—and the Soviet Union—and maintain a new European balance of power under the aegis of the dollar.

When the First World War ended, there was no possibility that the United States would assume an isolationist (in the sense of complete withdrawal) position in world affairs. Economic factors alone demanded otherwise. Between 1914 and 1919, the United States changed from a debtor nation, owing $3.7 billion to foreign creditors, to the world's leading creditor, to which was owed some $12.5 billion, including $10.3 billion in Allied war debts. By the end of the decade, this foreign indebtedness had swollen to $21 billion. Further, by 1919 the United States alone accounted for nearly half the world's manufactured goods, a

44

sixth of the world's total exports, and an eighth of its imports. The roster of American corporations with extensive overseas subsidiaries and investments was very long, including Standard Oil, General Motors, Ford, International Business Machines, Singer, and International Harvester. By 1929, American national income equaled the aggregate of twenty-three other nations, including Great Britain, France, Germany, Canada, and Japan. Assessing it all in 1930, the liberal theologian Reinhold Niebuhr said that the United States had become "the real empire of modern civilization," whose legions were not arms but dollars, and that the ultimate question was whether America could "develop a political genius equal to the responsibilities thrust upon us by our imperial power."

The Republicans who ruled in the 1920's understood—or claimed to understand—the nature of the problems confronting America in that decade and the solutions required. Certainly they recognized the interrelation between political and economic affairs, and the way in which the material and financial needs of the war had moved the United States into a dominant position, while making Europe's war-torn societies—England and France as much or more than Germany—dependent on American capital. Government and financial leaders sought to preserve and expand America's economic and financial primacy while using the nation's vast material and monetary resources to create a favorable international political climate, which in turn would reinforce economic opportunities. In Europe, this meant underwriting German political and economic stability, while shielding it from French political and economic demands. At the same time, Republican statesmen eschewed not only political commitments (such as Article X of the League Covenant) that might have involved the United States in European or Asian conflicts but any international arrangement that they thought might infringe upon American prerogatives. Correspondingly, the Republicans also pursued domestic economic policies that were intensely nationalistic.

For a while, these procedures seemed to work well, and the United States appeared to have achieved the best of two worlds: economic primacy in a world of industrial and financial interdependence and virtual freedom from political responsibilities or liabilities in an increasingly nationalist world. By the early 1930's, however, the contradictions implicit in Republican policies were laid bare. Combined with the abundant lack of political and economic good faith elsewhere in the world, they led to consequences of catastrophic proportion.

Several factors provided an atmosphere conducive to Republican policy. First, there was the political effect of the 1920 elections. The Republicans' triumph was not surprising, for they had been the majority party from the Civil War to the formation of the 1930's New Deal coalition. Wilson had been elected a minority President in 1912 only because of the split between regular and Bull Moose Republicans, and then he barely won re-election over Hughes despite being an incumbent campaigning on a record of peace and prosperity. But the magnitude of the Republican victory in 1920 was enormous. Warren G. Harding and Calvin Coolidge swamped James M. Cox and Franklin D. Roosevelt by some 16 million popular votes to 9 million and 404 electoral votes to 127, winning every state outside of the Democratic Solid South. The Republicans also won 26 of 32 Senate contests, 300 of 435 seats in the House of Representatives, and 23 of 27 gubernatorial races.

The extent to which the vote can be taken as a direct repudiation of Wilson's foreign policy or commitment to the League of Nations is difficult to measure. The Democratic platform called for immediate ratification of the Treaty of Versailles and the League Covenant "without reservations which would impair its essential integrity." Cox and Roosevelt were fairly vigorous and consistent on that point, although by the end of the campaign they made clear that to achieve ratification they would accept almost any Senate reservation consistent with the League and legitimate congressional Constitutional demands. The Republicans muddled the issue. Lodge set somewhat the tone of Republican policies in his convention keynote address when he said "we must be now and ever for Americanism and Nationalism, and against internationalism." He, George Harvey, and the Irreconcilable Senator McCormick of Illinois were dominant figures among the coterie that achieved Harding's nomination and blocked an effort by less imperialist-oriented Republicans to have a platform plank advocating entry into the League of Nations with reservations. Instead, the platform called for "no acceptance of Mr. Wilson's treaty without reservations," an emphasis that was more than semantic.

During the campaign, prominent Republicans like former President Taft and Elihu Root insisted that Harding favored entry into the League with reservations, and thirty-one leading Republicans, including Root, Taft, Hughes, Hoover, and President Nicholas Murray Butler of Columbia University, signed a public manifesto on October 14 stating that the best way to ensure American entry into the League was to vote for Harding. Other Republicans, such as Borah and Johnson, said that Harding favored outright rejection of the League. Harding himself had twice voted for the League with Lodge reservations, but that was as much out of party regularity as out of conviction. During the campaign, he took not less than fourteen different positions on the League, although he probably expressed his truest sentiments on October 7, 1920, when he said he did not want to clarify America's obligations under the League Covenant and Article X but to forget about them.

Harding's position received support from such unlikely sources as both the *New Republic* and the *Nation,* which opposed Article X of the Covenant and supported not Harding or Cox for President but, respectively, the Socialist and Farmer-Labor candidates. Politics in 1920, especially the League, was making strange bedfellows. Generally, liberals believed that the Treaty of Versailles was too harsh, and that the League of Nations, and especially Article X, was a British and French imperial institution to maintain the *status quo.* Conservatives like Root feared that Article X emphasized the *status quo* at the expense of inevitable change, but basically conservatives were concerned less about the moral basis of the Treaty of Versailles than that it would ensure French (and British) hegemony over Germany (and therefore Europe) at the expense of American economic interests, and that American obligations under the League Covenant, especially as envisioned by Wilson, were too extensive.

The Treaty of Versailles and the League Covenant were assailed from the Left and the Right, for different reasons. Further, in 1920 domestic issues were intertwined with those of foreign policy, which led to an across-the-board repudiation of the Wilson administration. The postwar era was marked by severe economic dislocation, including bitter strikes in major industries such as coal and steel, rising unemployment, rapid inflation yet a sharp decline in the price of farmers' products, severe urban housing and credit shortages, race riots, and the Red Scare, or Palmer raids, of 1919, which exacerbated political and social tensions.

The effect of these factors was well illustrated in New York State. Between March 1919 and April 1920, Senator Clayton R. Lusk from upstate Cortland headed a committee that carried out a series of investigations and police raids on institutions like the Rand School of Social Science and made much propaganda about subversive activities but failed to achieve a single conviction. At the end of his witch hunt, Senator Lusk carefully burned his committee's papers. The state was affected, too, by the major industrial strikes of 1919, and in New York City, where the housing shortage was acute, the consumer price index rose 28 percent during 1919–20.

The state of New York voted overwhelmingly for Harding, and so did 61 of New York City's 62 assembly districts. Most revealing were the results in the Twenty-third Assembly District in Kings County (Brooklyn), the Eighth and Seventeenth in New York County (Manhattan), and the Third and Fourth in Bronx County. The populace in these districts was at least four-fifths immigrant (or children of immigrants)—German, Irish, Italian, and Jewish—and very poor. All five districts had voted for Wilson in 1916. In 1918, they had elected Socialists to the State Assembly, who were expelled by the Assembly for their anti-war attitudes. In September 1920, in a special election, these five assembly districts re-elected these same five Socialists by even wider margins over fusion Democratic-Republican candidates.

In November 1920, however, these poor immigrant and "radical" districts voted overwhelmingly for Harding (by 4 to 1 against Cox), while giving a strong second place to the Socialist presidential candidate, Eugene V. Debs, then in a federal penitentiary, convicted under the 1917 Espionage Act for opposition to the draft. These districts also split their tickets and voted overwhelmingly for Democrat Al Smith for governor over the Republican candidate and winner, Judge Nathan Miller. In short, people whose politics had little in common with the Republicans of 1920 now voted for Harding because they wished to repudiate the Wilson administration for what they considered its failure both at home and abroad.

Prevalent also was deep-seated disillusionment among the intelligentsia. Of course, they recoiled at the bloodiness of war; as the hero of Ernest Hemingway's *A Farewell to Arms* (1929) said, he "was always embarrassed by the words sacred, glorious, and sacrifice, and the expression 'in vain,'" because he had seen nothing sacred on the battlefield, and the sacrifices resembled the Chicago stockyards. Even more, intellectuals now felt that they had either been naïve—or deceived—to have believed, as so many once did, that the Great Crusade would serve not only as the means to defeat autocracy but also as the catalyst that would persuade men of good faith to democratize, liberalize, and humanize societies everywhere. Between 1914 and 1918, intellectuals had "put their science, art, and reason into the service of their governments," lamented the French writer Romain Rolland in 1919, only to discover that "the states as well as their social parties make intellectuals into servants and instruments. Such was the case in the autocracies; such is the case in the bourgeois democracies; and such will be the case in the proletarian revolutions." Or, as F. Scott Fitzgerald would later recollect, his generation of the 1920's had grown up "to find all Gods dead, all wars fought, and all faiths in man shaken."

The results of the war, then, stood in disrepute almost from the moment the war ended, and shortly afterward there began to appear a rash of journalistic and historical "revisionist" literature, encouraged by the Bolshevik release of Czarist government documents, which questioned whether Germany had been responsible for the outbreak of the war in 1914. In the United States in 1922, Albert Jay Nock's *Myth of a Guilty Nation* blamed the war on the French and the Russians, while John Kenneth Turner's *Shall It Be Again?* said Wilson had led the United States into war to preserve Wall Street investments. In December 1923, Senator Robert Owen, a liberal Democrat from Oklahoma, delivered a forty-thousand-word speech in the Senate that said the French and Russians were responsible for the outbreak of hostilities, and in 1926 the sociologically oriented historian, Harry Elmer Barnes, published *The Genesis of the World War,* which argued that Germany had been neither as nationalist nor as imperialist and militaristic as the Triple Entente of England, France, and Russia. In 1928, Sidney B. Fay, a highly regarded historian, published his two-volume *The Origins of the World War,* which, while not exonerating the Germans, contained enough criticism of the French and Russians to allow revisionist defenders of Germany to claim that their arguments had been vindicated.

Paralleling these developments was the revival of popular sentiment for Germans and Germany. German-Americans were the largest "hypenate" group in America, and while sometimes harshly treated during the war, they had stood high prior to 1914, owing largely to their success in adapting to the values of middle-class society and making the most of their opportunities for political, economic, and social upward mobility. After the war, they wasted no time in forming organizations such as, in 1919, the Steuben Society (appropriately named after Friedrich Wilhelm Steuben, who had been Inspector General of the American Army during the Revolutionary War), which promoted cultural exchanges, distributed revisionist literature, and reprinted such classic works as Albert Bernhardt Faust's *The German Element in the United States: With Special Reference to Its Political, Moral, Social and Educational Influence* (1927), two volumes that extolled the contribution of German immigrants to abolition, civil service reform, sound money, peace congresses, and personal liberty.

At the same time, American officials abroad sent back glowing reports about the rehabilitation of Germany under the Weimar Republic. As early as 1922, the British Ambassador in Berlin, Viscount D'Abernon, was complaining that American businessmen were "pro-German" and not only opposed reparations but even denied Germany's war guilt. The first postwar American Ambassador to Germany was Alanson B. Houghton, chairman of the board of Corning Glass Works, who had done graduate work study at Göttingen. Houghton was sympathetically disposed toward Germany and had a keen eye for the possibilities of American investment. At the outset of his stay in Berlin, he was somewhat concerned about radicals and the antireparations, anti-Western-powers sentiment in Germany, but by 1925 he was convinced that Weimar Germany aimed only at economic rehabilitation and would be a bulwark against Bolshevism. Houghton's successor in Berlin from 1925 through 1929 was Jacob Gould Schurman, who had been president of Cornell University for nearly thirty years and during 1921–25 had been minister to China, which was torn by civil war and not nearly so attractive to him as the Weimar Republic. Schurman, too, had studied in Germany, at Heidelberg, and he moved easily and was received cordially in the highest political, economic, and academic circles. He became enamored of Germany, which was doing "wonderfully well," he wrote to a friend in 1925. The authorities were meeting their obligations, the people were working hard, and "the whole land today looks like a garden." Schurman got along very well with President Paul von Hindenburg, greatly admired Foreign Minister Gustav Stresemann, and did everything in his power to promote political and cultural relations between the United States and Germany—and above all, American investment in Germany. The German people, he told the New York Chamber of Commerce in 1928, wanted and needed American friendship, and those who advocated a return to the ways of the Old Empire, or a new socialism, were voices in the wilderness. The people of Germany were bearing a colossal burden "bravely, heroically even," but radicalism there would never succeed.

Schurman's successor as ambassador during 1930–32 was Frederic M. Sackett, a lawyer, businessman, and banker from Kentucky, who had served the Wilson administration in wartime, and was elected to the Senate in 1928. Sackett proved to be a very poor analyst of the political scene, but this did not dissuade him from encouraging American investment in Germany and from becoming a sympathetic, if sometimes indiscreet, spokesman for the German Government in its battle to end reparations.

The German Government was extremely grateful for American assistance and sought to encourage American good will. Their first ambassador to the United States in the postwar period was Otto Wiedfeldt, a member of the board of directors of Krupp Works, who was chosen because it was felt he would get along well with the big-business mentality of the administration in Washington and interest America in investing in Germany. Wiedfeldt encouraged his government's tendency to seek American good will as a means of protecting Germany from French political and economic demands. His successor in 1924 was a career diplomat, Ago von Maltzan, who had been closely associated with the eastern, or Russian, orientation in German foreign policy in the 1920's. Nonetheless, he also quickly saw the value of the United States as a counterbalance to French demands, and he skillfully courted American opinion. When, for example, President Friedrich Ebert died in 1925 (his passing was lamented in popular and diplomatic American circles, and many newspapers compared him to Abraham Lincoln) and was succeeded by Paul von Hindenburg, Maltzan, at Foreign Minister Gustav Stresemann's behest, waged a skillful and successful campaign to persuade American officials that their fears of a revival of militarism were unfounded.

Hindenburg, he insisted, was a man of duty and honor who would not endanger the Republic. In a short time, Maltzan reported to Berlin with evident satisfaction that President Coolidge had let him know that Hindenburg was not a barrier to improved relations between the United States and Germany, and that Americans were already referring to "dear old Hindy."

In 1928, Friederich W. von Prittwitz und Gaffron became ambassador to the United States. Prittwitz was a career diplomat, more liberal than most of his colleagues (he would resign from the diplomatic service as soon as Hitler became Chancellor in 1933). More than most, he pursued good relations with the United States as an end rather than as a tactic to escape the French or the Treaty of Versailles. Between 1928 and 1933, he and his staff, and numerous German consuls general, won great favor in the United States and successfully encouraged American investment in Germany. In turn, they insistently reported to their own government, as one consul general, Otto Vollbehr, said in late December 1932, that the United States was "not only the best friend but actually the only friend which the Reich has in international society."

The attitudes that prevailed in the 1920's, from the liberal disillusion over the origins and outcome of the war and its effect upon domestic as well as international affairs to the good favor in which Germany stood (a contrast as well with the seeming intransigence of the British, and especially the French, over matters political and economic, especially war debts), were politically and socially nonpartisan. They provided also an atmosphere that was far more hospitable than hostile to the aims of Republican diplomacy, rooted in an essentially conservative world view. This is not to say that, in many respects, there was not as much continuity as change in policy between the Wilsonians and the Republicans of the 1920's, many of whom had served the previous Democratic administration in wartime administrative agencies or in advisory capacities at the peace negotiations. Certainly the Wilsonians and the Republicans shared something of a consensus, or similar viewpoint, with regard to the perfidy of the Allies, the almost divine-right assumption about the legitimacy and necessity of maintaining American economic primacy in a world that would be receptive to, and ordered by, American capital and capitalists, and the need to reintegrate Germany politically and economically into the mainstream of the Western world.

But there were important differences between Wilson's conceptions and those of his successors. For Wilson, the League of Nations and Article X were not intended solely to maintain a *status quo* for the benefit of the imperialist powers. They were the first steps toward creating, if not a parliament of man, then a forum for the rational argument and adjudication of international disputes, a way to ensure that change, however slow, would occur by peaceful means and have the benefit of multilateral guarantees. Wilson recognized the extent to which this marked a departure from the imperial or balance-of-power ideas that had prevailed in thinking about international affairs. He also recognized the extent to which the American people would have to be educated to new responsibilities—one reason, perhaps, that he opposed any compromise in the fight over the Treaty of Versailles.

From the Republican standpoint, political guarantees were as undesirable as they were superfluous, not merely because, as men like Hughes sometimes charged, they held nations to the *status quo,* but because they might limit the choices open to the United States in a conflict and might even be used against the United States in areas where Americans presumed the right to act unilaterally to preserve special interests. The Republicans really had little interest in educating the public either to new responsibilities or to abridgment of traditiónal American "rights," especially when they felt the public might be bothered by such responsibilities. They believed that their superior management techniques would allow them to achieve all of their own, and certain goals of the Wilson administration, without any political or economic cost or surrender of old ways.

President-elect Harding had taken the earliest occasion he could to signal his administration's intention to avoid any political commitments or multilateral guarantees when, two days after his election, he declared the vote a mandate that made the issue of American entry into the League of Nations as "dead as slavery." In his inaugural address in March 1921, he said his administration would shun virtually any overseas responsibility, and in his first address to Congress, in April, he declared, in typical hyperbole, that "in the existing League of Nations, world-governing with its superpowers, this Republic will have no part." Secretary of State Hughes, a man of more worldly views, was given to more cautious and legalistic language. But from the moment he took control of the State Department in 1921 he abandoned the position he had taken in 1919–20. At that time, he felt that the United States should seek entry into the League on modified terms. Now, however, he turned his back on the League and its related activities, even to the point of advising American judges not to join its affiliated, but virtually powerless, Permanent Court of International Justice, popularly known as the World Court.

With the Treaty of Versailles and the linked League Covenant dead issues in 1921, the United States remained technically at war with Germany until a congressional resolution of July 2, 1921, authorized an end to hostilities and conclusion of a separate peace. By August 25, 1921, American and German diplomats had negotiated the Treaty of

Berlin and exchanged ratification on November 11, 1921, three years after the Armistice. Germany granted to the United States all the rights accorded to other nations by the Treaty of Versailles. Thus, confiscated German property in the United States was mortgaged against American financial claims on Germany, and Americans were guaranteed treatment equal with that of citizens of other countries in the settlement of claims. However, the United States had none of the political or military responsibilities of the Treaty of Versailles. The Treaty of Berlin reflected the highly nationalist attitude of "having your cake and eating it" prevalent in the United States, and even Hughes admitted that the arrangements had to be swallowed with a "wry face." As Hugh R. Wilson, a very cautious and conservative career diplomat of the time later recollected, such a one-sided arrangement was unprecedented and virtually unbelievable. No one in the administration, of course, even wished to think about reviving the Treaty of Guarantee—which Wilson had negotiated in Paris, and which obligated the United States and Great Britain to aid France in the event of German aggression. This provision had died in the Senate Foreign Relations Committee during the fight over the Treaty of Versailles.

Nothing could have been further from the Harding administration's mind than to involve the United States in any system of collective security. In 1923, the European powers attempted to augment the power of the League Council through the Draft Treaty of Mutual Assistance, which would have authorized the League Council to designate an aggressor in the event of hostilities. The treaty's signatories would have been obligated to offer financial or military aid to the nation or nations under attack. Hughes responded coolly when the prospective treaty was presented to American officials early in 1924 and in June of that year said flatly that the United States's Constitutional machinery, combined with the fact that the country did not belong to the League of Nations, made acceptance impossible.

Another reason for American rejection of multilateral guarantees was revealed in the discussions in 1924 and 1925 over the Geneva Protocol for the Pacific Settlement of International Disputes. Article XII of the Covenant permitted a nation to resort to war if the League Council failed to reach a unanimous decision on resolving a dispute within ninety days, while Article XV exempted domestic questions from League jurisdiction. The Geneva Protocol envisioned strengthening the Covenant by providing for compulsory arbitration in disputes that the League Council could not settle, and it sought to extend the jurisdiction of the World Court to some allegedly domestic issues. A nation that signed the Geneva Protocol but refused to abide by League Council arbitration rulings would be judged an aggressor and subject to League sanctions. If one of the nations in a dispute was not a signatory of the Geneva Protocol, it would be invited to accept the Protocol; if it did not, and the ruling went against it, that nation would be subject to League sanctions. This latter aspect, however, did not extend the jurisdiction the League already had but sought to clarify it and perhaps give it more force.

The State Department solicitor, Charles C. Hyde, told Hughes in November 1924 that he felt compulsory arbitration and inclusion of nonsignatories threatened not only the American neutral rights to trade with all nations (even aggressors) in a dispute but also America's exclusive right of intervention in Latin America under the Monroe Doctrine and the Roosevelt Corollary. And the American Ambassador to Italy, Henry P. Fletcher, after talks with various European officials, told them and Hughes that he felt the Geneva Protocol so restricted American action "that it might easily be made to appear a new Holy Alliance." Hughes held to the Hyde-Fletcher view, and in a series of talks with the British Ambassador in January and February 1925, insisted that the Geneva Protocol threatened the Monroe Doctrine and the Roosevelt Corollary, as well as American neutral rights, and was even "a proposal of a concert against the United States."

These ideas bordered on the absurd. European nations had neither the capacity nor the desire to intervene against the United States in the Western Hemisphere, especially at the risk of upsetting European security. Nor, the State Department knew by its own soundings, did such signatories of the Geneva Protocol as Brazil, Chile, and Uruguay intend to seek redress against America by summoning the Old World to redress the balance of the New. In short, the administration raised the specter of iniquitous and cunning Europe in order to obscure its own determination to avoid any multilateral system of adjudication and guarantees. The consequence of this action was to allow the British, already wavering on the Geneva Protocol, to kill the proposal.

The Labour government of Ramsay MacDonald had undertaken the first negotiations for the Protocol with enthusiasm, partly to reassure the French and partly to get the French accustomed to negotiating and not be intransigent about every issue involving the Treaty of Versailles. But the Conservative government under Prime Minister Stanley Baldwin and Foreign Secretary Austen Chamberlain that came to power in November 1924 felt that the Protocol was too broad a commitment of British power and determined to push instead for faster revision of the Treaty of Versailles. The American response to British inquiries about the Protocol then reinforced their premises and principles. Thus, in March 1925, Foreign Secretary Chamberlain could tell the League Council that the Geneva Protocol was unacceptable because, so long as the United States did not sign it and remained outside the League of

Nations, sanctions against an aggressor would be useless and in case of war would only create an even more favorable balance of trade for the United States.

Even in a matter as relatively minor as the World Court, American policy offered no encouragement. From the turn of the century, leading Republicans, such as John Hay, Elihu Root, and Hughes, had favored American membership in an international tribunal, and in 1920 Root helped write the statute for the World Court, which functioned through a protocol separate from the Treaty of Versailles and was limited to matters of minor importance because it had jurisdiction only in cases where all parties to a dispute authorized it. In 1922, the World Court opened membership to all nations, including those not in the League, and with Harding's approval Hughes drafted a proposal for entry that included four reservations. These said that by joining the World Court the United States did not assume any League obligations. The United States also insisted that it be granted equal voice in the election of Court justices, that it determine its own financial obligations to the Court, and that the World Court statute not be amended without American consent.

Harding's death in the summer of 1923 delayed matters, but President Calvin Coolidge, after both his own election and Senator Lodge's death in November 1924, supported membership in the Court. His message to Congress of December 1924 and his inaugural address of March 1925 indicated this, while a fifth "reservation" was added that the United States not be bound by any advisory opinions handed down in matters that it had not voluntarily submitted for judgment. Led by the recalcitrant Borah (now chairman of the Senate Foreign Relations Committee), the fight in the Senate over adherence to the Court was bitter, and at times various Senators called out the names of foreign justices on the Court as if to indicate the Court would be hostile to American interests. There was also considerable, and predictable, public opposition, led by Colonel Robert McCormick's *Chicago Tribune;* even some thorny legal questions were raised by eminent jurists. But the Senate finally approved the legislation for adherence to the Court with Hughes's original four reservations and a slight rephrase of Coolidge's fifth, which stated that the Court could not hand down an advisory opinion in advance of a settlement on any matter affecting American interests without American approval. The Senate also insisted that all forty-eight nations then adhering to the World Court agree separately to all five American reservations.

Not only had Coolidge demanded almost literally as much as the most ardent opponents of World Court membership, but he proceeded in a lackadaisical manner to secure foreign agreement to the American reservations, rejecting in the spring of 1926 a League proposal for a con-

ference on the matter. Eventually, all forty-eight members approved the
first four reservations, and in September 1926 twenty-one offered to
negotiate on the fifth. But rather than risk any argument in the Senate,
Coolidge rejected the offer, thus ending prospects for American membership in the World Court. In 1929, Root worked out a new compromise
of the reservation arrangement whereby the United States would withdraw from the Court if it disapproved an advisory opinion, and President Herbert Hoover submitted the proposal to the Senate Foreign
Relations Committee. But there it remained bottled up until 1935, when
the Democratic leadership would make a final but futile effort to secure
American adherence. The better chance for membership was lost in the
1920's, however, not merely because of isolationist opposition, but because the Republican administration agreed with the fatal fifth reservation and demonstrated no leadership on the issue.

The international political achievement in which the Republican administration of the 1920's seemingly took most pride was the Kellogg-
Briand Pact (or Pact of Paris) of August 1928. Throughout the 1920's,
there had been sentiment among many public figures concerned with
international politics that the Western world's system of international law
served chiefly to legitimize and institutionalize war, and that it was
necessary instead to find some way to outlaw war. One exponent of this
effort, who coined the phrase "outlawry of war," was Salmon O. Levinson, a wealthy Chicago lawyer with many political contacts, including
Borah. In the spring of 1927, while visiting Paris, Levinson mentioned
to French Foreign Minister Aristide Briand the idea of a pact to outlaw
war. Briand was as high-minded a statesman as Europe produced in the
interwar decade, given both to securing French interests through security
treaties with the Little Entente of Czechoslovakia, Yugoslavia, and
Rumania and to seeking rapprochement with Germany, as evidenced in
his famous friendship and negotiations with Stresemann. Briand was
also deeply concerned over the poor state of French-American relations,
which undercut France's position vis-à-vis Germany. Hence, for reasons
of national interest as well as world peace, on April 6, 1927, the tenth
anniversary of America's entrance into the World War, Briand publicly
declared that France would subscribe with the United States to any
mutual agreement that would outlaw war between those two states.

Coolidge and Secretary of State Frank B. Kellogg suspected that
Briand was after a bilateral arrangement that might be construed as
some form of alliance, and he made no reply until a groundswell of
publicity demanded it. On June 11, the administration agreed to informal
diplomatic talks that might culminate in a treaty, but which would take
a long time to conclude. Within ten days, however, Briand produced a
draft proposal of a bilateral pact whereby the United States and France

condemned and renounced warfare as an instrument of national policy toward one another and agreed to resolve all bilateral disputes by pacific means.

The Coolidge administration then used the absence of Ambassador Myron T. Herrick from France as an excuse to delay negotiations; at a press conference on November 25, Coolidge suggested that the proposed treaty might even be unconstitutional, because it would deny Congress the right to declare war on France. But by December 1927, everyone—including Borah, who distrusted the French and wanted no pacts with them—agreed that something had to be done, whereupon Borah and Kellogg concluded that a multilateral pact that extended to as many nations as possible would earn the United States the plaudits of peace-making while playing down the French connection and virtually absolving everyone of any real commitment. As Borah publicly stated in February 1928, such a pact (which Kellogg formally had proposed late in December 1927) would not interfere with any other commitments—such as France's alliances with the Little Entente—and inasmuch as the pact had no provision for determining an aggressor, nor any enforcement machinery, a resort to war by any of the signatories released all the others from the pact and freed them to take whatever action they wished.

The Americans had outmaneuvered the French, who had little choice but to go along with the diplomatic proceedings. So did all the other great and small powers (excluding the uninvited Russians), who on August 27, 1928, signed (and thereafter adhered to) the Pact of Paris and thereby solemnly renounced war as an instrument of their national policy and agreed to resolve all disputes by pacific means. To be certain that the pact was as innocuous as the Americans had indicated it could be, most powers exchanged interpretive notes (a euphemism for reservations), asserting their right to defend themselves from attack and to determine when circumstances required a war of self-defense. Further, just prior to the signing, Kellogg conceded that, as regarded imperial nations with far-flung holdings, "wherever any government has special interests, it has a right to defend them, *whatever that degree of interest is.*"

When the pact came before the Senate for ratification in the autumn of 1928, two members of the old nonpartisan Irreconcilable coalition, George Moses (Republican) of New Hampshire and James Reed (Democrat) of Missouri, proposed three reservations that stated that the pact did not impair America's right to act in self-defense or unilaterally under the Monroe Doctrine, that it did not impose obligations on the United States to act in concert with other nations against any violator of the pact, and that it did not obligate the United States to the conditions of any treaty (such as that of Versailles) that it had not signed. Administration officials said the reservations were superfluous and would complicate matters diplomatically. They arranged a compromise whereby Borah and the Foreign Relations Committee offered the reservations as an explanatory report that expressed the sense of the Senate, while Vice-President Charles G. Dawes told reluctant senators that the Kellogg-Briand Pact and increased naval appropriations were "the declared and unified policy of the United States." The Senate passed the pact by 85 to 1 on January 15, 1929. Symbolically, Coolidge's pen ran dry as he fixed his signature to the pact.

In the years to come, the Kellogg-Briand Pact proved worthless, except as a moral yardstick. This was not merely because of its inherent flaws but largely because of the ways in which nations defined their expanding national interests and wars of self-defense and because of a lack of good faith in international dealings. The onus for the failure of the pact surely does not rest entirely with the United States, but the Coolidge administration must share in the blame. As Assistant Secretary of State William R. Castle, Jr., wrote in his diary in February 1928, the administration had gotten involved in the diplomatic negotiations only to outmaneuver the French: "the political trick has been turned and now we should take a well-deserved rest." But, he continued in virtual disbelief, "the funny thing is" that Kellogg and others in the administration "seem to take it all with profound seriousness." Kellogg and his aides were undoubtedly caught up in the idealism of their undertaking, but they were also moved by the opportunity to "outcovenant" Wilson and take up the mantle of peacemaking for the Republicans. For both foreign and domestic political benefit, then, the Coolidge administration was less than candid about its purposes, which were not all idealistic.

European leaders were not necessarily more helpful in the general project that the French sometimes described as the organization of the peace. From 1919 onward, virtually all Germans and every political party from Left to Right regarded the Treaty of Versailles as unacceptable—especially those provisions relating to disarmament, reparations, Danzig, and the eastern borders with Poland and Czechoslovakia. They tended increasingly to blame the treaty for their domestic as well as foreign problems. The assassination of Foreign Minister Walter Rathenau in June 1922 was indicative of the vindictive nationalist attitudes toward a liberal foreign policy, and it reinforced the French image of a Germany bent upon revenge.

Germany and Russia used one another for purposes of political leverage—the Russians to extricate themselves from their pariah diplomatic status and from military and economic weaknesses, and the Germans to extricate themselves from the Treaty of Versailles. Germany and Russia both astonished and frightened the Western diplomatic world (which was partly deserving of it) in April 1922 by signing the Treaty of Rapallo, which re-established full diplomatic and consular relations and renounced their financial claims against each other, the latter consisting of German war reparations and Russian compensation for German property nationalized in the postwar era. There were also rumors of a political and military alliance, which proved untrue.

There was, however, extensive secret military and economic collaboration between the two countries that clearly violated the Treaty of Versailles. The earliest initiative was advanced in March 1919 by the Russian Communist agent Karl Radek, who had been active in the German Spartacist uprisings of that year. No real headway, though, was made until the German Army, or Reichswehr, started serious negotiations in 1921. Civil officials in the Weimar government at first were kept in the dark, but beginning in 1922 every Foreign Minister and Finance Minister was apprised of the secret military and economic collaboration, and while not all of them liked the policy, they all acquiesced in it. The Reichswehr was thus able to gain concessions for concerns such as Krupp, Stolzenberg, and Junkers to engage in heavy industrial production for Russian military purposes, as well as to establish in Russia experimental and training centers for the development and use of airplanes, tanks, poison gas, and sundry other war matériel forbidden by the Treaty of Versailles. In return for granting these privileges, the Russians earned not merely German good will but a share in the armaments industry and economic benefits that their ailing economy was not yet able to produce. The concern of German officials throughout the 1920's was not the propriety of these illegal activities but what might happen if the Western powers should decide to make an issue of them, or if one day Russia might use the acquired techniques and matériel against Germany. The latter was not likely to occur for many years at least. However, the more Germany moved toward political *rapprochement* with England and France in the later 1920's, the more the Reichswehr stepped up its military-industrial activities in Russia. British, and especially French and Polish, intelligence experts knew a remarkable amount about this Russo-German collaboration, and there were even public revelations, such as the stories in the *Manchester Guardian* during December 1926. But these seemed to make little impression or difference, while the British and French disagreed over the whole question of Germany, the Treaty of Versailles, and European security.

According to Georges Clemenceau, when he visited Lloyd George in the House of Commons shortly after the war's end he was asked whether he had anything to say. "Yes, indeed!" replied Clemenceau, "I have come to tell you that from the very day after the Armistice I found you an enemy to France." To which the British Prime Minister replied, as Clemenceau recollected, "Well, *was it not always our traditional policy?*" Clemenceau might have exaggerated, but it is indisputable that the British felt far more secure behind the Channel than the French did bordering the Germans. From almost the moment they signed the Treaty of Versailles, the British were prepared to revise it in Germany's favor, especially in matters relating to Eastern Europe. As early as 1921, Lloyd George told Briand that England was not concerned about Poland's disputes with Germany over Danzig, Upper Silesia, or other border areas, and that Eastern Europe was unstable, with fighting likely at any time, from which the British had to remain aloof. The British, as will be seen, also opposed the French occupation of the Ruhr in 1923 and used American hesitations to cover their own intentions of rejecting the Geneva Protocol of 1924–25.

Seen in this light, the principal political diplomatic achievement of the European statesmen of the decade, the Locarno treaties, would appear to have been illusory. The Germans, under Foreign Minister Stresemann, set the negotiations in process in February 1925 with an offer to the French to enter into a series of agreements that would guarantee Western Europe's boundaries and provide for the peaceful settlement of juridical and political conflicts with other states. The French, as ever, were suspicious, but the British, and particularly Foreign Secretary Austen Chamberlain, who would virtually dominate the forthcoming conference, were enthusiastic. Thus, the Locarno treaties, negotiated in October 1925 and signed in December, placed the boundaries between France and Germany and Germany and Belgium under an Anglo-Italian guarantee and established arbitration treaties, without the Anglo-Italian guarantee, between Poland and Germany and Czechoslovakia and Germany. It also recognized the validity of the Franco-Polish and Franco-Czech treaties for mutual assistance in case of German aggression. Germany's assent to the Locarno treaties marked a significant development: It had now agreed to give up claims to Alsace and Lorraine and to keep the Rhineland demilitarized. Locarno provided for Germany's entry into the League of Nations, delayed until September 1926, and went a long way toward reintegrating Germany into Europe. Statesmen and politicians everywhere, including President Coolidge, praised the so-called spirit of Locarno, which prevailed for the next few years. It is interesting, however, that the so-called spirit of Locarno, much referred to at the time, did not always seem the same to the principal signatories. A contemporary quip had it that there were three spirits: the spirit of Locarno, *l'esprit de Locarno,* and *der Locarnogeist.*

The Locarno treaties had certain structural flaws. In some ways, they provided as much against an effort by France to occupy or detach the

Ruhr from Germany (as in 1923) as they protected France against German aggression. Bringing Italy into the arrangements also had two drawbacks. First, it granted a certain moral legitimacy to the Fascist dictator Benito Mussolini. Mussolini came to power legitimately in October 1922, after he and his followers had created conditions of extreme social and political turbulence. In 1924, he had his chief parliamentary opposition leader, the Socialist Giacomo Matteotti, murdered, and he meted out castor-oil torture to other dissenters. He then assumed a dictatorship and full responsibility for everything that had occurred with his declaration in February 1925 that, "if Fascism has been a criminal conspiracy, then I am the leader of that conspiracy." Unfortunately, Mussolini and his Fascism, with its claim to establishing order and making the trains run on time, had a certain vogue and became attractive to disillusioned liberals as well as conservatives and figures as different in outlook and temperament as Mahatma Gandhi, Winston Churchill, and Austen Chamberlain (whose wife sported a Fascist party badge). Equally important, the inclusion of Italy as a guarantor of the Locarno arrangements tended to foster the idea that Italy could or would provide a counterbalance to Germany, a presumption that in later years led British statesmen to woo Italy in the Ethiopian crisis of 1935 and the German-Czech crisis of 1938, while pursuing a disastrous policy of appeasement.

Most important, while the Locarno treaties guaranteed the boundaries of Western Europe, the arbitration treaties for the eastern frontiers, where the disputed regions were, had no guarantees. This arrangement divided Europe's borders into first class and second class, and not even a man as dedicated to peaceful methods as Stresemann would accept the eastern boundaries as final. Shortly after his diplomatic initiative to the French, he stated publicly that Germany could not renounce its right to seek to alter, albeit by peaceful means, its eastern frontiers. The British acquiesced; Austen Chamberlain was entirely convinced that for the sake of the Polish Corridor "no British Government ever will or ever can risk the bones of a British grenadier." Thus, the statesmen who made the Locarno treaties included a reservation that the "military situation" and "geographical location" of every state be taken into account in determining what action should be taken in the event of aggression— effectively exempting Germany from any coalition against Russia *and* recognizing that Germany had not given up its territorial (or population) claims against Poland or Czechoslovakia. Locarno did not truly deal with the most troublesome region of Europe and the one that, ironically, would later provide the setting for another Great Power conflict.

The faster the British and French complied with the letter and spirit of Locarno—and hastened to reverse the Treaty of Versailles by withdrawing the control commission on disarmament in 1927, setting a limit to reparations in 1929, and removing the last of the French troops from the Rhineland in 1930, five years ahead of schedule—the fiercer German nationalist demands became. Then, in what to many would prove to be the cruelest irony, if not the ultimate tragedy, the economic structure that the United States had sought to erect as a firm underpinning for a stable world political order collapsed. All nations were rapidly trapped in a spiral of interrelated political and economic problems; politicians found that the domestic economic crises limited their diplomatic flexibility, and they also tended to take rigid and strident stands on foreign policy issues to try to compensate for, or obscure, the domestic problems they did not know how to solve.

If there was any realm in the postwar world in which Republican administrators believed that they possessed both the upper hand and the expertise with which to assist in permanent peacemaking, it was the economic realm. But here again, economic factors served not only to divide victors and vanquished but to separate the United States from its wartime associates. Wilson had largely set the American course at the Paris Peace Conference and in a letter of November 3, 1920, to Lloyd George, in which he insisted that every nation repay the money it had borrowed from the United States. He refused to make Allied payment of war debts dependent on either the amount of reparations Germany paid or the amount of money the United States might contribute toward European reconstruction. With variations, this was the basic executive stance from Wilson, through Harding, Coolidge ("They hired the money, didn't they?" he allegedly said), and Hoover, to Roosevelt. Congress was equally if not more adamant. In February 1922, it established the War Debt Funding Commission and stipulated that all war debts had to be repaid within twenty-five years at not less than 4.25 per cent interest, and that there could be no debt cancellation except through payment. When the British, in August 1922, proposed writing off their share of German reparations against the entire inter-Allied indebtedness, the Harding administration was infuriated as well as worried about congressional reaction. In July 1923, the British agreed to pay off their $4.4 billion war debt over sixty-two years, with an average interest rate of 3.3 per cent. The terms were more generous than those Congress had wanted, but the interest rate was higher than that charged other countries (Italy paid .4 per cent interest) and much more than the 2 per cent Ambassador Harvey had led the British to anticipate. The British agreement was followed by thirteen more agreements of varying terms with America's wartime associates and the successor states of the Austro-Hungarian Empire.

For several years, the French remained intransigent about their debt.

They wanted war debts and reparations linked, with the United States guaranteeing German payments or perhaps even paying—directly or through debt cancellation—that portion of the reparations Germany did not meet. This view caused Under Secretary of State Norman Davis to comment in 1920 that the French "still have the idea that the United States is Santa Claus." The French believed they were being over-charged. Their total debt was $3.4 billion, but they had borrowed only $1.9 billion during the war and had spent almost all of it at high prices in the United States. They had obligingly purchased $400 million worth of American war supplies in 1919. The remaining $1 billion of the debt was for postwar relief aid. They were not assuaged by the fact that during this time the United States agreed to forego interest on the debt, or by the fact that Treasury Secretary Andrew Mellon and the men Harding appointed to the Debt Commission took, in the perspective of their era, a moderate view with regard to collecting from the French. The French rejected the British agreement as a model for their negotiations and foolishly prevented the United States from receiving German repara-tions funds to cover the small cost of American occupation forces in Germany. In turn, the State Department dissuaded J. P. Morgan and Company and other bankers from floating postwar loans for France.

Late in 1924, the Americans and the French tried to reach agreement, but tentative negotiations were marred by acrimony and two major stumbling blocks: the interest rate and French insistence on a "safe-guard" clause that would allow them to reduce their payments if the Germans did not pay their reparations in full. Serious negotiations did not begin until mid-1925, and final terms were not agreed upon until the spring of 1926: payment of the debt in full over sixty-two years at an average interest rate of 1.6 per cent. The French were still furious over the lack of a safeguard clause and the inclusion of another clause that would have allowed the United States to exchange bonds, which the French Government sold specifically to raise money to pay its war debt, for different marketable French securities. These securities might then be sold to anyone, including the Germans. Secretary of the Treasury Mellon insisted this latter development would never happen, but the French remained skeptical. There followed public and private French denunciations of protests against the United States, and former Premier Clemenceau wrote publicly to President Coolidge, in the summer of 1926, that "France is not for sale even to her friends." French ratifica-tion of the debt settlement was delayed until the summer of 1929, when the French Senate expressed its anguish through an informal reservation —which Briand acknowledged was not part of the contract—stating their right to "safeguard" France by reducing debt payments if Germany did not meet its reparations in full.

The rancor and dissension between the United States and its erstwhile friends over war debts was equally present in the reparations issue and carried over in a substantial way into the international political realm. At the Paris Peace Conference, the Americans and Allies had clashed over whether Germany's bill should be based on a capacity to pay or on the absolute "costs" of the war. The United States's failure to ratify the Treaty of Versailles meant that there was no official American representative on the Reparation Commission—comprised of British, French, Italian, and, alternatively, Belgian and Japanese delegates—and in January 1921 President Wilson, convinced that American advice was neither wanted nor being heeded, withdrew an unofficial observer. In May 1921, the Reparation Comission fixed Germany's bill at the equivalent of $33 billion, to be paid over an as yet undetermined period, with annual installments of $375 million during 1921–25 and rising to $900 million thereafter. These terms reflected both Anglo-French vindictiveness and Germany's attitude of negotiating reparations with a "stiff upper lip."

For a variety of political and economic reasons, the reparations schedule could not work. In May 1922, the commission granted Germany a year's moratorium and then in January 1923, for the second time, declared Germany in default on its scheduled coal and timber deliveries to the French, who, along with the Belgians, were preparing to occupy the Ruhr in an effort to secure by bayonet what could not be gotten through negotiations.

Secretary of State Hughes tried to forestall the crisis when, in a speech to the American Historical Association on December 29, 1922, he said that distinguished Americans, in private capacity, would be willing to serve on a new committee that would reassess Germany's financial liabilities. (Hughes apparently told one State Department official it was the "voice of God" that directed him to talk about Europe; more likely it was the strident tones of French Premier Raymond Poincaré.) Then, on January 8, 1923, he privately warned the French that, if they sent troops into the Ruhr, the United States would withdraw its occupation forces—while, conversely, the government of Chancellor Wilhelm Cuno appealed for American troops to remain to protect the Germans from the French. When the Franco-Belgian forces marched into the Ruhr two days later, Hughes undercut their action by withdrawing the remaining American forces. The British, convinced that the French gamble was futile, remained aloof. The Cuno government thwarted the French effort to collect through a policy of passive resistance and reckless inflation. The latter wiped out the value of the mark, along with the savings and economic security of millions of middle-class citizens who were traumatized by the experience, and also allowed German industrialists and the German Government virtually to wipe out their internal debts.

Public opinion in the United States and Great Britain divided over the Ruhr crisis, although the majority view was probably that of antipathy toward the French as Europe's new militarists and sympathy for the beleaguered Germans. The French gamble failed. A French-inspired separatist movement in the Ruhr failed, and financial collapse in Germany precipitated devaluation of the French franc. By September 1923, the French began negotiations with the Ruhr mine owners, while a new German Government under Gustav Stresemann (who was Chancellor for three months before becoming Foreign Minister until his death in October 1929) ended passive resistance and inaugurated Germany's policy of "fulfilling" its treaty obligations.

The Reparation Commission organized two new committees to reassess Germany's financial status and reparations obligations, and at Germany's suggestion that Americans serve on the committees, Hughes nominated former Brigadier General Charles G. Dawes, who was also a wealthy banker and big contributor to Republican campaign coffers, and Owen D. Young, president of the General Electric Company.

Between January and April 1924, the negotiators in London devised the so-called Dawes Plan, which stabilized the German mark, reorganized the Reichsbank under Allied supervision, and arranged a five-year interim reparations schedule under which Germany's payments, based on its capacity to pay, would range from $250 million to $625 million annually. To meet these obligations, Germany would have to bond and mortgage principal railways and industries, while the Allies agreed to provide Germany with an immediate loan of $200 million, over half of it from Americans. Coolidge publicly supported the Dawes Plan, and Secretary Hughes, traveling in Europe in the spring of 1924 for a meeting of the American Bar Association, campaigned for its acceptance. When the French politicians proved reluctant, he told them that "if you turn this down, America is through." Everyone agreed to the Dawes Plan, which worked smoothly for the next five years. Then, in the summer of 1929, Owen D. Young returned to Europe to draw up a final reparations settlement. The Young Plan set Germany's total obligation at $8 billion, to be paid over 58.5 years at 5.5 per cent interest. Germany's minimum, or "unconditional," payments were set at $153 million annually—far less than under the Dawes Plan but, interestingly, equal to the annual Allied war-debts obligations to the United States—while the remainder of Germany's "conditional" obligations would be based on its capacity to pay.

The Republicans' 1920's version of dollar diplomacy appeared enormously successful. Americans were glad to invest in Weimar Germany. Indeed, their $110 million share of the Dawes Plan loan was oversubscribed by 10 to 1 and bankers had to apportion subscriptions among eager applicants. Between 1924 and July 1931, Americans invested at least another $2.6 billion in a wide variety of German public and private enterprises. Germany, meanwhile, flourished almost as never before: by 1928, production in basic industries exceeded the 1913 level by 50 per cent, and per capita income for the same period rose from $178 to $279. Equally, if not more, important, American money seemed to have transformed Europe politically as well as economically, providing the firm foundations for the Franco-German *rapprochement* represented in the Stresemann-Briand negotiations and the Locarno treaties and, ultimately, the Kellogg-Briand Pact of 1928.

But the economic basis of the peace was as structurally flawed as the political basis. The connection between German reparations and Allied war debts is obvious. The system of payments was entirely dependent on a continual outflow of dollars. American creditors lent money to the German Government, which used it to pay reparations to the British and French, who in turn paid their war debts to the U.S. Government. Along the way, some American creditors profited from their interest-bearing German bonds, but basically the American citizen wound up providing the capital to pay off war debts owed to his own country. If the private loans were defaulted, he lost both the loans and the defaulted payments of the Allies to the U.S. Treasury. Further, American banking investment firms, too anxious to make their middleman profits by sponsoring German loans and bond issues, were overzealous in pushing American citizens to invest in Germany despite repeated "unofficial" State Department warnings about Germany's shrinking ability either to absorb loans or to pay them back. The extent to which banking institutions ignored or did not perceive the rotting of both political and economic foundations in Germany in the late Weimar years is illustrated by the National City Bank's advice to its clients, circularized as late as June 14, 1930, that there was never a more opportune time for the purchase of German bonds.

Unhelpful, too, were the highly nationalistic and protective Fordney-McCumber (1922) and Hawley-Smoot (1930) tariffs. They pushed rates beyond even the 38–40 per cent rates of the Payne-Aldrich tariff of 1909, and by placing the highest levies on certain manufactured goods and raw materials (china, cutlery, woolen manufactures, silk, rayon, and textiles), closed American markets to the very nations that needed to raise money through exports in order to pay war debts or reparations. The Republican tariff-makers, it is true, introduced reciprocity, allowing the President to negotiate with individual countries to lower, or raise, tariffs mutually, with the hope of generally reducing rates. However, in thirty-two of thirty-seven instances in the 1920's, tariffs were raised under reciprocity, while lowering was restricted to such unimportant items as millfeed or paintbrush handles. In 1930, over a thousand members of the American Economic Association urged President Hoover not to sign the Hawley-Smoot tariff, while many nations protested that it would set off a tariff war amidst the rapidly declining world trade and rising unemployment that came in the wake of the October 1929 stock-market crash. But Hoover bowed to nationalist business pressures and consoled himself that a commission would revise tariff laws. The result was retaliatory tariffs by thirty-one nations and, ironically, a desire on the part of many Americans with investments in foreign businesses to cut back on further credit. This only contracted the international money market, with bankers on both sides of the Atlantic quickly calling in short-term loans amidst mutual recriminations and further weakening of the war debts–reparations structure.

The German Government was partly responsible for the mounting financial mess. Weimar officials did not accept the legitimacy of reparations and would not even try to levy taxes to pay them. Instead, Weimar governments resorted to foreign borrowing, which was often reckless and amounted to far more than was paid in reparations. Stresemann warned in November 1928 that Germany was too dependent on foreign credits. Then, in 1929, a powerful bloc, spearheaded by big business and Adolf Hitler's National Socialist Party, waged a bitter if losing campaign to secure approval first in the Reichstag, and then by national plebiscite, of a "Law Against the Enslavement of the German People," which would have subjected government officials to charges of treason if they fulfilled treaties or agreements, such as the Young Plan, that accepted a "war-guilt" hypothesis.

The Reichstag ratified the Young Plan in March 1930, but the new government of Chancellor Heinrich Brüning immediately embarked on a very risky course. Brüning was an able if highly conservative nationalist of the Catholic Center, whose government was in a minority in the Reichstag. He wanted to deal with the domestic consequences of the depression by deflationary techniques—cutting the budget by reducing public spending, social services, and tax incentives—even though these steps increased unemployment and raised the general level of discontent. To offset this, he looked toward success in the foreign-policy realm, especially the reduction—really elimination—of reparations. Thus, in the Reichstag elections of September 1930, the Brüning government praised neither the Young Plan nor the recent (June) French evacuation of the last occupied zone of the Rhineland but instead demanded further revision of the Treaty of Versailles on such matters as the Polish Corridor, the Saar, and the demilitarized Rhineland. Brüning's tactics allowed him and his party to maintain a grip on the government, but they contributed much to the atmosphere that aided the startling growth of the National

Socialists, who increased their elected deputies from 12 to 107, and the Communists, who jumped from 53 to 77, making these parties, respectively, the second and third largest in the Reichstag. Thus those forces that sought to destroy the Republic were now larger than those that wished to bolster it, or, like Brüning, that would have preferred to restore the monarchy.

Brüning continued to pursue his foreign policy and persuaded the American Ambassador, Sackett, to press President Hoover to call a world conference to re-evaluate the war debts–reparations tangle. Hoover, however, rejected the idea in January 1931 and remained adamant into the spring of 1931, even though both the Treasury Department and American bankers interested mainly in protecting their private investments in Germany urged action to reduce the intergovernmental flow of war debts and reparations. The Germans continued to press the British and made no effort to stop the flight of capital from Germany—as if to demonstrate that financial weakness made reparations payments impossible—while, in March 1931, the French blocked a proposed German-Austrian Customs Union. In May, Austria's largest bank, the Kreditanstalt, was near collapse, and later that month German officials told American diplomats that reparations would have to cease. Then, on June 6, the eve of Brüning's departure for negotiations with the British, his Cabinet published a long-planned manifesto, which had to have a disastrous effect on international credit, announcing that the conditions under which Germany had agreed to the Young Plan and reparations no longer existed.

President Hoover would take no action to acknowledge the link between war debts and reparations until mid-June 1931, when his policy of inaction became demonstrably hopeless. American officials therefore contrived to have the obliging Germans send a letter of appeal from President von Hindenburg, which arrived too late to be used and was far too despairing. On the weekend of June 20–21, Hoover issued a call for a year's moratorium on intergovernmental debts and reparations. The French were furious at not being consulted and feared more than ever for the future of the Treaty of Versailles. They resisted the moratorium. But by July 6 American pressure prevailed, causing Under Secretary of the Treasury Ogden Mills to remark that the United States had just made the world safe for Germany.

Hoover's moratorium gave Germany some relief, and at a conference in London in July, Secretary of State Henry L. Stimson prevailed over what he called the "God-damned folly" of nervous international bankers who wanted to call in their short-term loans to Germany and got them to refrain from doing so under a "standstill" agreement. Brüning also persuaded Germany's creditors to agree to a conference scheduled for

January 1932 in Lausanne to review Germany's obligations, but when word leaked of his ultimate intention to seek cancellation of reparations, the French forced postponement of the meeting until June 1932. Eventually, the Lausanne conferees agreed virtually to cancel German reparations—lowering them by 90 per cent—contingent on a similar reduction of war debts, to which the Americans never agreed.

After Hoover's crushing defeat at the polls in November 1932, he was persuaded by his advisers to invite President-elect Roosevelt to the White House to discuss war debts–reparations problems. At the meeting on November 22, Hoover was sullen, suspicious, and somewhat contemptuous of Roosevelt, who, on his part, was wary of being entrapped by an outgoing administration. Both finally agreed that, in principle, war debts were separate from reparations and should be paid. Roosevelt afterward insisted that application of these principles was "not his baby," and that any settlement the Hoover administration made in the next three months was its own responsibility. On November 23, the Hoover administration justified its position on war debts and demanded payment in a long public note, which Herbert Feis, then the State Department adviser on international economic affairs, said was "as devious a document as has entered the debt negotiations. Our diplomacy—under a most honest secretary—has been anything but honest. It has been craven throughout the period from the moratorium." In December 1932, the British paid their debt installment but warned that this did not mean they could or would continue to pay in full. The French defaulted. Hoover and Roosevelt met again on January 20, 1933, but agreed only that war-debts negotiations should continue. To no avail. The British made token payments in 1933 but thereafter, along with French and every other country except Finland (also Cuba, Liberia, and Nicaragua, who had paid their entire debts), defaulted permanently, causing an aroused Congress in 1934 to pass a Debt Default Act, sponsored by Senator Hiram Johnson, that forbade loans to, or the purchase of securities or bonds from, nations that had defaulted on their war debts.

Small matter. By January 1933 events had far outstripped dollar diplomacy. For almost fifteen years the United States had pursued a war-debts and reparations policy that, however well intentioned, was shot through with contradictory and unrealistic assumptions. British policy over reparations from Lloyd George's time was scarcely better, while the French were usually as intransigent about reparations and their own war debts as they were about everything else. German attitudes were perhaps worst of all. Brüning's risky foreign and domestic policies had secured certain gains but at high cost. Germany did not create the international credit crisis of 1931, but the international community came to feel, with justification, that the Germans exploited the crisis and their debtor position to the full. Ironically and tragically, Brüning himself never benefited from his policies, for right-wing intrigues against him had persuaded President von Hindenburg to secure his resignation on May 29, 1932, weeks before the long-delayed Lausanne Conference. Brüning was replaced with the wily and highly conservative Franz von Papen. But the downward spiral of German politics only accelerated thereafter. It culminated, on January 30, 1933, with the accession to power and the Chancellorship of Adolf Hitler, who repudiated all the traditions of Western diplomacy, as well as reparations payments. Far more than anyone then realized, and owing as much to the war debts–reparations tangle as any single issue, the Western world had entered a new and extremely bleak era in international politics.

4

The Search for Order

In the Far East, just as in Europe, the First World War catalyzed or revolutionized transformations that had long been under way. Prior to 1914, Japan was emerging as a great power in its own right and the predominant one in Far Eastern international politics. The Japanese compressed a century or more of Western industrial revolution into the last thirty years of the nineteenth century and demonstrated their strength and modernity first by defeating China in a war in 1894–95, and thereby acquiring Formosa and the Pescadores, and then by defeating Russia in 1904–5 and taking the Russian-held concessions of Port Arthur and Dairen on the Liaotung Peninsula in China and the southern half of Sakhalin Island, stretching between the north of Japan and southern Siberia. In 1905, the Japanese also established a virtual protectorate over Korea, which President Theodore Roosevelt recognized at once, and proceeded to exploit that land ruthlessly for the next forty years. Japan's achievements or prowess was also acknowledged by the Anglo-Japanese Naval Agreement, originally signed in 1902, revised in 1905 and 1911, and renewable every ten years. Under its terms, Great Britain and Japan recognized each other's special interests in China and Korea, respectively, and the right of both Allies to protect their interests from internal or external threats. Both countries pledged neutrality if either went to war in defense of its interests, and to intervene in behalf of one another if a third power became involved in a war against either England or Japan. Secret terms provided that each country would try to maintain a naval force in the Pacific larger than that of any third power.

In succeeding years, Japan became the leading imperial economic power in Manchuria, China's largest, richest, and northernmost region. This was done chiefly at Russian expense, but not without also undercutting American investors such as Edward H. Harriman, and later Jacob Schiff, who looked to Manchuria as a New West (Harriman's phrase) that would absorb American railroad investments and manufactures. During the World War, Japan used the occasion of aiding England under the Anglo-Japanese Alliance to seize the German-held Mariana, Caroline, and Marshall islands and the German concessions on the Shantung Peninsula and Kiaochow Bay. In 1915, Japan pressed its Twenty-one Demands on China, which would have turned it into a virtual economic and political satellite, but Wilson succeeded in moderating the most obnoxious aspects of these. In November 1917, Secretary Lansing and Ambassador Viscount Kikujiro Ishii exchanged diplomatic notes that stipulated that geography created special relations between Japan and China and special interests for Japan in China. In an attached protocol (kept secret at Japanese insistence out of fear of infuriating military extremists), the United States and Japan pledged not to seek special rights or privileges in China that would abridge those of "other friendly states." At the Paris Peace Conference, Japan formally acquired Germany's Shantung concessions and mandates over its former Pacific islands north of the equator.

The major objectives of Republican diplomacy in the 1920's, as had been the case with the Wilson administration, was to prevent Japan from establishing either political or economic hegemony over any other area in the Far East and to reassert the Open Door doctrine, which was concerned primarily with maintaining equal commercial opportunity for all nations in China (including Manchuria) and only secondarily with maintaining China's territorial and administrative integrity.

At the same time, the Republicans recognized that the current, or real, value of American commercial and trade relations with Japan far exceeded that with China, notwithstanding that omnipresent lure to American investors and manufacturers of China's unearthed mineral riches and the potential market of its 400 million inhabitants. At the start of the 1920's, the United States supplied Japan with approximately 75 per cent of its automobiles, lumber, and building materials and 50 per cent of its oil and machinery needs. It purchased 90 per cent of Japan's raw silk exports, and 40 per cent of its exports, while providing 40 per cent of the foreign capital invested in Japan. In short, Japan had to be contained, but without jeopardizing America's lucrative commercial and trade relations with this rising new empire.

The Republicans also had to face the issue of China itself. The long-tottering Manchu Dynasty had finally given way to the revolutions of 1911 and the subsequent establishment of the Republic of China. But the "revolution," inspired partly by a growing sense of nationalism and Western liberal ideas, never really succeeded, and from 1912 to 1916 the government in Peking was presided over not by the Republic's spiritual or intellectual leader, Sun Yat-sen, but by a former Manchu strong man, Yüan Shi-kai, who named himself Emperor in 1916. He died that same year and was succeeded by Li Yuan-hung, who was recognized as the legitimate head of state by the Western powers, while in 1917 Sun Yat-sen's Kuomintang (or National People's Party) set up a rival government in the south in Canton. Sun's followers were deeply embittered by the Shantung settlement, and the ultimate aim of the nationalist Young China and May Fourth movements was to end all foreign privilege in China.

The especial targets of this new nationalism were the foreign powers' control over China's tariff structure and the century-old (dating to 1844) and constantly expanding system of extraterritoriality. Under the rights, or privileges, of extraterritoriality, the foreigners who lived, worked, and employed one another and Chinese in all kinds of commercial and industrial enterprises in the increasingly large concession areas were subject only to the laws of their own countries and maintained their own postal, banking, social, and commercial systems. Foreign powers justified extraterritoriality as the only way in which enterprise could flourish in a China that was more a geographical expression than a unified nation with a government capable of administering a uniform system of laws. But as late as 1937, when extraterritoriality was still being debated, the American Minister to China, Nelson T. Johnson, urging that the United States end its extraterritoriality, pointed out to his State Department superiors that extraterritorial privileges had grown far beyond anything envisaged at the inception of the system and created a privileged class of Americans (this applied to all foreigners as well) who were immune from Chinese law, committed serious and inexcusable violations, and then got government officials to intervene in their behalf.

The problem that confronted the United States and the other Great Powers at the start of the 1920's, then, was how to deal with a weak and divided China—the "sick man" of Asia, whose weakness made it an irresistible lure for every nation's trade or imperial ambitions, a nation that was also becoming increasingly nationalistic and self-assertive. What American diplomats proposed was to do away with traditional forms—gunboats, balance of power, and exclusive spheres-of-influence diplomacy—and yet preserve the substance of foreign privilege and opportunity in China that had grown up under the treaty system.

Then there was the matter of the Anglo-Japanese Alliance, originally designed to contain Russia, which had made great inroads into Manchuria after the Boxer uprisings of 1900. But the Russo-Japanese war and the revolution of 1917 had curbed or ended the Russian imperial threat, and the outcome of the World War ended the imperial ambitions of Germany, which in May 1921 signed an agreement surrendering its extraterritorial privileges and granted tariff autonomy to China. The

Anglo-Japanese Alliance remained in effect, and the question of whether it could be invoked against the United States was debatable. The 1911 revision of the Alliance exempted application of it to any nation that concluded an arbitration treaty with either England or Japan. In 1911, the United States concluded, but did not ratify, an arbitration agreement with England. To allay American fears, Japanese Foreign Minister Count Uchida said publicly in February 1921 that nonratification made "no particular difference," and that both England and Japan understood there should be no application of the Anglo-Japanese Alliance against the United States.

Distrust of the Anglo-Japanese Alliance persisted among Americans; they regarded it as a symbol of the "old" diplomacy, a challenge to the Open Door policy, and an indication that England and Japan might at some time strike a bargain recognizing the primacy of their special interests in China proper and Manchuria to the exclusion or at the expense of all third powers, including the United States. In March 1920, Wilson's Secretary of State, Bainbridge Colby, had told the British that the United States opposed renewal of the Alliance, and later the Republicans under Harding indicated their disapproval of it as well, largely by suggesting privately that it might encourage militaristic leaders in Japan to breach the Open Door.

The question that remained, however, was not merely how to end the Alliance but what, if anything, to substitute for it, and how then to deal with both the advantages and liabilities inherent in Japan's rise to power and China's weakness and inability to resist foreign encroachments.

The Republican answer to these questions was the Conference on the Limitation of Armament, which met in Washington between November 1921 and February 1922. The origins of the Washington Conference can be traced to the Anglo-American-Japanese naval race that developed during the World War. Wilson's administration had inaugurated the "navy second to none" policy in 1916 and by 1918 was prepared to achieve that distinction. The United States then possessed sixteen battleships, with an aggregate of 400,000 tons displacement, approximately half of Great Britain's thirty-three battleships, with one million tons displacement. But the Navy Department plans presented to Congress at the end of 1918 proposed expansion by 1925 to thirty-nine battleships and twelve battlecruisers, making the American Navy superior to the British in every way. Secretary of the Navy Josephus Daniels moved the main body of the fleet, including fourteen of the newest battleships, to the Pacific, placing the United States at parity with the Japanese in that region; opened the dry dock at Pearl Harbor; and sought money, which Congress would not appropriate, to fortify Guam and expand American facilities in the Philippines. Daniels insisted that, in order to fulfill its destiny as a leader of democratic impulse, the United States had to be "incomparably strong in defense against aggression and in offense against evil-doers."

In September 1921, the General Board of the Navy, defining the framework of world politics that would determine American naval needs (and congressional appropriations), argued that Japan aimed at commercial and political domination of the Far East, with concomitant territorial expansion and naval domination of the Yellow Sea, China Sea, and Sea of Japan. The Japanese governing classes, the Board said, were inspired by "militaristic" and "feudalistic" traditions, and the Japanese Government was "aggressive." The contrast with American governmental traditions and institutions, it argued, therefore meant that the permanent adjustment of controversial problems was virtually impossible "and will be maintained only by force." The Japanese in 1920 appropriated funds for sixteen new capital ships—equivalent to Congress's 1919 authorization—and by 1921 Japanese naval expenditures not only were triple their 1917 level but constituted one-third of the imperial budget. Meanwhile, Japanese troops remained in the Russian Maritime provinces and the promise to restore political sovereignty to China in Shantung remained unfulfilled.

Amidst these escalating tensions, Senator Borah in December 1920 introduced a resolution calling for the United States, Great Britain, and Japan to summon a conference to end the naval race. The resolution was not voted upon, and Borah reintroduced it in April 1921. The Harding administration had at first made clear its intention to continue with the Wilson naval-building program, which meant delaying any naval limitation conference at least three years, but the public response was so unfavorable that even an imperialist like Senator Lodge recognized by the spring of 1921 that naval appropriations would have to be reduced. The Harding administration withdrew its opposition to Borah's resolution of April 1921, and the Senate (74–0) and the House of Representatives (332–4) passed it and the current naval appropriations as a package. Harding did not sign the bill into law until July, by which time events had moved toward a Great Power conference.

For some time, the British had been indicating interest in a Great Power conference. They wished to avoid an outpouring of funds for naval building. They also wanted to resolve the internal conflict between those who advocated renewing the Anglo-Japanese Alliance and those who favored scrapping it in favor of cooperating with the United States. Moreover, most British leaders, including Prime Minister Lloyd George and the Foreign Office, recognized in 1920 that, whereas the Alliance had been successful with regard to limiting Czarist Russia and Imperial

Germany, it had been a notable failure in its more subtle but equally crucial purpose of restraining Japan. The British now sought to avoid terminating the Alliance, and thereby offending the Japanese, by enlarging the agreement into a tripartite pact with the United States, thus gaining American cooperation while inoffensively "containing" Japan. The British abandoned this strategy after Harding's election, however, not simply because they felt that the United States was about to slip into isolation, but because they believed there were too many outright imperialists or Anglophobes in the Senate who would refuse to cooperate with England. More impetus toward an outright end of the Anglo-Japanese Alliance now came from Canada, where Prime Minister Arthur Meighen and his associates saw the Alliance as "obsolete" and ineffective in restraining Japan, while it antagonized the United States and possibly compromised Canada's commercial and missionary interests in Korea. Prime Minister Jan Smuts of South Africa took a similar view of the Alliance's shortcomings, and in February 1921 Meighen proposed to Lloyd George that Great Britain end the Alliance, work toward Anglo-American accord, and call a conference among the United States, Britain, Japan, and China to reconcile everyone's position in the Pacific.

Britain's War Ministry, the Admiralty, and the Exchequer, and men like Winston Churchill, Austen Chamberlain, and the Foreign Secretary, Lord Curzon, favored renewal of the Alliance, while limiting its initial tenure to five years and prohibiting its application against the United States. This view was strongly supported by the governments of Australia and New Zealand for purely imperial reasons. At the Paris Peace Conference, they had opposed a Japanese-sponsored statement of racial equality, which was defeated when Wilson ruled that it did not have unanimous agreement, and they bitterly opposed Japan's retention of Germany's island possessions in the North Pacific. Now they felt that only the Anglo-Japanese Alliance would restrain Japan's movement into the South Pacific, a view that was widely held in France and the Netherlands, where there was great concern over their respective holdings in French Indochina and the Dutch East Indies. After considerable discussion, on May 30, 1921, the British Cabinet elected to continue the Alliance but to modify it to meet American objections and to support the American idea of summoning a conference of Pacific powers. The British thrashed out their arguments again at their Imperial Conference in June 1921 and determined to encourage the Americans to call a conference, while deciding that the Anglo-Japanese Alliance should remain in force (it was now discovered that, technically, the Alliance was not due to lapse that summer) until or unless the proposed conference reached some new treaty arrangement to stabilize the Great Power relations in the Far East.

In further discussions, American officials demonstrated their adamant opposition either to continuing the Anglo-Japanese Alliance or to signing a new tripartite pact, while the British still pressed for a conference. Consequently, in the wake of this and the Borah resolution, Harding and Secretary of State Charles Evans Hughes, on July 8, 1921, stepped out in front of the British and indicated their intention of convoking a conference. Formal invitations went out to England, Japan, France, Italy, and China in August and to the Netherlands, Belgium, and Portugal in October. The Russians were furious at being excluded. The Japanese feared that Anglo-American cooperation would curb their imperial ambitions, and they indicated that they would accept the invitation only on condition that problems that were "of sole concern to certain powers or such matters that may be regarded [as] accomplished facts" would not be discussed—in short, Japan's position in Manchuria and Inner Mongolia. Hughes ignored this reservation, however, in issuing the formal invitation, although he did promise that the United States would maintain an absolutely impartial role between China and Japan at the conference. The Japanese then agreed to come, and Hughes presumptuously announced that all acceptances were unconditional. The Japanese, as Hughes knew, were prepared to counter any American pressure on their special interests by raising embarrassing questions about the exclusive American position in the Philippines, Hawaii, and the Panama Canal Zone and the American interpretation of the Monroe Doctrine toward Latin America.

Secretary Hughes opened the Washington Conference on November 12, 1921, with his well-known declaration that "the way to disarm is to disarm." Then, to the amazement and discomfort of British and Japanese admiralty officials, he demonstrated his thorough knowledge of the current status of every nation's navy, and precisely how many and which ships ought to be retained, scrapped, or not built in order to establish an equilibrium of naval power. There followed several weeks of hard bargaining, and the result was the Five-Power Naval Limitation Treaty. The United States and Great Britain were each allowed a total of 525,000 tons in capital ships (in battleships each was limited to a maximum of 35,000 tons, with 16-inch caliber guns), Japan was allowed 315,000 tons, and France and Italy 175,000 tons each. This 5:5:3: 1.75:1.75 ratio accorded approximately with the current naval situation —taking account of ships that were then only partially completed—and was more favorable from the American point of view than the 10:10:7 ratio Japan wanted. The Japanese were allowed to keep their most powerful and nearly finished battleship, the *Mutsu* (which Hughes knew from intercepted messages they would never agree to scrap), the United States continued building two of its most advanced ships while scrapping two older ones, and the British were allowed to build two entirely new ships and scrap four old ones. All further naval building of capital ships was ended for a period of ten years. Additionally, Article XIX of the treaty provided for maintaining the *status quo* on fortifications in the western Pacific, which included Guam and the Philippines, British Hong Kong, and Japan's adjacent Kurile and Bonin islands, Formosa, and the Pescadores but exempted Hawaii, Singapore (where the British planned a great new naval installation), and the Japanese mainland. Allotments for aircraft carriers were set at 135,000 tons each for the United States and Great Britain, 81,000 tons for Japan, and 60,000 tons each for France and Italy, while, much to French anger, nothing was said about ground forces.

The naval agreement did not include auxiliary ships—submarines, destroyers, and cruisers of fewer than 10,000 tons, with guns of maximum 8-inch caliber—and this almost immediately set off a five-year building race in these categories of ships that was as fierce between the United States and Great Britain as between either of these two powers and Japan. President Coolidge concluded in 1926 that the time had come for a new settlement, and he summoned a conference to meet in Geneva in 1927. But preparations were poor, and naval advisers tended to dominate on all sides. Anglo-American conflict was especially acute. The United States, with relatively few and widely spaced bases, wanted a low total tonnage allotment (250,000 to 400,000 each). It wanted the right to use this allowance to build cruisers with greater cruising range and fire power (10,000 tons and 8-inch guns) than preferred by the British, who had more bases but a far-flung empire and wanted a cruiser allotment of 600,000 tons, consisting of smaller cruisers limited perhaps to 6,000 tons and 6-inch guns. The deadlock was complicated by the British desire to eliminate submarines—their nemesis in the World War—and Japan's insistence on a 10:10:7 ratio for auxiliary ships. The conference failed, and the next two years were marked by a rapid increase in naval building on all sides and highly strained Anglo-American relations.

By mid-1929, the new administration under President Herbert Hoover and Secretary of State Henry L. Stimson determined that neither naval officials nor technical matters should dominate Great Power relations. In Great Britain, the new Labour government under Prime Minister Ramsay MacDonald, who was very much at heart a Wilsonian idealist and believer in Anglo-American cooperation, was much more disposed to agreement than had been its predecessor Conservative regime under Prime Minister Stanley Baldwin, which bowed to the more imperial and "big-navy" views of men like Churchill. Anglo-American agreement on naval matters was furthered by diplomatic exchanges and a highly successful visit to the United States in October 1929 by MacDonald, who told the Senate in florid and eloquent language, "There can be no war; nay, more; it is absolutely impossible, if you and we do our duty in making the peace pact effective, that any section of our army, whether land, or sea, or air, can ever again come into conflict. . . .What is all this bother about parity? Parity? Take it, without reserve, heaped and flowing over."

Diplomacy and good will smoothed the way to the London Naval Conference of January–April 1930. The United States sent a strong delegation dominated by the civil side, including Secretary Stimson, Secretary of the Navy Charles Francis Adams, Senators Joseph Robinson of Arkansas and David Reed of Pennsylvania, Ambassador Dwight Morrow (recently acclaimed for his mediating work in the civil war in Mexico and resolving difficulties over oil concessions), and Charles G. Dawes, Coolidge's Vice-President and now ambassador to Great Britain. The British, too, were willing to override their big navy enthusiasts, and the result was an Anglo-American compromise, and parity, on total auxiliary tonnage—327,000 tons each for cruisers, 150,000 tons for destroyers, and 53,000 tons for submarines. The United States also scaled down its demand for heavy cruisers (10,000 tons each, with 8-inch guns) from twenty-three to eighteen, with a delayed schedule of construction.

The Anglo-American agreement, then, provided an edge for Senator Reed in two months of hard bargaining with Japan's Ambassador to Great Britain, Tsuneo Matsudaira, and produced a compromise that allowed the Japanese twelve heavy cruisers, or 66 per cent of the American total, 70 per cent on light cruisers and destroyers, and parity for submarines—a 10:10:6.975 ratio, which was virtually what Japan sought. The 5:5:3 ratio on capital ships still prevailed, and the ten-year holiday on their construction agreed to at the Washington Conference was extended to 1936.

Secretaries Hughes and Stimson, and the civil side of the American Government, were delighted with the limitation agreements of the Washington (1921–22) and London (1930) conferences. Predictably, the navy was not. Its basic objection, aside from the inevitable bureaucratic criticisms stemming from the loss of ships, command posts, and congressional appropriations, was that the United States was not using its financial superiority to build a navy that would outstrip any Japanese fleet. The navy was upset at not being able to turn Guam and the Philippines into impregnable redoubts and perhaps to construct in the Philippines a battleship base that could be used for offensive action against Japan. From the naval standpoint, articulated by the General Board at least as early as 1921, Japan was the enemy and the United States should maintain a navy at least twice Japan's size (which the 5:3 ratio virtually provided). Strategy and tactics rested on that assumption. Thus, the navy reorganized the fleet in 1922, stationing the Scouting Fleet in the Atlantic and the Battle Fleet in the Pacific. In 1923, the General Board drew up a blueprint for action, which it incorporated into its "Orange Plan" of 1924 (predicated on a war with Japan). This included fortifying Guam and the Philippines as much as possible, making all vessels capable of transpacific operation, and keeping mobile expeditionary forces in readiness to recapture Manila, seize Japanese-mandated islands, blockade Japan—and then carry through an offensive island-hopping campaign against the Japanese mainland. The navy lobbied vociferously against independence for the Philippines, even though these islands were indefensible—a fact the navy never denied, shifting instead to the more believable (however mythical) argument that the Philippines were of enormous commercial value as an entrepôt to Far Eastern trade.

The navy's policy was clearly that of diplomacy through a porthole, but historians have tended to accept its military arguments, viewing Japanese policy as a progression from the Twenty-one Demands of 1915 to the attack on Pearl Harbor in 1941. The most serious criticism of the naval point of view has been strong doubts that Congress would have appropriated funds to meet the navy's objectives, for as late as 1934 American naval building remained below the prescribed treaty limits and a serious effort to build a dominating force did not begin until 1938. However, taken in concert, British and American naval forces clearly predominated over Japan's, while controlling the waters in the North and South Pacific through which 70 per cent of Japan's seagoing commerce passed. As for Guam and the Philippines, they were more secure after the Washington Conference than before, especially as the terms of a Four-Power Treaty signed at the conference provided a guarantee of the sanctity of insular possessions.

Moreover, a naval race in the 1920's was unjustifiable from the standpoint of America's real national security and national interests and might have provoked a Japanese-American clash. Japanese governments often depended on their ability to strike fair bargains with the West in order to protect themselves from chauvinistic and military assaults at home, and even then Premier Hamaguchi was shot in November 1930 (he died six months later) because of his strong defense of the Reed-Matsudaira compromise of 1930. Thus, it would have been virtually unthinkable for any Japanese government to agree to allow the United States to build to a level of overwhelming naval superiority in the Pacific. This is not to say that American policy ought to have been based on protecting other governments from their own extremists, but as the conservative, interwar career diplomat Hugh R. Wilson properly recollected, not only was the idea of a heavily fortified Guam amidst the Japanese mandate islands an unacceptable threat to Japan, but "security is a double concept. There may be security for one party by domination, but security for both parties can only be achieved by some form of balance, by a mutual belief that the situation has been so arranged that the home areas are safe from attack."

Naval "diplomacy" in the 1920's was out of step with the purpose and design of Republican foreign policy in the Pacific. Great publicity attached to naval limitation agreements, which not only were popular with budget-minded governments everywhere but contributed to an atmosphere of détente. And it was in the Four-Power and Nine-Power pacts that emerged from the Washington Conference that American diplomats believed that, by their lights, they had achieved their signal triumphs.

On the eve of the Washington Conference, the British made a final effort to salvage at least the intent of the Anglo-Japanese Alliance by proposing that the United States enter into a tripartite "arrangement." The signatories would respect one another's territorial rights in their island possessions, consult about the best means to protect them if they were threatened, and allow any two signatories to form a military defensive alliance, which had to be communicated to the third signatory, to combat any threat. But Hughes flatly rejected American participation in a scheme that had too many political overtones and resembled too closely an old-fashioned alliance.

The Japanese had anticipated the American response and proposed instead to turn the Anglo-Japanese Alliance into a tripartite consultative pact drawing upon the Root-Takahira agreement of 1908, which provided for the United States and Japan to respect each other's Far Eastern possessions and to support the *status quo*. The pact would also draw upon the Lansing-Ishii agreement of 1917, which recognized Japan's special relations with China. In November 1921, the Japanese proposed that the United States, Great Britain, and Japan agree to consult on the best means of "jointly or separately" defending their respective "territorial rights or vital interests . . . in the region of the Pacific Ocean and of the Far East" if another power threatened them. If any two of the three signatories had disagreements, each might obtain the other's permission to invite the third signatory to a conference to resolve the dispute. The British disliked the implications of Japan's "vital interests," and Hughes would not agree to extend even a consultative pact to the Far East for fear that such an arrangement would recognize Japan's special (or vital) interests in Manchuria and Inner Mongolia.

The result of these deliberations was the Four-Power Treaty, which accorded with American intentions. The United States, Great Britain,

Japan, and France agreed to respect one another's insular possessions in the Pacific Ocean, to refer any dispute among the signatories to a conference of the four powers for "consideration and adjustment," and in the event of a threat to the possessions by any other power, to consult about measures to be taken "jointly or separately." The treaty was to run ten years, and upon ratification it formally ended the Anglo-Japanese Alliance—a major American objective. The United States succeeded in gaining a specific guarantee for its own island possessions (e.g., the Philippines). It avoided acknowledging Japan's special interests in Manchuria and Inner Mongolia (or elsewhere on the Asian mainland), and by including the French (as Hughes said afterward), it ensured that American interests would not be compromised in any tripartite agreement by a 2-to-1 Anglo-Japanese decision. The United States also got a guarantee of free access to the Japanese-mandated island of Yap, a link in the transpacific cable system.

The third major agreement of the Washington Conference was the Nine-Power Treaty signed by the attending nations. The four principles of the treaty were largely the work of the Republican elder statesman Elihu Root. The first three principles pledged the signatories to respect the sovereignty, independence, and territorial and administrative integrity of China; to provide the "fullest and most unembarrassed" opportunity for the growth of a stable Chinese government; and to maintain equal commercial and industrial opportunity for all of the signatory powers in China. The fourth principle, or Root "security clause," pledged the signatories neither to seek special rights or privileges in China that would abridge those of citizens of other states nor to take any action "inimical to the security of such States." The signatories pledged not to sign any treaty that ran counter to the Nine-Power Treaty or to support any of their nationals who entered into agreements seeking to create spheres of influence or mutually exclusive opportunities. The Chinese were not to discriminate among foreign commerce in charges for the use of railroad and other facilities. The British agreed to return to China the port of Weihaiwei on the Shantung Peninsula (an action delayed until 1930), while the Japanese returned to China sovereignty over Shantung. Japan's action was of major importance: because the question of sovereignty over the Peninsula was a burning issue to the Chinese; and because the British felt, as stated by their chief delegate to the conference, Arthur Balfour, that Japan's sovereignty there gave it exclusive control "of one of the most important means of peaceful economic penetration into the vitals of China." Concurrently, the Japanese withdrew their remaining troops from Siberia.

Harding and Hughes regarded the Nine-Power Treaty as a triumph for the United States, which achieved formal recognition of the Open

Door policy in China enunciated in Secretary of State John Hay's famous notes of 1899–1900. Moreover, Harding informed the Senate in March 1922, the Nine-Power Treaty by definition superseded the ambiguous Lansing-Ishii agreement of 1917, which was only an expression of executive policy. And then, as if to minimize further the importance of that agreement, the President added that previously the United States had recognized Japan's special interests in China as being different from every other nation's interests in degree (by virtue of proximity and heavy investment) rather than in kind.

The Japanese thought otherwise. Apparently, they had readily accepted the principles of the Nine-Power Treaty for three reasons. First, its chief draftsman, Root, was known to be favorably disposed toward Japan and a spokesman for bankers and industrialists with heavy interests there. Second, the Japanese believed that the Root "security clause" recognized Japan's special interests in Manchuria and Inner Mongolia, interests they deemed vital to their country's security. And third, Root had indicated to the Japanese that the United States acquiesced in this latter point of view. The Japanese at once queried Harding's assertion that the Nine-Power Treaty superseded the Lansing-Ishii agreement; or as they put it, they wanted to know why the agreement was dead, even though it did not conflict with any treaty? Hughes replied merely by reiterating Harding's points, and then in May 1922 he told the Japanese that if they still regarded the Lansing-Ishii agreement as being in effect it would also be necessary to publish the protocol, kept secret at Japanese insistence, under which the United States and Japan had pledged not to seek privileges in China that would abridge the rights of other nations. Diplomatic exchanges on this issue continued until December 1922, when the Japanese declared that their special interests in China existed "with or without express recognition embodied in diplomatic instruments," and that their concurrence in the cancellation of the Lansing-Ishii agreement was "not to be taken as an indication of a change in the position of Japan relating to China." Hughes replied that he was "happy" the Japanese did not claim any special rights prejudicial to China or to other foreign powers and had agreed to cancel the Lansing-Ishii notes.

In accepting the Nine-Power Treaty and terminating the Lansing-Ishii agreement, the United States and Japan either talked past one another or deliberately obscured their differing views on whether the treaty applied to China's northernmost regions, Manchuria and Inner Mongolia. Despite these diplomatic obfuscations, however, the Harding-Hughes administration hailed the Four-, Five-, and Nine-Power treaties as inaugurating a new era of stability and peace in the Pacific region, and the treaties readily won consent in the Senate. The Nine-Power

Treaty gained unanimous consent, while there was only one dissenting vote cast against the Five-Power Naval Limitation Treaty. Only the Four-Power Treaty ran into difficulty. Ironically, the leading challengers or skeptics, such as Senators Borah, Johnson, and La Follette and the Democrats who were seeking retribution for Woodrow Wilson's difficulties, usually asked the wrong questions. Their main line of questioning was directed toward ascertaining whether the United States had entered into some form of alliance with an imperial power, which might necessitate American military involvement in China. Nothing could have been further from the minds of American statesmen. Hughes had told the American delegation to the Washington Conference in December 1921 that his policy was predicated on the presumption that the United States "would never go to war over any aggression on the part of Japan in China." But that only half explained American policy, for even more basic to the strategy of the Republican statesmen in 1921–22 was their determination to avoid or negate the old-fashioned, particularistic alliance systems of the pre-1914 era and to replace the spheres-of-influence policy—always supported by force—with the commercially competitive and advantageous American Open Door policy. And in this they had succeeded, or so they thought, at the Washington Conference.

Thus, it could fall to the man the Harding administration had chosen to steer the Four-Power Treaty through the Senate, the old imperialist and sometime Anglophobe Henry Cabot Lodge, to assure his colleagues in good conscience that the treaty had been concluded "without alliances or penalties or the sanction of force lurking in the background," while President Harding could argue that the United States had preserved the Senate's and the American people's desire "for freedom from entanglements, for preserved traditions, for maintained independence." Appeased, the Senate approved the Four-Power Treaty by 67 to 27, and then, as if to reassure itself, voted 91 to 2 for a reservation stating that under the treaty the United States incurred "no commitment to armed force, no alliance, no obligation to join in any defense."

The Washington Conference marked the end, at least in outward form, of the old era of imperial alliances and policies in Far Eastern international relations and inaugurated a new and relatively stable era of multinational agreements and peaceful coexistence among the Great Powers. Almost unanimously, however, critics of the new Washington treaty system have argued that it contained at least one fatal flaw: that, whereas the Nine-Power Treaty pledged the signatories to respect China's sovereignty and territorial and administrative entity, it did not provide enforcement or coercive machinery that could be used in the event any power violated China's sovereignty or territory. The Nine-Power Treaty rested on good faith rather than good works.

There is another and perhaps better way of defining and analyzing this problem. If the Washington treaty system contained a fatal flaw it was that, whereas it sought to regulate relations among the Great Powers and the way in which they operated in China, it did not come to grips with the problem of China itself, as China was, or, perhaps more important, as it aspired to be.

As in the case of the Paris Peace Conference, the Chinese delegates came to the Washington Conference with high hopes that the assembled nations would grant their country full sovereignty and equality of status. On November 16, 1921, the Chinese delegates put forward a Ten Point statement, or "Bill of Rights," that asked not only that the powers recognize China's sovereignty and territorial and administrative integrity, but that they declare null and void all their special rights, privileges, and immunities in China and review all others to see that they accorded with the conference's principles, and that they terminate all restraints upon China's "political, jurisdictional, and administrative freedom of action." In return for providing the assembled powers with equal commercial opportunity in China, the Chinese were demanding an end to the century-old system of extraterritoriality, foreign control over China's tariff system, foreign leases on port cities, and foreign control of the so-called international settlements. For Chinese nationalists the entire system of "unequal treaties," with its clearly implied status of inferiority, was a gross, unacceptable affront to Chinese dignity, an infringement on China's sovereignty, and a mechanism whereby foreign powers inhibited China's quest for national unity and corresponding respect and power abroad.

Whether agreeing to all of China's proposals at the Washington Conference would have saved China from the following three decades of civil and foreign wars, and spared the Great Powers a war as well, is a moot question. Whatever the answer, in 1921 the Great Powers were not willing to grant China the status it craved. The reasons for this were a complex and overlapping combination of racial and imperial political and economic factors. Indisputably, neither by Western, or Anglo-American, standards (if indeed these ought to have applied) nor by Japanese standards, nor in comparison with the reality of a strong and unified Japan, did China possess a government that represented the whole country and was willing or able to deal efficiently with the myriad political, economic, legal, and technical problems that were a function of the sprawling foreign investment and delegations resident in China.

From 1920 to 1924, the recognized provisional government in Peking was controlled by the Chih-li military party and its chief *tuchun* (loosely, warlord), Wu P'ei-fu, who determined to unite China, and who had a relatively good reputation for honesty. His Chih-li faction was anti-Bolshevik and more nationalist than the Anfu party it had displaced, which was more given to cooperating with Japan. Manchuria was dominated by its famous *tuchun,* Chang Tso-lin, who held no office in Peking but strongly influenced successive governments there. He was an enemy of Wu P'ei-fu, and finally defeated him in September 1924 and brought the Anfu party back to power under Tuan Ch'i-jui. In the south, at Canton, since 1917 Sun Yat-sen's Kuomintang regime had rivaled the one in Peking, with Sun the nominal "President" of China. Sun was devoted to his three principles (largely Western-inspired) of National-ism, Democracy, and the People's Livelihood, all of which suggested nothing more radical than social democracy. Throughout the rest of China, *tuchuns* held sway in their respective provinces, exercising far more control than any central government and constantly shifting their loyalty, however nominal, to whichever faction, north or south, they felt would best serve their interests. China's administrative chaos spilled over into the question of exactly what constituted its territorial integrity, for Chang Tso-lin felt that his Manchuria was not really a part of China (a view, ironically, that the Japanese shared), even if he wished to dominate it from his headquarters in Mukden.

From the British point of view in 1921, the provisional government in Peking had to be dealt with carefully. Sun Yat-sen was regarded as a wholly impractical visionary, and all the warlords were too quick to steal the cash boxes and use the funds in an attempt to buy the loyalty of their troops. Stated succinctly a dozen years later by Sir John Pratt, the Far Eastern adviser for the Foreign Office during 1925–38, the Chinese were "endowed with almost every gift except a sense of political reali-ties and a capacity for centralized government." Under these circum-stances, the British were wary of changes that might jeopardize their extensive investment in, and trade with, China, which by 1931 amounted to about $700 million. Relatively, this sum was not so significant, for China took only 2.5 per cent of the total of British exports and consti-tuted 5 per cent of British investment abroad. Moreover, in forming policy toward and in China, the British had to take several other, often conflicting, factors into account. They had strong commonwealth ties to Australia and New Zealand, which were highly fearful of Japan and therefore anti-Japanese, while India, the "crown jewel" of the empire, had to be protected from any foreign encroachment. Nonetheless, the British admired the Japanese for having moved from feudalism to modernity in fewer than fifty years, and felt that Japan (also a vigorous island empire) needed markets and resources that China could supply. Hence, while British interests had to be preserved, it was necessary to allow for Japan's interests, provided these did not become exclusive.

The Japanese view of the "China problem," if somewhat less racial or patronizing than the British, was no less imperial. The manner in which the Japanese ruled and exploited Korea, and then moved in on Shantung and Manchuria, inspired little confidence in both Chinese and foreign observers. In Shantung in 1919, the Japanese, having seized the German concessions, took over the entire railroad system, set up their own wireless systems, and, as one British observer noted (in inimitable Victorian style), flooded the province with "disreputable" Japanese who allied with bandit chiefs and trafficked heavily in "drugs and other lures to disturb the public order and to debauch the manhood of the people," while some 1,500 Japanese officials, aided and abetted by the government in Tokyo, ran the province as a virtual colony. Expressed in another way, between 1921 and 1931 China absorbed a fourth of Japan's total exports and nine-tenths—about $1 billion—of its total foreign investment. The Japanese thus took a dim, if not aggressive, view of any government in Peking, warlord regime in Manchuria or elsewhere, or any foreign government that in any way jeopardized Japan's interests in China, including Manchuria.

The American attitude toward China was a composite of many factors. Long-standing missionary endeavors combined with Wilsonian idealism and protectiveness inclined Americans to be sympathetically disposed toward Chinese nationalism and aspirations, but these led to the presumptuous and patronizing view that the Christian, capitalist, and treaty systems that had been imposed upon China really worked for its ultimate benefit. The American Government by no means wanted to involve itself in the civil war in China and tried to remain aloof from the constant strife. But there was a preference for regimes that maintained order, and "impartial" dislike for those whose policies, whether properly perceived or not by American officials, could be construed as jeopardizing Western interests. American officials, like their British counterparts, were gravely skeptical about Sun Yat-sen, and in May 1921 the State Department pointedly told a consular official who was conveying information from Sun not to serve as "a vehicle of official communication for an organization in revolt against a government with which the United States is in friendly relations." The minister in Peking, Jacob Gould Schurman, thought Sun was "the one outstanding obstacle" to unification of China under Wu P'ei-fu (seen to be more favorably disposed toward Western business interests), and when an internal revolt overthrew Sun's regime in 1922, Schurman hoped that the revolt, or Wu's forces from Peking, would eliminate Sun. Schurman also counseled against foreign mediation of the dispute lest it "dignify and magnify Sun Yat-sen and assure him of prestige in the future." The Harding administration agreed and even refused Sun the use of an American vessel for safe escort from Canton.

The "market mentality" was another significant factor affecting the

American perspective. As General Leonard Wood, the imperialist governor-general of the Philippines, expressed it in 1922 in a widely held view, China was "the greatest future trade area in the world." Indeed, American trade with China in the 1920's was sizable although it accounted for only about 3 per cent of the total of American exports. American investment in China, which by 1933 was approximately $120 million, was about 40 per cent the size of Japan's and 15 per cent the size of England's investment. But whether trade and investment figures were (or are) treated absolutely or relatively, in terms of the present or future prospects the result was always the same. As Sir John Pratt remarked in 1933 with seeming timelessness, "China has always . . . been the occasion of political activities by Japan and the Great Powers of Europe and America out of all proportion to the volume of trade passing over her borders."

This combination of Anglo-American-Japanese racial-imperial attitudes toward China and Great Power distrust of one another led to a mixed reception in 1921 for China's Bill of Rights—its demand for sovereignity and termination of the unequal treaties. No doubt the United States thought of itself as China's "friend," but as Secretary Hughes told Minister Schurman on December 7, 1921, Schurman should inform the Peking government that there was a "very real danger that a policy of insisting upon impractical points of view may defeat the hopes of China and of China's friends that the Conference may help in ameliorating some at least of the existing unfortunate conditions." China might progress only according to the judgment and standards of foreign powers.

The Americans, British, and Japanese agreed to the Nine-Power Treaty, which recognized China's sovereignty and territorial integrity and promised to provide conditions that would help create a stable central government, but specific Chinese requests were brushed aside or evaded. Foreign troops would not be withdrawn until the Chinese could guarantee foreign lives and property. Foreign radio stations were placed under Chinese control—except where they counted, in the sprawling leased territories and the Japanese-controlled South Manchurian Railroad zone. Foreign postal services were limited to leased areas, provided the Chinese maintained efficient services elsewhere and a foreign codirector of the postal system. Most important, the Chinese demand for an end to extraterritoriality was rebuffed. Instead, the Great Powers agreed to form a special commission to investigate Chinese legal and administrative systems and suggest reforms that, if adopted by the Chinese, might warrant the Great Powers' relinquishing, "progressively or otherwise," their respective extraterritorial privileges. China's request for tariff autonomy was refused: The Great Powers agreed to grant China a 2.5 per cent surtax increase in customs rates for revenue purposes—but only at some future conference that would meet "as from such date, for such purposes, and subject to such conditions" as the Great Powers themselves would determine.

Because of many factors, including French failure to ratify the Washington treaties until July 1925, the conferences on tariff autonomy and extraterritoriality were delayed until 1925 and 1926, while momentous developments occurred in the meantime. The Peking regime was as disappointed with the Washington Conference as the Chinese had been with the Paris Conference, yet nationalist antipathies toward the Peking regime increased because it was seen as a vassal of the imperial powers. Further, Sun Yat-sen's Kuomintang in Canton now had nowhere to turn for assistance except toward Soviet Russia, which was deliberately excluded by the United States and the other powers from the Washington Conference. In 1922, Sun agreed to Sino-Soviet management of the Chinese Eastern Railroad in Manchuria and the maintenance of Russian troops in Outer Mongolia, although, in truth, he had no control in either region. In 1924, upon the recommendation of Chiang Kai-shek, who had been to Moscow for training, Sun agreed to allow the Russian adviser, Mikhail Borodin, to restructure the Kuomintang along Communist Party lines. They formally allied the Kuomintang with the small Communist Party in China and issued a joint declaration calling for the end of the unequal treaty system and all foreign concessions. The Peking regime in turn could respond to these nationalist and anti-imperialist pressures only by giving *de jure* recognition to the Soviet Union in May 1924 and granting it virtually the same control—which its armies had taken already—over Outer Mongolia and the Chinese Eastern Railroad that Sun's regime had.

The marriage between Moscow and the Kuomintang in Canton was purely one of convenience. Sun disliked communism, which he thought inapplicable to China, and distrusted the Russians. The Russians likewise thought China scarcely ripe for communism, but they were interested in a Chinese lever to counter Western hostility toward the Soviet Union. Nonetheless, the Moscow-Canton relationship virtually negated the intent of the Washington Conference system and lent organization and virulence to the antiforeign or anti-imperial drive among Chinese nationalists. Western powers remained complacent, and their preoccupation remained, as Hughes expressed it in December 1922, the way in which the Chinese Government made recompense for damages to foreign property or lives. This 1920's version of "strict accountability" was indicative of the Western failure to appreciate the full and ultimate significance of the raging civil wars in China and the way in which antiforeignism and anti-imperialism fueled the fires. John V. MacMurray, head of the State Department's Far Eastern Division, and then minister to China from 1925 to 1929, was perhaps the least favorably disposed of his colleagues toward China or its nationalism, but his comment of November 1924 was typical: "We have no favorites in the dog fight in China: they all look alike to us." He added that the State Department's only hope was that "somebody, whoever it may be, licks his rivals completely," so that he would become the recognized authority.

American and Western complacency was shaken in 1925. During the previous autumn, the Anfu party under Tuan Ch'i-jui, abetted by Manchuria's Chang Tso-lin, ousted the Chih-li faction under Wu P'ei-fu in Peking, and in January1925 Sun Yat-sen, too, arrived in Peking to negotiate with the Tuan government, vowing to liberate China from its status as a "secondary colony." But Sun died of cancer on March 3, and the more militant, or left-wing, members of the Kuomintang, including Chiang Kai-shek, opposed *rapprochement* with the Tuan regime, while antiforeign agitation and labor disputes in foreign-owned factories in the treaty ports reached new heights. In May, one laborer was killed in a Japanese-owned cotton mill, and on May 30, in Shanghai, British police killed seven and wounded many unarmed Chinese students.

The "Shanghai incident" caused the Peking government to demand indemnities for the killings and revision of the unequal treaties. The British felt their soldiers had done their best to maintain public order. The Americans were of two minds. In Peking, Minister MacMurray took a dim view of granting the Chinese demands, although he expressed surprise at the depth of Chinese national self-consciousness and the way in which the Shanghai incident had "awakened instincts and passions hitherto dormant, and given an element of fanatacism to what were behind the somewhat unsympathetic and desultory aspirations of the small articulate portion of the Chinese people." In the United States, however, men such as Senator Borah demanded an end to the unequal treaties, and a significant portion of the newspaper world, including the *New York Times,* suggested a conciliatory posture, as did the new chief of the Far Eastern Division in the State Department, Nelson T. Johnson. It is clear, too, that the new Secretary of State, Frank B. Kellogg, not only felt that the problem called for conciliation but feared that recalcitrance would lead to increased Bolshevik influence within the Chinese nationalist movement. He determined, he said, to meet the "demands of the conservative elements of the Chinese people."

Kellogg convoked the long-awaited Special Tariff Conference, which met from October 1925 to April 1926. He was prepared to grant the Chinese the 2.5 per cent tariff increase provided by the Washington Conference, plus an additional increase of up to 12.5 per cent in return for Chinese abolition of the *likin*—transit taxes imposed upon goods in China at various stages from time of import until their sale in retail shops—which foreigners found bothersome and erratic. In addition, he was ready to set a date for tariff autonomy for China, and he suggested that the conference consider the issue of extraterritoriality. Although the British were willing to grant the Chinese tariff increases if the *likin* were abolished, they considered foreign control over the collection of customs revenue—the British-run Maritime Customs Administration—essential, for they felt that the Chinese were incapable or too corrupt to handle this matter efficiently. Because they thought that China was or ought to be a federal rather than a centralized nation, the British preferred to distribute the proceeds to the provincial governments rather than to a central administration.

The Japanese opposed a 12.5 per cent tariff increase because they feared it would endanger their cotton exports to China and encourage reckless Chinese borrowing (on the basis of increased revenue), which would diminish the value or jeopardize repayment of earlier long-term Japanese loans to China. The Japanese also opposed discussing extraterritoriality. The conferring nations agreed only to grant China tariff autonomy by January 1929 in return for China's pledge to abolish the *likin* by then. They spent the rest of their time wrangling over proposed but never adopted tariff schedules. Any interest in further negotiations ended when the Tuan government collapsed in April 1926. The final effort under the Washington treaty system to achieve multilateral agreement on a new economic status for China was dead.

In January 1926, the Great Powers convened a conference on extraterritoriality but concluded in September that no changes were possible until the Chinese adopted a uniform system of laws and revamped their judiciary and penal systems. This decision rested in part on conditions in China that the civil war exacerbated, but it just as strongly reflected the condescending attitude that, unless China conformed to foreign standards, foreign nations would not surrender their privileges there.

Meanwhile, the Kuomintang, which had proclaimed itself a national government in July 1925, began the first phase of its so-called Northern Expedition in May 1926 and formally convened operations on July 4, 1926. Led militarily by Chiang Kai-shek, but with strong political impetus from the Communist leadership, the Kuomintang's purpose was to defeat the armies of Wu P'ei-fu, Chang Tso-lin, and other northern leaders and unify China, being rid at once of the "aggression of the imperialists" and the "nation-selling warlords," as the Kuomintang manifesto put it. Throughout this period, American officials adopted a "watchful waiting" attitude, not giving *de jure* recognition to any faction and limiting the use of troops to protecting lives and property in the international settlements, despite the preferences for forceful military intervention to reassert treaty "rights" of men like MacMurray and the British, who felt most threatened and at times seemed to bear the brunt of antiforeign nationalism. In March 1927, the United States sent five thousand Marines to Shanghai, but the administration and their field commander, Brigadier General Smedley D. Butler, insisted that their sole purpose was to protect lives. Any effort to pacify the Nationalist movement, Kellogg warned, would require not less than a million and a half troops in the first year alone.

Kellogg sought to appease the Chinese when he issued a statement on January 27, 1927, saying that the United States asked only that its citizens and property in China be protected, that Americans wanted only "equal opportunity" to live and work in China, and that in return the United States would negotiate on tariffs and extraterritoriality with Chinese delegates who represented "the authorities or the people of the country." The Chinese were not assuaged: Tariff and extraterritoriality issues had already been subject to negotiation, and China's problem, which foreigners had done little to resolve, was that it did not possess a government or delegates who could speak for the whole nation. Kellogg's statement offered no new initiative and could be dismissed as intended more for the American public than to deal with Chinese problems or realities.

The virulence of nationalist feeling became evident on March 24, 1927, when Kuomintang soldiers in Nanking rampaged through the city and killed six American, British, and Japanese nationals, including John E. Williams, the American vice-president of Nanking University. The offended nations at once demanded punishment of those responsible, as well as a full apology and reparations. The Kuomintang regime replied that it would afford reparations but could not accept blame, or apologize, until a commission investigated the affair. At this same time, on April 12–13, 1927, Chiang Kai-shek now turned on his Communist allies and began a bloody purge that, in its way, marked the beginning of the intermittent civil war that would plague China for the next quarter century.

Chiang's purge of the Communists had two important effects, both immediate and long range. The West (and Japan) no longer saw him as the "red general" but as a moderate who might overcome China's tendency toward radical nationalism; the British viewed his coup against the Communists as signaling the "revolt of the *bourgeoisie*," as one official said, and at once sought to discourage any sanctions against China for the Nanking incident, blaming it on the Communists. Similarly, both Coolidge and Kellogg saw Chiang as the leader of a new moderate force, and they insisted on a soft line in the Nanking-incident negotiations. The result was an agreement in March 1928 whereby the Kuomintang would express its regret over the episode and assign a mixed commission to assess reparations.

Chiang's purge of the Communists, resting upon an alliance with traditional capitalist Chinese (bankers and landlords), also led to a reign of terror against all opponents and rapid evaporation of whatever zeal for reform had ever existed. As early as August 1927, the British Minister, Sir Miles Lampson, was reporting that the Kuomintang's success against its northern opposition owed more to bribery, extortion, and corruption than to military superiority, while in 1930, just two years after the Kuomintang had established itself as the government of China, the new and favorably disposed American Minister in Peking, Nelson Johnson, was insisting that, if the Kuomintang ultimately prevailed over its opponents, it would be because it had more money "and not because it has ideals that are inspiring the people."

The domestic failings of the Kuomintang were so great that as early as August 1927 Chiang had to retire momentarily from the leadership of the party. In December 1927, he married Wellesley College–educated Soong Mei-ling, whose father was a wealthy Christian Shanghai businessman and former supporter of Sun Yat-sen. Chiang now also converted to Christianity, thereby wedding missionary support to his new capitalist affiliations. Then, in January 1928, he resumed leadership of the Kuomintang, and following the Nanking incident negotiations in March, resumed the Northern Expedition. The Kuomintang finally occupied Peking on July 3, 1928 (which it renamed Peiping, or "northern peace," while retaining the capital at the Kuomintang stronghold in Nanking) and announced that it would end the unequal treaties. The United States recognized Chiang's Nationalist government and concluded a treaty on July 25, 1928, granting China tariff autonomy in return for most-favored-nation status. American officials urged all other powers to open negotiations on extraterritoriality.

Foreign officials were universally hostile to the idea, however, and unconvinced that the Kuomintang ruled all of China. The United States would not relinquish its privileges unilaterally but proposed, in the summer of 1929, that a conference negotiate unilateral gradual relinquishment. Nothing came of this, and in December 1930 the Chinese gave everyone three months to end extraterritoriality. The extraterritoriality issue was soon overshadowed by the outbreak of the undeclared Sino-Japanese war in September 1931. Nonetheless, some American diplomats, such as Minister Nelson Johnson in China, were still arguing as late as 1937 that the United States ought to terminate its extraterritorial privileges, for "we can no longer travel this road and be true to ourselves and our ideals." Few, if any, persons paid attention. Not until

1943, in the middle of the Second World War and the Anglo-American effort to defeat Japan, did Western governments assent to terminating extraterritorial privileges and accord China that long-sought equality of status. By this time, it could have little effect on the outcome of the soon-to-be-renewed civil war in China between the Kuomintang and the Communists or on the succeeding two decades of the Western nations' relations with Mao Tse-tung's People's Republic of China.

Whatever the countless short- or long-run domestic failures of the Kuomintang, in 1928 Chiang's regime, though never free from challenges by provincial leaders and political factions, ruled China at least nominally and restored a measure of its sovereignty. But now China's problems were compounded by the foreign response to its new unity.

One of Chiang's overriding aims was to destroy the Communists, but he also wished to bring Manchuria entirely under Kuomintang rule. Beginning in the spring of 1928 and increasing through 1929, therefore, Kuomintang and loyal forces in Manchuria under Chang Hsüeh-liang (son of Chang Tso-lin, whom the Japanese military had murdered on June 4, 1928) raided Soviet offices in Manchuria, expelled Russian employees, including the assistant manager of the Sino-Soviet-run Chinese Eastern Railroad, and, in July 1929, took control of the railroad and the Russian-controlled telegraph and telephone lines. Russian civilians were placed in concentration camps under wretched conditions; the Chinese in Nanking rejected all diplomatic protests; and Sino-Soviet relations were broken. In August 1929, Soviet forces bombarded and eventually seized Manchurian border towns, and by November the Chinese were appealing for diplomatic assistance, perhaps a conference, to the signatories of the Kellogg-Briand Pact.

Foreign response was unsympathetic. The British thought China's difficulties would provide a breathing spell on the extraterritorial issue. The Japanese, who had thought Chiang Kai-shek and Chang Hsüeh-liang had tacitly agreed to preserve Japan's special economic status in Manchuria, had been disappointed when Manchuria formally reunified itself with China under Kuomintang rule in December 1928. The Japanese also did not favor any multilateral intervention in the Sino-Soviet crisis of 1929 lest it set a precedent that might be invoked if Japan acted unilaterally to defend its interests in Manchuria.

American officials were very upset over the reports on conditions in the concentration camps, and the State Department indicated that the Chinese should end the entire conflict by accepting the Russian offer to appoint new personnel for the Chinese Eastern Railroad. From the American vantage point, the Chinese were violating their 1924 treaty arrangements, and they would do well to settle before the Russians, now on the offensive and determined to maintain their treaty rights, imposed severe losses. The United States was concerned that the intent of Chinese action had been to establish a precedent for the forcible overthrow of other treaty rights, especially extraterritoriality. Finally, in late November 1929, Secretary of State Stimson, who wished to restrain China as well as Russia, chose not to invoke the Kellogg-Briand Pact formally but to call it to the attention of both powers through diplomatic notes. By this time, the Chinese had recognized their diplomatic isolation and collapsing military situation and had agreed to direct negotiations. This led to an agreement on December 22 that restored the *status quo ante bellum,* or all of the Soviet Union's 1924 treaty rights in Manchuria.

But the Sino-Soviet agreement ended only the first phase of the crisis over Manchuria. Japan's stake in this region, rich in timber, coal, gold, iron, soybeans, and grains, was enormous, and for reasons of national interest and prestige no government in Tokyo would relinquish Japan's holdings or claims to special status in Manchuria. Throughout the 1920's, civil officials had sought to avoid the overt use of force and to protect Japan's Manchurian stake through multilateral agreements with other Great Powers or bilateral negotiations with the Chinese. By the end of the decade, however, Japan's Manchurian—or Kwantung—Army and South Manchurian Railroad and territorial officials constituted an entrenched bureaucracy, with a life and commitment of its own. The army especially feared the rise of Chinese nationalism, Russian incursions, and foreign competition. In June 1928, some senior officers of the Kwantung Army decided on their own to assassinate Manchuria's ruler, Chang Tso-lin, not only because they thought his son, Chang Hsüeh-liang, would prove more malleable, but because they hoped the assassination would throw Manchuria into chaos and provide a pretext for a military takeover. The governments in Tokyo and Nanking, however, combined to prevent further action, although Premier Giichi Tanaka had to resign because he wanted to prosecute the officers. The army refused because it feared its plans would be exposed, thus creating a domestic as well as foreign crisis.

Kwantung officers persevered, however, and during 1930, in concert with the War Ministry in Toyko, agreed upon a three-stage "solution" of the Manchurian problem. The military sought, first, to get the Mukden officials to guarantee Japan's rights in Manchuria; failing that, they hoped to establish a pro-Japanese regime in Mukden; failing that, they determined to conquer Manchuria by force. The military's boldness was increased by the fact that it had direct access to the Emperor and tremendous influence over the civil government, as General Tanaka's resignation showed. The military was a potent political force in Japan, where parliamentary government rested on a shaky foundation. The younger, more ambitious, more restless military officers were not in the tradition of the *samurai,* nor did they come from the older, aristocratic (or more cautious) classes. Often, they were men of rural background with strong attachment to, and influence over, their peasant conscripts and the peasant masses. And as the Great Depression wore on after 1929, the peasantry suffered enormously. They were easily roused to assaults on the so-called civilian elites and civil government, and they acquiesced in or espoused ultranationalist or chauvinistic acts, such as the shooting of Premier Hamaguchi in November 1930 for accepting the compromises of the London Naval Conference.

Further, Sino-Japanese relations seriously deteriorated during 1928–31, as the Kuomintang sought to end extraterritoriality, built railway lines in Manchuria to compete with the Japanese-owned South Manchurian Railroad, harassed Japanese and Korean citizens in Manchuria, and boycotted Japanese goods. In those three years, there were some 120 cases of alleged Chinese violation of Japanese rights and interests in Manchuria, ranging from excessive taxation to infringement on property rights and unlawful detention. The Japanese concluded that the Chinese intended to force them to abandon their special status in Manchuria, and in the spring and summer of 1931 conditions reached the flash point, first, when Chinese peasants destroyed part of the work of a Korean rice-cultivating community, and, later, when Chinese troops apparently captured and shot a Japanese intelligence officer.

Key military officials in Manchuria and in Japan now agreed to act. The only question was whether to strike in September 1931, as the Kwantung officers wanted, or to wait until spring or summer 1932, as the Tokyo military preferred, in order to build public support. There was also some disagreement over whether a struggle in Manchuria should be coupled with a *coup d'état* in Tokyo and the establishment of a military dictatorship. The "Manchuria first" advocates, however, forced abandonment of this latter idea, but on the night of September 18, 1931, Kwantung officers claimed that Chinese troops had destroyed a piece of track on the South Manchuria Railroad just north of Mukden, and within hours the army occupied the capital city. Three days later, Japanese troops began to chase "bandits" in the direction of Tsitsihar, some 370 miles northwest of Mukden, and occupied that area on November 9. They bombed Chang Hsüeh-liang's headquarters at Chinchow, 175 miles southwest of Mukden near the Great Wall, and occupied it on January 2, 1932. Japan was now in military control of Manchuria, and in February the Tokyo government, acquiescing in the military's pressure and *faits accomplis,* established the state of Manchukuo with Henry Pu-yi, heir to the throne of the collapsed Manchu Dynasty of 1911, serving as Regent.

The Chinese had offered no military opposition. Chiang Kai-shek, partly because he believed that domestic political opponents had to be destroyed first and partly because he felt Chang Hsüeh-liang's 400,000-man army was not a match for the smaller but better-trained and -equipped Japanese forces, had ordered a strict policy of nonresistance and appealed to the League of Nations on September 21. Foreign response again was tepid. Western nations admired neither the Chinese Nationalist challenge to the treaty system nor Chinese weakness and inability to resist the Japanese, whose mirroring of Western strength and purpose inspired resentment yet admiration. Manchuria was "a long way off," as French Premier André Tardieu said, and his country's primary concerns were its investments in Yunnan province in south China and Indochina, and Germany and the war debts–reparations issue. The primary concerns of the British in the Far East were their investments in China proper, from Peking south to Canton and the Crown Colony of Hong Kong, and seething political unrest in India. Throughout the Manchurian crisis (and after), the British aimed, as Foreign Secretary John Simon noted at a Cabinet meeting on November 11, 1931, to be "conciliatory" toward Japan, against which "we don't want to apply sanctions," while the Chinese would be told not to rely on others but to play their part and to avoid seeking sanctions under Article XVI of the League Covenant. The world economic crisis was crucial too. The British had to leave the gold standard in September 1931, a psychological blow nearly as crushing as the unemployment lines. And as Chancellor of the Exchequer Neville Chamberlain insisted in March 1932, "We are no more in a position financially and economically to engage in a major war in the Far East than we are militarily."

Domestic and foreign political Anglo-French concerns, shared by the Great Powers, were reflected in the cautious policy of the League of Nations, whose Council requested, on September 21, 1931, that Japan and China end hostilities. A few days later, on September 30, it expressed approval of Japan's intent to withdraw its troops to the railway zone, while the Chinese pledged responsibility for life and property. The League Council invoked the Kellogg-Briand Pact in October. Watching the continued deployment of Japanese troops, it set a November 16 deadline for their withdrawal but proposed no means to enforce this. Officials in Toyko insisted that withdrawal could not begin until after the Chinese gave guarantees for Japan's subjects and treaty rights in Manchuria. But as a show of faith at the end of November, the Japanese halted their attack on Chinchow and proposed an inquiry into the conflict. On December 10, the League established a commission under Lord Lytton that included French, German, Italian, and American representatives.

American views of the crisis were similar to those of other foreign observers. Nelson Johnson, now minister to China, viewed Japan's military action as a premeditated "aggressive act," but even after the total occupation of Manchuria in January 1932 he felt that Chinese revocation of treaty rights had provoked it all. Japan's error was tactical: that is, using force instead of seeking legal redress through the International Court at The Hague. Above all, Johnson felt Congress and public opinion should not and would not approve any sanctions, which would only wreck the Japanese economy to the detriment of American trade, while creating revolutionary conditions in Japan.

Secretary Stimson was also sympathetic toward the Japanese, or at least the civil government in Tokyo. He hoped that the military action beginning in September 1931 was just another local "mutiny," and that the Japanese would soon be "crawling back into their dens," as he confided to his diary. He viewed favorably the reassurances given by Ambassador Katsuji Debuchi in Washington, and the Secretary's earliest formal diplomatic responses (to the embitterment of the Chinese) expressed only "regret" or "great concern" over the crisis. Stimson opposed any plan for a neutral commission and instructed the American Minister in Switzerland, Hugh Wilson, that the United States favored resolution of the conflict through direct negotiations between Japan and China. Failing that, the Americans next preferred that League machinery be used to effect a settlement; or, finally, that negotiations be held either under the 1922 Nine-Power Treaty or in accordance with the provisions of the Kellogg-Briand Pact.

On October 8, 1931, Stimson told the Chinese that the United States was discussing neither right nor wrong, nor was it taking sides. "We are playing no favorites." The object was "to let the Japanese know we are watching them and at the same time to do it in such a way which will help [Foreign Minister] Shidehara, who is on the right side, and not play into the hands of any nationalist agitators." Shortly thereafter, Stimson allowed the American consul in Geneva, Prentiss Gilbert, to attend League Council meetings as an "observer," but he worried about Japanese opposition to this: "It lines us up vis-à-vis Japan, just the position that I have been trying to avoid." After the Council invoked the Kellogg-Briand Pact on October 17, Stimson agreed, only after British insistence, to allow Gilbert to continue sitting at "the damned table," provided he would "keep his mouth shut." Stimson's endorsement of the League's resolution of October 24 was communicated to Japan only two weeks after the Council's action, without mention of the November 16 deadline for the withdrawal of troops. In sum, American policy not only sought to play no favorites and not antagonize Japan but also reflected American determination to prevent the League of Nations or anyone else from "leaving any baby" on the American "doorstep." In all these matters, Stimson, the State Department, and President Hoover thought and acted in virtual unanimity and agreed, as Hoover said, that America could not go beyond "moral pressures," and that military or economic sanctions were only "roads to war."

Stimson's attitude began to change in late November, when the Japanese taking of Tsitsihar suggested to him that the situation was "in the hands of virtually mad dogs." But early in December, President Hoover ruled out any thought of sanctions as producing only "incurable hatreds" and being like "sticking pins in tigers." Stimson was further upset when the Japanese Cabinet fell on December 11 (only a day after establishment of the Lytton Commission) and was replaced by another under Premier Inukai Tsuyoshi and Foreign Minister Yoshizawa Kenkichi that appeared to be more susceptible to military influence. Japan's final occupation of Chinchow on January 2, 1932, brought matters to a climax, and Stimson determined to state in advance that the United States would not recognize any changes in territorial status brought about by force.

Stimson had three sources for this inspiration. Secretary of State Bryan's notes had taken this position over the Twenty-one Demands in 1915, Hoover had made a similar suggestion on November 7, 1931, and in December 1931 the columnist Walter Lippmann had proposed such a course in lieu of military action. The result, with Hoover's approval, was Stimson's note of January 7, 1932, to the Chinese and Japanese governments, stating that the United States would not admit the legality of any agreement or treaty that impaired "the treaty rights of the United States or its citizens in China, including those which relate to the sovereignty, the independence, or the territorial and administrative integrity of the Republic of China, commonly known as the open door policy." Nor would the United States recognize agreements brought about contrary to the Kellogg-Briand Pact.

The United States had acted unilaterally, and Stimson had expected the British to follow suit. However, they opposed any action that might further offend or antagonize Japan and believed that neither the League nor the United States had any more business in Manchuria than it did in India. Equally important, in January 1932 Foreign Office personnel felt that the United States was "unreliable," "quite capable of backing out after we had agreed to give our support, leaving us to clean up the resulting mess." Or, as Stanley Baldwin, Lord President of the Council and a leader in the Cabinet, said in February 1932, "You will get nothing out of Washington but words, big words, but only words." Instead of endorsing the Hoover-Stimson doctrine of nonrecognition of January 7, 1932, the British reiterated their support for the open door in Manchuria and requested that Japan reaffirm its intention to abide by this policy. Stimson was piqued and convinced that with "No. 1 . . . backing out" so would everyone else. Nonetheless, Stimson still looked upon his notes of January 7 as urging a negotiated settlement of the Sino-Japanese conflict rather than presaging sanctions against Japan. Thus ended the first phase of the Sino-Japanese crisis in Manchuria.

The second phase began on January 28, 1932, when the Japanese, in response to a Chinese boycott of Japanese goods and general harassment, bombarded the Chinese district of Chapei in Shanghai and thereby shifted the geographical basis of the conflict from Manchuria to China proper. The United States and Great Britain moved land and naval reinforcements to the area, but this was only to protect lives and property. In Cabinet meetings on January 26 and January 29, Hoover insisted that it would be "folly" to get into a war with Japan, and that the United States should try to end the fighting in Shanghai by conciliatory methods. Stimson was less certain, but when the Japanese requested American good offices on February 1, he formulated a five-point program for a cease-fire and simultaneous resolution of the Manchurian and Shanghai crises. But the Japanese refused to link the two, insisting Manchuria was a special case.

Stimson again turned toward Great Britain. In a series of telephone calls during February 11–16, in which poor connections hindered conversation, he told Foreign Secretary John Simon that "there is no further opportunity for conciliation." He proposed a joint invocation of the Nine-Power Treaty, which provided for consultation in case of disputes, but which also might be interpreted as implying some form of sanctions in the event talks failed. Stimson was determined to link Manchuria with Shanghai in order "not to lose the moral issue," and also so as not to rouse Chinese nationalists against all foreigners who might otherwise be seen as appeasing Japan in Manchuria to salvage their investments in China proper.

Simon responded as warmly as he could about his intent to "go hand in hand with you" and "do my best," but at least two factors made the British wish to delay. First, Simon said, they held "a more hopeful view of things being stopped," and second, the British, as League members, had to act in concert with that body and not pronounce judgment "alone right away." Where British policy really diverged from Stimson's was in looking toward a settlement of the Shanghai (or Chinese proper) crisis without linking it to Manchuria. And where Stimson now was prepared to resort to sanctions, Simon told the Cabinet on February 15, 1932, that he "never for one moment favoured the adoption by the League of any kind of sanctions, not even of an economic kind . . . we might provoke a situation that precipitated Japanese resentment." Moreover the British thoroughly distrusted the Americans.

By February 16, Stimson concluded that the British would not accede to his proposed demarche—they had "let us down"—and instead, with Hoover's approval, released a public letter of February 23, 1932, to Senator Borah, chairman of the Senate Foreign Relations Committee. In this letter, Stimson reviewed the Open Door policy, reaffirmed the nonrecognition policy of January 7, recommended that other nations adopt it, and made the "new" point that the Four-, Five-, and Nine-Power Washington treaties were "interdependent and interrelated," and that to violate one would be to release the signatories from their obligations under the others. In short, if Japan violated China's integrity, the United States might feel free to construct battleships and fortifications without limit.

Aside from keeping straight the long-run legal and historical record, Stimson intended his statement to "keep the Japanese guessing" about whether the United States might use sanctions. Hoover, however, adamantly opposed them and but for Stimson's protests would have publicly ruled out sanctions when the letter to Borah was published. Then, when Stimson went to Europe in May 1932 for disarmament talks, Hoover had Under Secretary of State Castle make two speeches precluding economic or military sanctions against Japan.

Stimson's letter to Borah achieved no immediate purpose, although the League, led by the British, adopted the nonrecognition policy on March 11, 1932. The British otherwise remained determined not to be "dragged" into any action by "American rashness," as Sir Francis Lindley, their ambassador in Tokyo, said, while the Japanese were embittered. Nonetheless, cease-fire and troop withdrawal arrangements were worked out for Shanghai in March 1932, and peace was restored two months later, notwithstanding the fact that military extremists assassinated Japan's Finance Minister in February and Premier Inukai on May 15, 1932.

The Manchurian crisis dragged on. The Japanese recognized Manchukuo in September 1932. In October, the Lytton Commission report blamed Chinese nationalism for stirring difficulties in Manchuria, negated Japan's claim to have acted only in self-defense, and recommended an autonomous regime in Manchuria, under Chinese sovereignty, with safeguards for Japan's special interests. The British were delighted. As their Foreign Office adviser on the Far East, Sir John Pratt, observed, many harsh things were left unsaid about Japan, which would no longer be treated as "a criminal in the dock," face sanctions, or be driven from the League.

The British guessed wrong, for, mild as was the Lytton report, the Japanese were infuriated when the League adopted it in January 1933, and in February they announced their withdrawal from Geneva. They promptly overran Jehol province, just north of the Great Wall, and then in May marched into Hopei province, establishing a military zone thirty to forty miles wide between Peiping and Tientsin, from within which Chinese troops were barred. On May 31, the Chinese agreed to the so-called Tangku Truce, virtually dictated by the Japanese, who were left in full control in Manchuria and Jehol. They gained extensive rights in Hopei and were a military threat to much of North China. Characteristically, Chiang Kai-shek simultaneously launched his Fourth Bandit Suppression campaign against the Communists with a quarter-million of his best troops.

In retrospect, American (really Secretary Stimson's) policy has been sharply criticized. Stimson has been viewed, properly enough, as a patrician elitist (Andover, Yale, a protégé of Elihu Root), with a strong legalistic and moralistic bent, given to viewing the world from a "Christian vs. lion" perspective. His nonrecognition policy resulted in the application of a standard of behavior toward Japan's vital interests that was unrealistic (and hypocritical, given Stimson's advocacy of retaining the Philippines and a strong American presence in the Pacific) and that served to hasten Japan's entry into the "community of the damned" while not altering the realities or the balance of power in Far Eastern politics. Moreover, while Stimson was prepared to consider economic or military sanctions against Japan in February 1932, Hoover would not, and both Congress and the public would probably have opposed sanctions. Finally, fifteen years after the event, Stimson admitted that the policy of nonrecognition was a failure.

Nonetheless, Stimson had sought to appease the Japanese from September to December 1931, and he turned to nonrecognition only after Japan's assault on Chinchow and occupation of Manchuria in January 1932. He looked to sanctions only after the Shanghai bombing, and less because he wished to pillory the Japanese than because he believed that Japan's action undermined the Washington treaty system (and the Kellogg-Briand Pact), and because he worried that Japan's goal was, or would become, by will or by impetus, the conquest of all China. As Stanley Hornbeck, who was chief of the State Department's Division of Far Eastern Affairs and who opposed sanctions against Japan, noted on May 9, 1933, the Japanese "are making 'war' in fact (though not in name) an instrument of national policy." Stimson believed that only collective action could stop the assault on both China and the treaty system. He stood, as he noted, like a man with a shovel in his hands before a breaking dam, and he sought means to halt the impending flood.

The British drew different conclusions from the same evidence. They sought to minimize conflict by conciliating or conceding as much as they could, while aiming first to preserve their empire. They were not cynically pro-Japanese, but as the Foreign Office specialist Victor Wellesley said in February 1932, Manchuria was never wholly identified with China, and he questioned whether a country of China's "size and wealth . . . is justified in obstructing the economic development of her more active and enterprising neighbour to the general detriment of world interests." Or as Simon said amidst the Shanghai crisis, "From the point of view of the security of the Settlement, it appeared better that the Japanese should succeed than the Chinese." Admiring Japanese capacities, and disdaining the Chinese and the implications of their nationalism, the British intended to afford Japan hegemony in Manchuria in return for the preservation of their imperial interests elsewhere in China and the Pacific. Seen in this light, British policy, especially that of Foreign Secretary Simon, once criticized for vacillating (or even "weaseling," as Stimson had said in 1931) and too quickly appeasing Japanese aggression, has begun to enjoy a new vogue. The British went as far as they could within the political, economic, and military limits of the era while also seeking to maintain a delicate balance between their desire to cooperate with the (unreliable) United States and their obligations to the League and to British imperial, or commonwealth, interests. Whether such policy was more realistic than Stimson's, or would succeed in "containing" Japan any more than had the Anglo-Japanese agreement between 1905 and 1921, time would tell. For the immediate future, the locus of the crisis in world politics again seemed to shift back to Europe.

5

The Era of
Appeasement

Between 1933 and 1939, Adolf Hitler's diplomacy and saber-rattling destroyed the political and military structure established at the Paris Peace Conference in 1919 and moved Germany to a position of virtual superiority in Western and Central Europe. The response of the administration of President Franklin D. Roosevelt to this dramatic shift of power was extremely cautious and aloof. Several factors were obviously responsible for this. Undeniably, Roosevelt's overriding concern throughout the decade was to deal with the Great Depression, and domestic policy took priority over foreign affairs at least until 1939.

Public and congressional attitudes also circumscribed the administration's alternatives. Revisionist literature in the 1920's had discredited traditional explanations of the origins of the First World War. Publication in 1934 of such best-selling works as Helmuth C. Engelbrecht and Frank C. Hanighen's *Merchants of Death: A Study of the International Armaments Industry,* and George Seldes's *Iron, Blood, and Profits: An Exposure of the World-Wide Munitions Racket,* combined with the publicity generated in 1934–36 by Senator George P. Nye's committee investigation of the munitions industry, challenged the propriety of relationships between bankers, munitions-makers, and government officials and the forces that might have led America to war in 1917. This sentiment manifested itself in the Neutrality Act of August 1935, which empowered the President to prohibit sale or shipment of arms, munitions, and implements of war to all parties involved in a conflict. Congress extended the law in February 1936, and in January 1937, at the administration's behest, it passed special legislation to cover the Spanish Civil War. The Neutrality Act of May 1937 allowed the President to embargo nonmilitary goods. It also contained a provision for the next two years that, if the President had to invoke the Neutrality Act, he might also, in the name of national security, place all trade on a "cash-and-carry" basis, thereby favoring the British with their large navy and merchant marine. But the primary purpose of the 1937 law was to allow Americans to maintain their neutrality and to carry on a lucrative war-time trade without the risk that commercial debts, or the loss of ships at sea, might lead to the circumstances that had inclined the United States toward intervention on behalf of Great Britain in 1917.

Minor administration efforts at international cooperation were often stymied by ultranationalist sentiments. In January 1935, the Senate Foreign Relations Committee approved a measure proposing that the United States join the World Court, and Roosevelt sent a special message to Congress to urge its passage. But a group of senators, led by Borah, Johnson, and Huey P. Long, and then a last-minute radio and telegram campaign, led by the chauvinistic publisher William Randolph Hearst, the now anti–New Deal "radio-priest," Father Charles E. Cough-lin, and the philosopher of the homespun, Will Rogers, caused crucial defections among supporters of the measure. It failed by seven votes (52–36) to gain the necessary two-thirds majority, despite the fact that the Democrats held 68 Senate seats. Secretary of the Interior Harold Ickes noted shortly thereafter that this defeat cut Roosevelt "pretty deeply," and that even the usually cautious and acquiescent Secretary of State, Cordell Hull, felt bad enough to consider an open fight with the Senate.

The administration was embarrassed in January 1938, one month after the Japanese had sunk the American gunboat *Panay* in the Yangtze River, when Representative Louis Ludlow of Indiana sought to force out of committee his proposed constitutional amendment that would have made a national referendum on a declaration of war mandatory in all instances except those involving direct attack upon the United States, its territories, or the Western Hemispere. Roosevelt had to commit his presidential prestige to prevent the bill's discharge from committee, and the administration prevailed by only the slim margin of 209–188. The World Court and Ludlow episodes were perhaps as much symbolic as real issues, but they indicated the intense opposition the administration would meet if it sought to intervene in the growing world crisis. Roosevelt no doubt had this opposition in mind when he ruefully remarked at mid-decade that it was "a terrible thing to look over your shoulder when you are trying to lead—and to find no one there."

But neither domestic economic concerns, nor congressional and public noninterventionist attitudes, nor the neutrality legislation, sufficiently explains American foreign policy in the 1930's. The emphasis accorded to these events in the past may have obscured analysis of the way in which New Deal officials viewed European developments and the rationale that underlay their strategy and tactics. Past analysis has also overlooked two important factors: (1) intra-administration arguments between those who wished to resist German demands and those who believed that peace was possible only if Germany were properly appeased; and (2) the embittered state of Anglo-American relations, which hampered cooperation at every level and facilitated the adroit exploitation by Hitler of the fears, weaknesses, and divisions in the Western world that ultimately led to war.

Roosevelt was a patrician internationalist; he had admired cousin Theodore Roosevelt's worldly tradition, imbibed Woodrow Wilson's principles for eight years as Assistant Secretary of the Navy, and in 1920 campaigned hard for the League of Nations. By the end of the decade, he deferred to practical and Democratic party politics by urging only "wholehearted cooperation" with the League, and in 1932, to placate the Hearst faction in the Democratic party, he flatly opposed American entry, a view he reiterated before the Woodrow Wilson Foundation in December 1933. All subsequent private talks, such as with Canadian Prime Minister MacKenzie King in the summer of 1936, concerning possible American entry into the League presumed that the League Covenant would be separated from the Treaty of Versailles, which Roosevelt, along with most other American and European diplomats, believed was more the cause of international instability than any single nation or leader.

Roosevelt believed Europe's problems were basically, or exclusively, European, and that the United States could do little to resolve them other than afford moral exhortation. His speech to the Wilson Foundation in December 1933 deplored the fact that 10 per cent of the world menaced the peaceful inclinations of the other 90 per cent, and his January 1936 annual message to Congress assailed nations seeking to redress injustices springing from past wars by reverting to the "law of the sword." But, he always hastened to add, the American response to foreign conflict would always be "a well-ordered neutrality."

Reinforcing Roosevelt's unwillingness to involve the United States in European politics was his dislike or suspicion of the British, and the ambivalent state of Anglo-American relations. Roosevelt disdained the British upper classes, whose political and economic views he considered too narrow, empire-oriented, and at the root of many of the world's past and present problems. He especially disliked the financial or commercial leaders he referred to as "the Bank of England crowd," including Neville Chamberlain, who was Chancellor of the Exchequer from 1931 to May 1937 and then Prime Minister until May 1940. When

Secretary of the Treasury Henry Morgenthau, Jr., asked in 1936 whether he might open talks with the British on stabilization of the exchange rate of the dollar and pound, the President replied that "the trouble is that when you sit around the table with a Britisher he usually gets 80 per cent of the deal and you get what is left. Tell them that. Tell them that if we got 45 per cent we think that would be doing well. As long as Neville Chamberlain is there we must recognize that fundamentally he thoroughly dislikes Americans." Roosevelt also believed, as he said in 1935, that the British Foreign Office needed "a little more unselfish spine," and he always suspected the British were trying to "thrust leadership on me" in order that the United States might bail them out of their European or Far Eastern difficulties, or both.

Secretary of State Cordell Hull also took a dim view of American involvement in European politics, and he, too, was suspicious of British intentions. As a congressman and senator, he had been a prominent champion of a low tariff and Wilson's League of Nations, but as Secretary of State he usually favored taking the path of least resistance at home and abroad, which often meant doing nothing or opting for neutrality. With a repetitiveness that exasperated foreign diplomats, he argued that world peace was possible only by expanding world trade through reciprocal, most-favored-nation agreements, as opposed to the exclusive agreements in the fashion of British imperial preferences or Germany's bilateral agreements with Eastern European countries. In his postwar *Memoirs,* Hull cited the failure of the United States and Great Britain to conclude a trade agreement before the autumn of 1938 (he put the onus on the British) as a major reason war was not averted. This was nearly as much his genuine conviction as retrospective blame-tossing.

Most of Hull's State Department subordinates were not as zealous as he was about increased international trade as the panacea for peace, but they shared similar viewpoints. Career diplomats such as William Phillips, Under Secretary of State from 1933 to 1936 and then ambassador to Italy until 1940, and Jay Pierrepont Moffat, Chief of the Division of Western European Affairs during 1932–35 and 1937–40, were always highly skeptical about American involvement in European affairs, except to encourage the process of appeasement. They were unhappy at Germany's announcement of rearmament in 1935 and its reoccupation of the Rhineland in 1936 but accepted these developments as inevitable. Phillips thought Chamberlain's flights to Germany in September 1938 during the crisis over Czechoslovakia were "fine and courageous," and he also favored American recognition of Italy's conquest of Ethiopia.

Even stronger views came from Hugh R. Wilson, minister to Switzerland 1927–37 (and a trusted go-between for the State Department and League officials), Assistant Secretary of State in 1937, and ambassador to Germany in 1938. Wilson's colleagues considered him a "realist," in contrast to those who held more liberal or "messianic" views and who also took a stiffer attitude toward German and Italian aggression. Not only did Wilson believe that Germany had to be economically satisfied and integrated into Europe's political mainstream, but he admired Germany's internal regimentation and was convinced that its "Strength Through Joy" program would benefit the world. Although he did not approve of German persecution of the Jews, he thought the "Jewish problem" and the American press were the reasons for increasingly bad relations between the United States and Germany. Hitler's plans, Wilson insisted in 1938, "do not necessarily involve the Western powers," and he thought the Munich settlement opened the way "to a better Europe." He also thought throughout the decade that Russia's urging resistance to German demands only endangered European peace. Three months after the Second World War had begun in Europe, he hoped the fighting would be ended so that Germany would be free to "take care of the Russian encroachment" and thereby further "the ends of civilization."

Then there was Sumner Welles, Assistant and later Under Secretary of State during 1933–43, and a close friend and confidant of Roosevelt. Welles's battles with Hull were well known and led to Hull's forcing his resignation in 1943, but their disagreements were personal and concerned diplomatic style and timing more than substantive issues. Welles and Hull agreed on American policy during the Italo-Ethiopian war, but in 1938 Welles favored recognition of Italy's conquest because he wished to appease Italy as the first step of a policy whose larger purpose was to appease Germany. In 1937 and 1938, Welles would make several proposals for achieving world peace that rested upon economic appeasement, and which, in the fashion of Hull's trade agreements, were intended to spill over into political appeasement. Hull opposed these schemes, not because he preferred a more militant stand against Germany, Japan, or Italy, but because he feared the United States was becoming too involved in world problems. Moreover, Welles also was suspicious of British purposes; for, while he would seek their approval to launch his projects, he did so more to prevent their scuttling of them than to confront anyone with an Anglo-American bloc.

By no means was the American emphasis on appeasement in the 1930's a unanimous or monolithic view. Roosevelt himself was torn with doubt about its usefulness in dealing with Nazi Germany, and as early as the spring of 1934 he asked the State Department to consider a multinational trade boycott against Germany if Germany refused to allow a commission to investigate its alleged infractions of the disarmament clauses of the Treaty of Versailles. But Moffat and Phillips persuaded the President that trade sanctions were a virtual act of war and inconsistent with a policy of neutrality. Roosevelt discussed similar proposals for sanctions or a blockade against Germany after its rearmament announcement in March 1935, and during the Rhineland crisis a year later told he told an English visitor that he thought the choice was between war then and in five years.

The American Ambassador to Germany during 1933–38, William E. Dodd, was quickly disabused of the alleged redemptive, or regenerative, aspects of Nazi foreign and domestic policies, and by November 1934 he became convinced that peace would last only "until Germany can be entirely ready to command Europe." He was always pleading with Roosevelt to find some means to avoid the general war that he felt would result from acquiescence in Hitler's demands. Similarly, George S. Messersmith, consul general in Berlin in 1930–34, minister to Austria in 1934–37, and then Assistant Secretary of State, and highly regarded by all his colleagues, concluded relatively early that Germany intended war, and in July 1936 he noted that Hitler's "burning ambition is to impose his will on Europe by force of arms." Messersmith disputed the common view that Germany's more conservative elements would moderate Hitler, for "Germany's so-called conservative elements are conservative in the sense that they believe Germany is not ready and must not take any precipitate action. They are by no means conservative in the sense that they do not share the political expansionist aims of Hitler and the more radical members of the Party." Likewise, Henry Morgenthau, Jr., Secretary of the Treasury from 1934 to 1945, and Harold L. Ickes, Secretary of the Interior from 1933 to 1946, both of whom represented progressive elements in the Democratic party, deplored Nazi foreign and domestic policies (perhaps intuitively as much as analytically) and were often at odds with the State Department, while they supported policies that urged Roosevelt toward a bolder course. But in every matter of importance the forces or circumstances favoring a policy of appeasement prevailed.

Finally, it should be noted that if the Americans took a jaundiced view of British policies, the British were equally hostile toward American policies. Foreign Office personnel believed New Deal economic policies were designed to appeal to the "less responsible" elements in American life. They belittled Roosevelt's "superficial" financial and economic knowledge and his proclivity for "yes-men" and "second-rate advisers" and disparaged his diplomatic aides. Secretary Hull was a "hot gospeller," Norman Davis, Roosevelt's disarmament negotiator and ambassador-at-large, was "suspect" as an internationalist, and Welles was an intriguer who would not improve Anglo-American relations. The British almost cavalierly, and caustically, dismissed every effort Roosevelt made to find some cooperative procedure that would lead toward economic or political appeasement of Germany, partly because they feared, as they said in 1936, that they would become the "prisoner in the dock" who would be forced to bear the cost of economic appeasement. The British no doubt had real reason to dislike aspects of American trade and monetary policies, but it is also inescapable that their attitude toward their American counterparts reflected a strong element of Victorian conceit or condescension and, as in the case of Chamberlain (who loathed the American efforts no less than the Americans), a conservative Tory, or imperial, view of world affairs.

The discordant elements that affected American and European diplomacy were acutely manifest in the spring of 1933. Bound by President Hoover's agreement of June 1932 for the United States to participate in a world economic and monetary conference (which would not discuss war debts, reparations, or specific tariffs), Roosevelt entertained a succession of foreign statesmen. Although he got along well with Ramsay MacDonald, Labour Prime Minister of the National (Coalition) government and a Wilsonian in world outlook, they reached no agreement on war debts, which the British, spurred by Chamberlain, insisted should be canceled outright. Roosevelt regarded the debts as too politically sensitive, and even the Foreign Office knew from informal sources that Congress was in no mood to transfer a $250 million yearly debt payment back to the taxpayers. Roosevelt would not allow the debts to be negotiated at the London Economic Conference—"that stays here with Pop," he told reporters—and was angry when Mac-Donald mentioned the subject in an opening address. Roosevelt tactfully avoided declaring the British in default when they offered a token payment of $10 million in June, but he would go no further, and numerous efforts to discuss the subject later in the decade ended abruptly and with recriminations on both sides of the Atlantic.

Stabilization of currency exchange rates was another divisive force. The British had left the gold standard in September 1931, causing the pound to plummet. Now they favored fixing the dollar-pound-franc rates, although whether they would return to the gold standard was problematic. The French were pressing everyone to return to the gold standard, although for their own particular political and economic reasons in April 1933 they did not favor immediate stabilization. Roosevelt's main concern was to raise American domestic prices—which might be achieved by devaluing the dollar—and on April 20 he took the country off the gold standard by prohibiting export of gold. At the

same time, he gave public and private assurances to the visiting statesmen that he would work toward restoring "some form of gold standard"
and achieving stabilization.

In succeeding weeks, Roosevelt became economically more nationalistic. The delegation he appointed to the London Conference included
politicians whose views ranged from inflationist, to support of the gold
standard, to, as in the case of Senator Key Pittman of Nevada, caring
about little except securing an international agreement on the price of
silver that would please his mine-owner constituency. Also, while the
delegation was en route, Roosevelt decided not to submit to Congress
the reciprocal trade agreement legislation that he and Hull had agreed
upon, and which the Secretary had hoped to use to bargain for tariff re-
ductions.

As the London delegates moved toward a stabilization agreement,
Roosevelt grew more cool to the idea. In late June, with fanfare that
raised great expectations, he dispatched Assistant Secretary of State
Raymond Moley to London but promptly rejected Moley's draft agreement that looked toward stabilization. Then, on July 3, 1933, Roosevelt
sent his famous "bombshell" message that flatly rejected international
stabilization. The French were furious. They were dissuaded from seeking a vote censuring the United States only by being reminded of their
earlier opposition to stabilization. The British were nearly as furious.
MacDonald felt his policy of diplomatic cooperation with the United
States was discredited, while Chamberlain left the conference to go
fishing in order "to forget the behavior of the American President and
the French delegation."

Roosevelt's action resulted primarily from his determination to raise
domestic prices and wages through a devaluation of the dollar, which
international stabilization and a return to the gold standard would
have prevented. Here he won plaudits not only from political and
economic nationalists but from such economists as John Maynard
Keynes as well, who publicly declared Roosevelt "magnificently right"
and others wrong for not thinking enough about managed currency.
Roosevelt's action also reflected his derisive attitude toward the "old
fetishes" (as he put it) of international bankers and his conviction that
the British were trying to keep their "favorable trading position absolutely liquid" by insisting that the United States return to the gold
standard without pledging to follow suit. This meant that there was an
unbridgeable gulf between the British desire to stabilize the pound at
$3.50, in contrast to its recent high of $4.50, and the American preference for a level of $4.00.

The collapse of the London Conference intensified the era's economic
nationalism, expressed in increasing resort to bilateral preferential

tariff agreements and trade quotas. It diverted attention from the deep embarrassment that the Germans were suffering as a result of their delegation's division between those who wished to cooperate with England, France, and the United States and such extreme nationalists as Minister of Economics Alfred Hugenberg, who wanted to forge a European bloc that would impose special duties on imports from the United States, France, and the Soviet Union.

Nationalism again manifested itself at the World Disarmament Conference, which had been meeting in Geneva since February 1932. The conference frequently bogged down between the French demand for security prior to a disarmament (or limitation-of-armaments) agreement and the German demand for equality of armaments. In December 1932, the major powers agreed to grant Germany "equality in a system which would provide security for all other nations," a resolution that stated the central problem rather than solved it. In March 1933, Prime Minister MacDonald proposed an agreement with three important stipulations. In event of a breach, or threatened breach, of the peace, any signatory could summon a conference—which would include the United States— to determine responsibility for breach of the peace. European armies would be standardized at 200,000 men each on the Continent and 200,000 more in colonial realms. And French forces would be scaled down over five years, allowing time to see whether Germany would behave.

Many technical points awaited resolution, but American officials were encouraged when Roosevelt's chief disarmament negotiator, Norman Davis, reported after an interview with Hitler in April 1933 that Germany's major objection to current matters was its inferior military status under the Treaty of Versailles, which the MacDonald Plan proposed to revise gradually. From the European standpoint, in fact, the crucial question appeared to be whether, in the event that the MacDonald Plan signatories voted sanctions against an aggressor, the United States would abide by the decision or insist upon its neutral trade "rights," as had been the case during the First World War.

Roosevelt, after pondering the matter and anticipating a truculent speech by Hitler to the Reichstag about Germany's inferior military status, declared on May 16 that all powers ought to accept the MacDonald Plan, agree on means to implement it, maintain current armament levels, and sign a nonaggression pact. Hitler's advisers now urged a moderate response upon him, and next day he announced that Germany would accept the MacDonald Plan, and, for the first and only time of the decade, Hitler welcomed Roosevelt's "magnanimous proposal of bringing the United States into European relations as a guarantor of peace." On May 22, Davis announced that, if the European nations reached agreement on disarmament, the United States would consult with other nations in event of a threat to peace, and, if it concurred with the decision, it would not interfere with sanctions against an agressor. The Roosevelt administration thus was abandoning traditional American neutral rights and going further than any administration since Wilson's to cooperate with a collective effort at sanctions under Article XVI of the League Covenant.

This maneuver quickly failed. In April, the House of Representatives had passed by a wide margin a bill, originally supported by Hoover and Stimson, allowing the President to impose an arms and munitions embargo against any nation threatening to commit or committing an aggressive act. But Senator Hiram Johnson demanded that the embargo apply to all parties in a dispute, and Key Pittman, the weak-willed chairman of the Senate Foreign Relations Committee whose swearing, heavy drinking, and vacillation increased with pressure, told Roosevelt that his committee would not pass the bill without Johnson's amendment. Preoccupied with the passage of the National Recovery Act and banking legislation, Roosevelt hastily acceded, and the amended embargo bill was reported to the Senate. Only after Hull, whom the President had not consulted, explained how the Johnson amendment negated the American pledges at Geneva to cooperate against an aggressor did Roosevelt grasp his error. Rather than reverse himself or risk a Senate fight, the President dropped the embargo proposal, and Hull had to admit to newsmen on May 29 that the administration's effort to cooperate in a collective effort against aggression was ended.

The disarmament conference suffered final defeat in the autumn. The Germans demanded the immediate right to build weapons prohibited by the Treaty of Versailles and to increase their 100,000-man army, while the French opposed any increment in German men or arms. Hitler hesitated to take decisive action because he feared Germany was still diplomatically and militarily isolated, but encouraged by all his normally cautious Foreign Ministry officials, he told his Cabinet on October 13, 1933, that the time had come to "torpedo the Disarmament Conference. . . . The path of negotiation is now closed." He declared that he was dissolving the Reichstag, setting new elections, and planning a plebiscite for the German people to ratify his decision to quit both the Disarmament Conference and the League of Nations. The next day, the German Government announced its fateful decision.

Foreign response was mixed. Even Mussolini believed that Hitler had overreached himself, while Americans like Davis thought that Hitler's action was intended mainly to have a "sobering effect" upon the recalcitrant French and to force an election that would rid him of the more radical Nazis. Roosevelt was determined above all, however, not to become involved in a collective response to Germany, and on October 16 Davis had to announce that the United States was concerned solely with disarmament, not the "political aspects of peace"—causing Neville Chamberlain to remark that "the Americans are chiefly anxious to convince their people they are not going to be drawn into doing anything helpful to the rest of the world."

Hitler meanwhile reassured his Cabinet that "the critical moment has passed. The excitement will presumably subside itself within a short time." Shortly, he told an associate, perhaps as much out of relief as glee, that the foreigners who opposed Germany's action "want war. Let them have it—but only when it suits me. . . . They don't dream of making war. . . . They'll never act. They'll just protest. And they will always be too late." On November 12, the German people elected by a 92 per cent majority the unopposed list of Nazi candidates for the Reichstag and approved by 95 per cent Hitler's decision to quit the League of Nations and the Disarmament Conference.

Hitler's diplomacy paid rich dividends. Disarmament negotiations were ended, and Western timorousness and division were laid bare. Hitler had at once struck a blow against the League system and the hated Versailles Treaty, and by doing what German diplomats had urged but never done themselves, he reduced their influence, enhanced esteem for his leadership, and reinforced his tendency to bluster or seize the moment rather than negotiate and compromise.

In January 1934, Hitler concluded a nonaggression pact with Poland, which asserted his peaceful intentions while also undercutting the French alliance system. German diplomats sought out men like Nicholas Murray Butler, head of the Carnegie Endowment for International Peace and president of Columbia University, to give the pact their stamp of approval. Hitler rid himself of the more voluble radical Nazis in the brutal Blood Purge of June 30—July 1, 1934, and then withstood diplomatic pressure and the embarrassment of Mussolini's mobilization of Italian troops at the Brenner Pass after Austrian Nazis murdered Chancellor Engelbert Dollfuss. In January 1935, residents of the Saar, voting in the plebiscite scheduled by the Treaty of Versailles, elected by 90 per cent to reunite with Germany. The huge mandate caused Ambassador Breckinridge Long in Italy to write that many people feared it would be "a big drink of Schnapps" for Hitler, and that it would encourage him "to pursue his Pan-Germanic ideas into the fields of former German territories and Austria."

The British and French apparently felt the same way, and in early 1935 they pressed Hitler to extend the 1925 Locarno guarantees of Western Europe to Central and Eastern Europe and to sign an agreement covering air attack. In return, Germany would be allowed to continue its rearmament program, which was an open secret in European diplomatic and intelligence circles. But Hitler thwarted negotiations. When the British tactlessly issued a White Paper on March 4, 1935, announcing an increase in armaments in response to German developments, Hitler announced on March 9 that Germany had an air force. One week later, despite the hesitation of his Cabinet and generals, he announced German rearmament: the reintroduction of conscription and creation of an army of 36 divisions, or half a million men.

Germany's action violated America's separate peace agreement of 1921 as well as the Versailles Treaty. But American officials steered clear of the current crisis. Roosevelt was still deeply depressed over his World Court defeat in January, and in April he would write that, while he hoped the European powers would institute a boycott or economic sanctions against Germany, "I feel very helpless to render any particular service to immediate or permanent peace at this time." Further, while most American diplomats deplored German tactics, like Davis they felt that the French had been "stupid" to think they could keep Germany in a permanent state of inequality. American officials believed that the British intended not to isolate or punish the Germans but to coax them back into the League of Nations and a collective security system. Ambassador Robert Bingham wrote from London that the real purpose of the Great Power conference that was scheduled to meet at Stresa in April to assess Germany's *fait accompli* was to allow the French and Italians to "blow off steam," and that the British would not let anyone interfere with their chances of "Christianizing" Germany. The State Department did not even send a note protesting German rearmament, and on March 22 Hull said he hoped continued negotiations would achieve a "general appeasement." Thereupon Roosevelt, as if to show his unconcern over recent events, went fishing off the Florida coast.

At Stresa, the British, French, and Italians issued a joint resolution on April 14, 1935, condemning Germany's action. The League censured Germany shortly after on April 17. The so-called Stresa Front vanished on June 18 with the signing of the Anglo-German Naval Agreement, which recognized Germany's right to build a fleet 35 per cent the size of that of the British. The British signed the agreement partly because their government was in a state of transition, with Stanley Baldwin replacing MacDonald as Prime Minister, and because they relied too heavily on naval, as opposed to political, advice. But it is clear that they hoped to preclude a German demand for 100 per cent parity and to set a precedent for forthcoming negotiations with Japan. Whatever the British intentions, the naval accord legitimized Germany's violation of the Versailles Treaty, brought Germany out of political isolation, and provided nearly a decade of construction projects and full employment for the German shipbuilding industry.

President Roosevelt thought the British had made a long-run mistake, and he, unfairly, suspected that the British had reached secret agreement on other issues. State Department officials also disliked England's unilateral treaty-scrapping and creation of a sixth naval power, but they concluded that the Pacific, not the Atlantic, was America's main concern, and that generally the agreement constituted "a constructive factor in European and world pacification."

The prospects for world pacification quickly dimmed on October 3, 1935, when Italy invaded Ethiopia. There had been numerous clashes between Italian and Ethiopian troops in the previous year, and from January through August both the French and the British had been trying to appease Mussolini by offering economic concessions in Ethiopia. The negotiations proved fruitless and, especially in the case of the French, probably signaled Mussolini that he could move freely. Following the invasion, however, the British encouraged the League Council to embargo, beginning November 18, 1935, the sale or shipment to Italy of a long list of war-related materials, not including oil, without which Mussolini's armored divisions could not proceed. Nor did the British or French consider blockading Italian ports or closing the Suez Canal to Italian ships, measures that probably would have brought Mussolini to heel. In sum, the British and French placed higher priority upon their intent to woo Mussolini—the guarantor of Austrian independence—as a counterbalance to Germany than they did upon Ethiopia's sovereign or moral rights. Nor would they jeopardize French possessions in North Africa or British navigation in the Mediterranean, the "life line" of the empire. British naval superiority over Italy was clear, but political and naval officials feared provoking Mussolini into a "mad dog" act that would damage their fleet and increase vulnerability to Japan in the Pacific. (The British argued similarly against action in the Pacific because of vulnerability in the Mediterranean and in Europe, thus creating a tightly reasoned circle of inaction.) Consequently, the British and French agreed in the autumn of 1935 to use the threat of economic sanctions, including oil, to induce Mussolini to accept what Foreign Secretary Sir Samuel Hoare and Foreign Minister Pierre Laval termed a "judicious mixture" of territorial and economic sanctions.

American officials wanted no involvement in the war. In August 1935, Roosevelt's request for a peaceful solution got only a brusque reply from Mussolini, and in anticipation of war the administration supported passage of the August 31, 1935, Neutrality Act. Roosevelt invoked it on October 5 and also warned Americans not to travel on belligerent ocean liners. These steps prevented the Italians from buying war materials in the United States and deprived them of passenger fares. The Ethiopians, in the meantime, had neither the money nor the need for modern war goods, nor submarines to sink Italian ships. The American embargo, like the League's, did not include oil, scrap iron, steel, or copper, and American businessmen made fast profits without regard for political implications. Oil sales to Italy in October were double the peacetime level, and triple in November, despite Hull's "moral" embargo of November 15, which pronounced the sale of oil and other vital materials contrary to the spirit of the Neutrality Act.

It is highly doubtful that the administration ever wanted to embargo oil, and when the British asked in early December whether the United States would embargo oil if England and the League did, Hull said only, "We have gone as far as we can." This evasive tactic reaffirmed the British contention that American diplomacy was "completely immoral and cowardly," and Prime Minister Baldwin could insist to his Cabinet that an oil embargo was inconceivable at least until the American Congress reconvened in January 1936 and took legislative action.

Meanwhile, Hoare and Laval negotiated a secret agreement proposing to give Italy political and economic concessions in Ethiopia, but the plan leaked to the press on December 9, 1935, and the adverse public response caused Hoare to resign and the Laval government to fall in January 1936. Roosevelt and the State Department professed their outrage, as though the Hoare-Laval plan represented that traditional old world imperial bargaining (and perfidy) they so despised. At the end of February 1936, Congress put the final preventive on American involvement by extending the Neutrality Act and refusing to allow the President discretion to apply the embargo solely against the aggressor, thus causing Mussolini to call the law a service to world peace. Anglo-French efforts to negotiate a settlement ended in March 1936, when German troops entered the Rhineland, making everyone even more unwilling to antagonize Mussolini, whose troops finally triumphed in Africa in May. Shortly thereafter, Italy annexed Ethiopia, and the United States and the League ended all sanctions.

The Italo-Ethiopian war discredited the Western democracies and increased Anglo-American mutual suspicions and recriminations. The war provided Hitler with the perfect opportunity to reoccupy the Rhineland and denounce the Locarno treaties. Plans to reoccupy the Rhineland were first drawn up in May 1935, when German military leaders argued that the recent Franco-Soviet Mutual Assistance Pact made the Third Reich vulnerable to concerted French, Russian, and Czech action. Hitler was uncertain how Italy, a Locarno signatory, would respond. But between September 1935 and March 1936 Anglo-French diplomacy fell between two stools: It was not resolute enough to force Mussolini to abandon his Ethiopian venture (and thereby serve as a warning to Hitler), but it did alienate Mussolini, who in late February 1936 assured Hitler that the Stresa Front was "finally dead," and that he would not support Anglo-French action against Germany's breaching Locarno. Thus reassured, Hitler now insisted that French ratification of the pact with Russia violated Locarno, and on March 7, 1936, German soldiers marched into the Rhineland.

Whether a concerted Western military response to Germany's action would have caused Hitler to withdraw his troops, and perhaps topple him from power, is arguable. German troops were under orders to meet a French advance by a tactical withdrawal to the eastern bank of the Rhine River and then to stand and fight. But Hitler did not think the French would respond, and he was right. The French were never prepared, politically or militarily, to oust German forces from the Rhineland. Nor would the British permit a showdown. In a series of hastily arranged conferences, they told the French that neither military nor economic sanctions could be considered.

American diplomats in London and Paris kept Washington well informed, and the State Department, with Roosevelt's acquiescence, immediately argued that, since the Versailles provisions relating to the Rhineland were not included in the separate peace with Germany of 1921, and since the United States was not a Locarno signatory, no American rights had been abridged and no further comment was therefore necessary. When Anglo-French discussions shifted to the League, American diplomats in Geneva were told not even to accept the customary visitors' tickets to Council meetings, and foreign diplomats in Washington were told the American position was strictly "hands off."

Ambassador Breckinridge Long summarized events, and implied their outcome, on March 21, 1936. Hitler, he said, would never remove his troops from land over which Germany was sovereign, and no one would fight. "Italy is not going to join England and France while under sanctions. Czechoslovakia is afraid. Russia is too far away. And France is not going in alone! So they will talk it to death—with England supporting Germany all she can." The next day, Roosevelt, as during the rearmament crisis, went fishing. And once again the League censured Germany, but this in no way compensated for the fact that, as an American diplomat wrote from Berlin, "by one single daring move on the political chess board" Hitler had "cut the military basis from under the whole series of French postwar alliances" and virtually ended the Versailles system.

The Rhineland crisis had barely subsided when the Spanish Civil War erupted on July 17, 1936, with rebel Nationalist forces, led by General Francisco Franco, attacking the loyal Republican government of Spain. For two years, Mussolini had been supplying the Nationalists with arms, and now Franco asked Hitler for air and convoy support to move his troops from Spanish Morocco to Spain. Hitler's affirmative reply was instantaneous and intuitive; he undoubtedly recognized that this might be an opportunity to ring France with a third hostile power, upset the Anglo-French balance of power in the Mediterranean, move England and France further apart from Italy, and gain access to Spain's new materials. Hitler's initial investment was small but might pay big dividends, and he was prepared to back off from his policy—at least until he formally recognized Franco's regime in November 1936—if the policy proved too risky.

Initially, the French Popular Front Government of the Socialist Léon Blum was inclined to sell the Spanish Government the planes and munitions they were legally entitled to buy. But French and British politicians and diplomats whose conservatism moved them to prefer Franco's "order" to Republican liberalism, and who feared to antagonize—or preferred to appease—Germany and Italy, thwarted this policy. The result was an Anglo-French strategy aimed at "containing" the Civil War by creating, by September, 1936, the International Nonintervention Committee. This committee, composed of twenty-seven nations, including Germany and Italy, was pledged not to intervene in the war in any way. The British and French persisted in this illusory policy for the next three years, even while knowing that Italy was expending $400 million and 50,000 troops and Germany an even more critical $200 million and 16,000 troops (including the air force Condor Legion, which bombed the Basque village of Guernica) in Franco's behalf. The Republicans, who probably would have won the Civil War had they received the aid to which they were legally entitled, got only slight technical support from Mexico and the Soviet Union, and some 40,000 poorly trained and equipped citizen volunteers from Europe and the United States, who made up the various International Brigades. The quantity and quality of military support supplied by Germany and Italy proved decisive and led to Franco's triumph in March 1939.

The United States never joined the Nonintervention Committee, but American policy was neither wiser nor more creditable than that of France and England. Even before the British and French announced nonintervention, Secretary Hull on August 7, 1936, declared that, while the Neutrality Act of 1936 applied only to conflicts between nations, American citizens should not involve themselves in any way in the Spanish Civil War. One week later, at Chautauqua, New York, Roosevelt reinforced this moral embargo with a graphic description of war horrors and a plea for Americans not to seek "fools' gold" by trading with either side. In October, Hull officially told the Spanish Government that the United States would not sell it arms, precedents notwithstanding. The State Department thwarted sales by private firms by insisting upon a licensing system and publicly labeling such sales unpatriotic. Then, on January 7, 1937, the administration steamrolled through Congress a special Neutrality Act prohibiting trade with either side in Spain, despite the argument of even such ardent isolationists as Senator Nye that this was not true neutrality. This fact was keenly appreciated by General Franco, who termed the law "a gesture we Nationalists shall never forget."

At the outset of the Spanish Civil War, American policy was determined by State Department officials who argued, first, that the United States could not advance a policy that might contravene whatever the British and French intended to do. By the same logic, they insisted, next, that it would be unthinkable to challenge Anglo-French policy once established—especially when it claimed to be averting a wider war. No less significant was the lack of sympathy for the Republican cause among State Department officials; Under Secretary of State Phillips, for example, believed the Republicans had "what amounts to a communistic government," whose victory would stimulate communism throughout Europe. Moreover, New Deal politicians in 1936 and 1938 greatly feared fracturing their domestic political coalition by offending the American Catholics—the Church hierarchy, press, most clergy and lay organizations—who were outspokenly pro-Franco and anti-Republican. This was most evident in May 1938, when Roosevelt inclined toward supporting a resolution sponsored by Senator Nye that would have ended the embargo and allowed the Spanish Republicans to buy goods on a cash-and-carry basis. But as Secretary of the Interior Ickes noted in his diary, the congressional Democratic leadership feared this policy "would mean the loss of every Catholic vote next fall. . . . This was the cat that was actually in the bag, and it is the mangiest, scabbiest cat ever."

Throughout the Spanish Civil War, the Roosevelt administration persisted in a policy that reinforced Anglo-French appeasement and served to secure Franco's victory, which constituted a cruel defeat for the Spanish people and demonstrated the political and moral bankruptcy of democratic foreign policy. Hitler, or course, never turned Franco into a faithful ally and could not persuade him to declare war on England in 1940, but his adventuristic Spanish policy helped him to secure Japan's signature in November 1936 on the Anti-Comintern Pact, which pledged Germany and Japan to collaborate against the spread of domestic communism and not to do anything to ease the position of the Soviet Union if it attacked either country. One year later, Italy, too, signed the pact. These arrangements were highly unspecific and more pretentious than real, but their purpose was to create the illusion of power that would facilitate Germany's advance in Europe and Japan's in Asia.

American officials recognized, by mid-1936, that Germany had seized the diplomatic initiative, but they were uncertain and divided over whether this meant that Germany should be appeased faster or resisted sooner, and their diplomacy was accordingly ambiguous. In the summer of 1936, Roosevelt began to consider calling a conference that would either resolve German grievances or serve as the starting point for collective action against aggression. In August, he instructed Ambassador Dodd to discover what might be achieved "if Hitler were asked personally and secretly by me" to outline German objectives over the next decade, but Dodd's inquiries were rebuffed by German diplomats and derided by the British. In February 1937, Roosevelt allowed Treasury Secretary Morgenthau, who was outspokenly anti-Nazi and critical of State Department cautiousness, to ask Chamberlain, then Chancellor of the Exchequer, for suggestions to lessen the financial burden of the arms race and to ask what a bold Anglo-American diplomatic initiative might achieve. The British downplayed any joint initiative and said, with evident sternness, that the best thing the United States could do was revise its Neutrality Act and help stabilize Far Eastern affairs. The Americans replied that their cash-and-carry policy helped the British, whose imperial preferences and production restrictions on rubber and tin in South Asia produced "extortion and crisis."

Concurrently, the State Department prepared a position paper that argued that Germany was bound by a political and economic *status quo,* and that the ultimate question was, "Can a compromise be found, or a price paid, which will satisfy the economic necessities of the German people, without war and without making Germany paramount on the Continent?" The Department advocated a general political and economic settlement and dispatched Roosevelt's emissary, Norman Davis, to London. Davis's talks were unproductive, but he pressed for a meeting between Roosevelt and Chamberlain, who had now become Prime Minister. Roosevelt invited Chamberlain to America for talks in the autumn, but Chamberlain refused, insisting the meeting could not produce results commensurate with its publicity.

Under Secretary of State Welles next stepped to the diplomatic fore, seemingly moved by Japan's resumption of undeclared war against China in July 1937 and Roosevelt's famous "quarantine" speech at Chicago on October 5, in which he said that "when an epidemic of physical disease starts to spread, the community approves and joins in a quarantine of the patients in order to protect the health of the community against the spread of the disease." Welles's concern was appeasing Germany permanently, and he did not think Japan would take part in the scheme he elaborated. On October 6, he proposed that Roosevelt sponsor a world conference to establish principles of international relations, laws and customs of warfare, neutral rights and obligations, and guarantees of equal access to raw materials. Roosevelt agreed but wished to sound other leaders through diplomatic channels and to have a small group of nations draft the international codes prior to a world conference, which would ratify them. He allowed Welles to expand the agenda to include proposing peaceful means to revise treaties—for Welles this meant getting rid of the "inequities" of the Versailles Treaty —with the understanding that the United States could not participate in any political readjustments.

Roosevelt prepared to announce his proposal to the diplomatic corps at the White House on Armistice Day 1937, but he abandoned it at the last moment because of Hull's opposition. Hull later said he believed that the project would have lulled the democracies into tranquillity instead of rousing them to rearm and resist Germany, but he really feared that the United States would be assuming too much responsibility—and British burdens—and resented Welles's influence with the President.

The Roosevelt-Welles plan remained dormant until January 1938, when the Under Secretary persuaded Hull to assent to it—provided British approval be secured in advance, so that the United States would not be left out on a diplomatic limb. Welles himself stipulated that, after the British approved, France, Germany, and Italy would be given advance notice to preclude charges of a secret Anglo-American deal. Welles confidently told Roosevelt that formulation and transmission of his projected codes of international behavior would aid the British effort to reach agreement with Germany on colonies (raw materials) and security, that it would appeal to Hitler's interest in offensive-arms limitation, and that it would obligate Germany and Italy not to aid Japan, which would have to make peace with China. Welles reiterated that on political matters the United States would serve only as a "channel of information."

The Roosevelt-Welles plan, with strong support from the British Ambassador, Sir Ronald Lindsay, was communicated to London on January 12, 1938. Foreign Office personnel thought it hasty and likely to interfere with their efforts to negotiate bilaterally with Hitler over colonies as a first step toward a general settlement and with Mussolini over *de jure* recognition of the conquest of Ethiopia in return for cooperation in Spain and elsewhere. But they recommended supporting Roosevelt's initiative if he insisted. Chamberlain, however, thought the project "woolly and dangerous," "fantastic," "preposterous," and "likely to excite the derision of Germany and Italy." On January 14, he told

Roosevelt that he "should consider holding his hand for a while" while the British negotiated with Italy and then Germany, and he expressed misgivings about America's insistence on maintaining freedom from political involvements.

Roosevelt and Welles unhappily agreed to delay and said that they opposed *de jure* recognition of Mussolini's conquest, except "*as an integral part of measures for world appeasement*," meaning that everyone would have to act together and not in bilateral agreements. Meanwhile, the British Foreign Secretary, Anthony Eden, had returned to London from a vacation. He, too, had doubts about Roosevelt's proposal and had been a proponent of appeasement of Germany in 1936 and 1937. But he also strongly advocated Anglo-American cooperation and was prepared to run risks jointly in the Far East and Europe, if only to increase American effort to redress the world balance of power in England's favor. In a series of bitter sessions of the Cabinet Committee on Foreign Policy, Eden persuaded Chamberlain to cable Roosevelt on January 21, 1938, that he would welcome his diplomatic initiative whenever he launched it. But Roosevelt continually delayed and finally told the British on March 12, the day of the German *Anschluss* with Austria, that he was abandoning his proposal.

Assessments of these developments have ranged from Winston Churchill's later charge that Chamberlain threw away "the last frail chance to save the world from tyranny otherwise than by war" to arguments that American isolationism made effective action impossible. The truth is more complicated. Chamberlain's initial rebuff both dissuaded Roosevelt from acting and rekindled his hostility toward Chamberlain and the alleged British desire to make bilateral deals at the expense of general principles and unwillingness to cooperate on an equal basis. Roosevelt might have acted after Chamberlain's more favorable second reply of January 21, but by then he was intimidated by events. Japan had ended efforts at a negotiated settlement with China on January 16, precluding a key benefit Welles argued would flow from European appeasement. In early February, Hitler gave German diplomacy a more outwardly radical appearance by making Joachim von Ribbentrop Foreign Minister; at the same time, he made himself commander in chief of the armed forces after purging some conservative generals. Then, on February 20, Hitler ended support for Chiang Kai-shek's Nationalists and recognized Manchukuo. Eden resigned the same day, at odds with Chamberlain over beginning negotiations with Italy as well as over the American proposal, causing American officials to worry that Chamberlain was going to "play ball with Hitler and Mussolini." The *Anschluss* provided Roosevelt with the occasion to abandon a proposal he now saw either as a hopeless deterrent to aggression or as affording too little chance of success to allow the American name to be associated with the increasingly risky policy of appeasement.

Despite the severe limitations of the American overture, Chamberlain's brusque dismissal of it was unwise and highly revealing, especially in light of his private view in January 1938 that "U.S.A. and U.K. in combination represent a force so overwhelming that mere hint of its use is sufficient to make the most powerful of dictators pause." Chamberlain's diplomacy demonstrated not only his conviction that he alone could negotiate peace but his unilateralist or neo-isolationist viewpoint as well: his determination to exclude the United States as well as the Soviet Union from European affairs. Chamberlain worried less whether Roosevelt's effort would appease Germany than about the consequent division of the world into "democracy versus dictatorship" blocs if American appeasement failed. The Prime Minister wished to preclude Anglo-American appeasement and collective action and to foreclose every option but conceding to German demands, neither thinking nor caring that this reinforced the American suspicion that all England wanted was for the United States to pull British chestnuts out of the Japanese fire.

For the remainder of 1938, American diplomacy floundered in the sea of appeasement, torn by doubts that the drift of events was wrong but unable to find any corrective. The result was acquiescence and complicity in developments later deplored.

In February 1938, Hitler had bullied Austrian Chancellor Kurt von Schuschnigg into lifting the political restrictions on the Austrian Nazis and appointing their leader, Arthur Seyss-Inquart, as Minister of the Interior. The Austrian Nazis soon undermined the government, and on March 9 the desperate Schuschnigg announced a plebiscite for March 13 to determine whether Austria would remain independent. Hitler used the threat of force to gain cancellation of the plebiscite and Schuschnigg's resignation and replacement by Seyss-Inquart, who in turn signed orders (dictated to him over the telephone from Berlin on the night of March 14, 1938) requesting German troops to restore order. Hitler had peacefully effected the *Anschluss* prohibited by the Versailles Treaty, although his diplomacy outraged everyone. Hans Dieckhoff, the German Ambassador in Washington, wrote Berlin repeatedly about the "malevolent bitterness" in the State Department and news reports about the "Prussian wolf raging amongst Austrian sheep." Nonetheless, American officials were no more prepared to act than Chamberlain, who told Parliament that nothing could have been done "unless we and others had been prepared to use force."

All eyes now riveted on Czechoslovakia, where in April the Nazi leaders of the 3 million ethnic Germans in the Sudetenland demanded autonomy, which threatened Czech sovereignty and defense. Hitler plotted with the Sudeten leaders throughout; his strategy was to have them demand more than seemingly could be granted, and by May 30 he had concluded that it "is my unalterable decision to smash Czechoslovakia by military action in the near future." The French, treaty-bound to aid the Czechs (as was the Soviet Union if France acted), suspected Hitler's design but were terrified to fight, and in April they deferred to Chamberlain's strategy of resolving the crisis by applying maximum pressure on the Czechs.

American policy remained divided and ambiguous. Ambassador Joseph P. Kennedy in London strongly favored Anglo-German accommodation and even had notions of improving American-German relations through economic concessions and a visit to Hitler. He believed the British would be routed in war and once proposed to state publicly that he could not see why anyone would fight in behalf of Czechs. The State Department deleted this, and Roosevelt said Kennedy needed his wrists slapped "rather hard." Ambassador William Bullitt in Paris feared above all that war would mean the slaughter of the French and the triumph of Bolshevism, and he, too, urged maximum pressure—almost blackmail —on the Czechs. He also thought firm statements might restrain Hitler, and twice in early September he was quoted in the French press as saying that the United States and France were "united in war as in peace," and that if war came no one could predict the American course. Roosevelt feared the clamor at home and the responsibility of urging French or Czech resistance and denied any American involvement in an anti-Hitler front.

Early in September, the Czechs agreed to give autonomy to the Sudeten Germans, who now demanded return to the Reich. Chamberlain thereupon surprised everyone by requesting a meeting with Hitler, and on September 15 he flew to Berchtesgaden ("The moral is: If you have enough airplanes you don't have to go to Berchtesgaden," Bullitt wrote), where Hitler granted time to achieve the peaceful transfer of the Sudetenland.

Roosevelt was of two minds. Intuitively, he felt that Chamberlain's procedures were wrong, and that the British and French intended to abandon Czechoslovakia and "wash the Judas Iscariot blood from their hands," as Ickes recorded. When word came that the British and French were going to force Czechoslovakia to cede all districts with fifty per cent German population, Roosevelt secretly summoned Ambassador Lindsay and said this was "the most terrible remorseless sacrifice" ever demanded of a nation. He added that he would be "the first to cheer" if British policy succeeded, and that he did not want to encourage the Czechs to "vain resistance." He proposed either a world conference, which he would attend, to "reorganize all unsatisfactory frontiers on rational lines," or that the British and French should refuse Hitler's demands and merely blockade Germany rather than fight a classical war. Surprisingly, the British were not interested in these suggestions, and on September 22 Chamberlain flew to Godesberg to tell Hitler that Czechoslovakia had accepted the "50 per cent plan"—only to have Hitler press Polish and Hungarian territorial claims on Czechoslovakia and insist that the transfer of all territory be completed by October 1, with all buildings, machinery, and military equipment left intact.

The Czechs were ready and able to resist, and it appeared that France and England would be drawn into war. Early on September 26, Roosevelt appealed directly to the heads of the German, French, British, and Czech states not to break negotiations, while the British and French worked furiously on a plan to turn over the Czech territories on a schedule approximating Hitler's. Then, on the night of September 27, Roosevelt cabled Hitler that it was senseless to go to war when the major points were already agreed upon in principle. He offered to take part in a conference at a neutral site, and he appealed to Mussolini to intervene with Hitler in behalf of a negotiated settlement. And when, on September 28, Chamberlain accepted Hitler's invitation to Munich, the President wired the Prime Minister two words: "Good man."

The Munich Conference of September 29–30, 1938—the Czechs were excluded, and neither the Soviet Union nor the United States was invited—provided that Czechoslovakia cede almost immediately the entire Sudetenland, with its 3 million ethnic Germans and 700,000 Czechs, and allow Germany to build a highway across Moravia to Vienna. Poland took the region of Teschen, with its railroad and minerals, and Hungary took part of southern Slovakia and Ruthenia. In all, Czechoslovakia surrendered nearly a third of its population and territory, leaving the state defenseless and politically unviable, as Hitler well understood. The American part in bringing about Munich had been minor. Mussolini had already acceded to British requests when he prevailed upon Hitler to issue his invitation to Chamberlain, although both dictators were aware of Roosevelt's September 27 messages before they acted. Taken *in toto,* Roosevelt's cables of September 26–28 show how strongly he supported appeasement and a conference whose outcome was foregone. A few American diplomats were distressed. Assistant Secretary Messersmith insisted that Czechoslovakia would not be Hitler's last territorial demand, and Ambassador to Spain Claude Bowers raged against the "rape of the Czechs" and the "Great Betrayal of Munich." But Under Secretary Welles stated in a national broadcast on October 3 that there was now more opportunity to establish "a new world order based upon justice and upon law," and Roosevelt rejoiced to Canadian

Prime Minister Mackenzie King that war had been averted and told Ambassador Phillips, "I am not one bit upset over the final result." He wrote Chamberlain that he shared the latter's hopes for achieving a new world order, and that he approved taking up still outstanding issues with Hitler.

Roosevelt perpetually inclined toward appeasement, but soon after Munich he began to view Germany more harshly, became more resigned to the eventuality of a European war, and determined to prepare America accordingly. In October 1938, he asked Congress for an additional $300 million for Hemispheric defense. The following month, he told his army and air force chiefs to think about establishing an air force of 20,000 planes and an annual production of 20,000 planes—enough to defend America and supply the British and French, whose combined annual production was only two-thirds Germany's 12,000 planes. In November 1938, Germany's brutal pogrom against its Jewish population further stiffened Roosevelt's attitude, and as a minor protest he recalled (permanently) Ambassador Wilson from Berlin. In his annual address of January 4, 1939, the President said that there were "many methods short of war" by which America could make known its sentiments toward "aggressor nations," and he lamented that the Neutrality Act might aid an aggressor against a victim. The next day, he proposed a $1.3-billion defense budget and shortly requested an additional $500 million for army and navy airplanes.

What Roosevelt desired, with the cash-and-carry provisions of the Neutrality Act due to expire in May 1939, was that Congress repeal the remaining arms embargo so that he might aid victims of aggression. But the President feared congressional opposition and was afraid to commit his prestige on this issue. So he left it to Key Pittman, the weak-willed chairman of the Senate Foreign Relations Committee, who continually delayed. Then, in mid-February, Senator Elbert Thomas of Utah proposed revising the law to allow the President to place an embargo on all war materials and to lift it solely for the victim of aggression, whenever any nation violated a treaty.

Politically, Roosevelt still remained in the background. Then, on March 14, Hitler, having inspired Slovak separatists to demand independence from rump Czechoslovakia, forced the Slovak Government to summon German troops (allegedly to ward off Hungarian designs on their territory), bullied the Czech leaders into making Bohemia and Moravia a German protectorate, and let Hungary take what remained of Ruthenia. Statesmen again were outraged, but Chamberlain insisted to Parliament that the final dissolution of Czechoslovakia was caused by internal events. Mussolini complained privately that "every time Hitler occupies a country he sends me a message"—whereupon, on

April 7, 1939, Italian troops occupied Albania. On May 21, Italy and Germany signed their "Pact of Steel," pledging mutual political and military support in the event either country was threatened or attacked.

Roosevelt immediately condemned Hitler's "temporary extinguishment" of Czechoslovakia's freedom and publicly called for revision of the Neutrality Act. Pittman proposed placing all trade on a cash-and-carry basis, but Roosevelt thought this might aid Japan over China, so the Senator suggested an embargo on exports to any nation violating the Nine-Power Treaty of 1922. At this Roosevelt deferred to caution and to the State Department, which supported cash-and-carry to maintain the facade of American neutrality.

Once again, Pittman delayed proceedings and finally in late May the administration had to turn to Representative Sol Bloom, chairman of the House Foreign Affairs Committee, who willingly introduced legislation to repeal the arms embargo then in effect. But the administration's strenuous efforts went awry when Republican John Vorys of Ohio amended the bill to restore the embargo on arms and ammunition, though not implements of war, and Republicans, with some Democratic support, pushed the bill through the House on June 29 by a vote of 159–157. An infuriated Roosevelt called the Vorys amendment a "stimulus to war" and even asked the Attorney General how far he might go in ignoring the Act. The administration tried to defeat the Vorys-amended Bloom bill in the Senate, but by a 12–11 vote the Foreign Relations Committee voted to postpone consideration of neutrality legislation until the next session of Congress, thus allowing the cash-and-carry provision of the 1937 law to expire and effectively placing an embargo on arms and munitions. Again an angry Roosevelt met with Senate leaders of both parties in the White House and talked about taking the fight to override the House and the Senate Foreign Relations Committee to the whole Senate. After an acrimonious discussion, the President had to abandon this idea when Vice-President John Garner bluntly told him: "Well, Captain, we may as well face the facts. You haven't got the votes, and that's all there is to it."

Amidst the neutrality legislation debate, and following Germany's occupation of Czechoslovakia and Italy's invasion of Albania on April 7, Roosevelt returned to his formula for appeasement. On April 14, he sent a long public message to Hitler and Mussolini, asking them to pledge that for at least ten years they would not attack the thirty-one nations of Europe and the Near East, in return for which the United States would enter diplomatic discussions aimed at achieving arms reduction and "opening up avenues of international trade" to provide equal access to raw materials and markets for all nations. At the same time, concerned nations, other than the United States, would enter into "such political discussions" as they deemed necessary.

Mussolini derided the President's "Messiah-like messages," while Hitler delighted a howling Reichstag audience on April 28 with references to American violence in 1776 and 1861, Germany's betrayal at Versailles by President Wilson, and the irony that the Americans, who had never joined the League of Nations, "the largest conference in the world," should propose one now. Moreover, a German poll of thirty-one nations had shown that none of them felt threatened by Germany, while it was British troops who currently occupied Iceland and Palestine. Hitler used this occasion to denounce the German-Polish Nonaggression Pact of 1934 and the Anglo-German Naval Agreement of 1935.

Senator Nye said that Roosevelt got the reply he deserved, and indeed the purpose behind the President's April 14 speech remains obscure, especially given his own observation the same day that "the two madmen respect force and force alone." The President's effort probably reflected his divided impulses. He never stopped hoping that one more effort in the fashion of Welles might produce economic appeasement, which would lead to political appeasement. Conversely, a negative reply from the "two madmen" might enlighten the public about differences between the so-called democracies and dictatorships and perhaps inspire Congress to neutrality revision.

Hitler was quietly pressing Poland to return the port city of Danzig and allow him to build an extraterritorial road across the Polish Corridor that divided East Prussia from Germany. Polish Foreign Minister Josef Beck, convinced that Hitler would not risk war, refused by silence and sought neither British aid (because he feared another Munich) nor Soviet aid (because of his anti-Russian views and his fear of provoking Hitler). He would accept only a secret bilateral defense treaty with England, which the British refused.

There matters stood until Germany destroyed Czechoslovakia and on March 23 forced Lithuania to return the port city of Memel. The British were enraged by this diplomacy. Fearing the embarrassment of another Munich, they were determined to dissuade Hitler from rash action that might provoke a war. Thus, in Parliament on March 31 Chamberlain pledged British support if Poland resisted a threat to its independence. Following Italy's coup in Albania, he extended this guarantee to Rumania and Greece.

Chamberlain's pledge could not be militarily meaningful without support from the Russians, whom he was loathe to involve in European affairs. Consequently, when in April the Russians initiated talks on European security and proposed an Anglo-French-Soviet guarantee of every state from the Baltic to the Black Sea, the British delayed talks until August, when it was too late. Whether the Soviets truly sought an agreement or were using negotiations as a lure for Hitler is uncertain. The Russians would not consider extending guarantees to the smaller countries of Western Europe. Further, while their insistence that Russian troops be allowed to operate in Poland, and that the British and French seize the Baltic ports to shut the sea to the Germans, was militarily sound, these steps were virtually precluded by political realities, since neither Poland nor the Baltic states (provinces of pre-1917 Russia) would accede to them. Simultaneously, the Soviets, who feared that the main objective of Anglo-French diplomacy was to turn Hitler eastward (witness Munich), made inquiries of Germany about trade talks.

Hitler, enraged by England's guarantee of Poland and encouraged by Ribbentrop, now warmed to an agreement with the Soviet Union that would permit him to wrest Danzig and the Corridor from Poland either by diplomacy or by force of arms. The result, after protracted negotiations and Vyacheslav M. Molotov's replacement of Maxim Litvinov (who had spoken so long for collective security arrangements with the West) as Foreign Minister in May, was a Russian-German trade agreement on August 19 and then the ten-year Nazi-Soviet Nonaggression Pact of August 23, 1939. The Nonaggression Pact publicly proclaimed that each country would remain neutral if the other went to war and secretly provided that in event of war they would divide Poland approximately in half. The Germans claimed a sphere of influence in Lithuania, and the Russians claimed one in Finland, Estonia, and Latvia and an "interest" in Bessarabia (in Rumania). The Russians were now at least temporarily free from a German assault, while Hitler was supremely confident that the British and French, with no prospect of Russian aid, would force the Poles to agree to his demands; otherwise, he could wage war against them without much opposition, after which everyone would adjust to the new reality. Whether Hitler preferred a military or diplomatic solution is difficult to discern. On July 4 and August 11–12, he brushed off Italian suggestions for a conference, insisting that if war came it would be local, or, in any event, that England and France could not harm Germany. And on August 22 he told his generals that he had Poland in exactly the position he desired, adding, "I am only afraid that at the last moment some swine or other will yet sumbit to me a plan for mediation."

Throughout this period Roosevelt, having met rebuff in Congress and abroad, inclined to abandon even whatever small part he might have liked to play in the diplomacy that was leading almost inexorably toward war. He offered no advice (nor was it solicited) to the British on their talks with the Russians, although he did pass along whatever information he had on the Russian-German talks. And on August 11 he told Russian Ambassador Constantine Oumansky to tell Stalin that if he "joined up" with Hitler it was as certain as night followed day that "as soon as

Hitler had conquered France he would turn on Russia." The President informed the Soviet leadership that he thought an Anglo-French-Soviet agreement against aggression was the best stabilizer for world peace. On the eve of the Nazi-Soviet Pact Roosevelt appealed to King Victor Emmanuel of Italy to avert war, and on August 24 he appealed directly to Hitler and President Ignacy Moscicki of Poland to solve their differences by direct negotiation, arbitration, or conciliation. Moscicki at once agreed to negotiation or conciliation, and Roosevelt forwarded the reply to Hitler, who remained silent. The President's original intervention was chiefly for the record, or, as Assistant Secretary of State Adolf A. Berle predicted, the messages "will have about the same effect as a valentine sent to somebody's mother-in-law out of season."

Hitler had set August 26 as the date for attacking Poland, but he moved it to September 1 when the British, reeling under the impact of the Nazi-Soviet Pact, hastily signed a mutual-assistance treaty with Poland, and the Italians indicated that they would not honor their commitment to fight under the Pact of Steel. The British also made a desperate effort to get Hitler to state his full demands on Poland, while pressing the Poles to open direct negotiations. Hitler made his demands known on August 26: the return of Danzig and a plebiscite in the Corridor. But at the last moment he insisted that the Poles dispatch a negotiator to reach Berlin the next day with full power to conclude an agreement, a condition that the Poles—wary of Hitler's tactic of always raising demands at the eleventh hour—would never accept. The British made futile last-minute efforts to bridge the gap, but on August 31 Hitler, while replying to Roosevelt that he had "left no stone unturned" in seeking a peaceful settlement, ordered his troops into Poland at dawn on September 1, 1939.

The next day, Mussolini sought a standstill cease-fire, but the British refused his intervention unless German troops were withdrawn from Poland. Chamberlain still hoped for some form of conference or negotiation and was prepared to state that, if Germany agreed to withdraw its troops, he would consider the peace restored. But he faced a revolt in the Cabinet and in Parliament, and at 9:00 A.M. on September 3 he stated that, unless the Germans called off their attack within two hours, England and Germany would be at war. Hitler was surprised by this resistance from the men who had given in over Czechoslovakia. "What now?" he said to Ribbentrop—but he did not relent as the British ultimatum expired and a state of war ensued. Late that afternoon, the French also declared war on Germany. The Second World War in Europe had begun.

Roosevelt and his aides despaired but were not surprised, and the President was fairly certain of what he wanted to do. In a fireside chat on September 3, he said that "this nation will remain a neutral nation, but I cannot ask that every American remain neutral in thought. . . . Even a neutral cannot close his mind or his conscience." While two days later he invoked the Neutrality Act, with its arms and ammunition embargo, he had told the Cabinet on September 1 that he intended to call Congress into special session to seek repeal of the neutrality legislation. Beyond that he was not prepared to go, although, as Berle wrote after meeting with the President on September 3, if the British and French were on the verge of defeat, and the American choice were between, on the one hand, entering the war and using England and France as outposts and, on the other hand, letting them go under and arming the United States to the teeth to meet the Germans in mid-Atlantic, the consensus was the latter course. This was a decision Roosevelt hoped not to have to make, and for this reason he saw no inconsistency between his desire to keep America neutral and out of war and his conviction that this could best be achieved by facing realities and supplying the British and French with materials they would need to resist the Germans. For the time being at least, there was still faint hope that a negotiated settlement might yet be possible.

6

Toward Armageddon

American foreign policy in the Far East during 1933–39 was as cautious and appeasement-oriented as it was in Europe. Once again the priority accorded domestic problems, the administration's fear of Congress and the public, and the innate caution and conviction of Roosevelt, Hull, and the State Department that economic appeasement was the surest route to peace circumscribed foreign-policy initiatives. Democratic leaders, like their Republican predecessors, balked at any action that jeopardized the nation's trade with Japan, which annually purchased about $225 million of American goods, constituting 8.5 per cent of the total American exports and greatly exceeding the average exports to China.

As Joseph C. Grew, ambassador in Tokyo from mid-1932 through 1941, wrote in the *Japan Times* in 1933, the economic interests that were the "principal basis of conflict among nations" did not harm American-Japanese relations. These two countries produced noncompetitive raw materials, and Japan's manufactures were chiefly those based on "manual dexterity," while the United States supplied goods manufactured in immense quantity by automatic machinery. Therefore, while the "jingoists" on both sides of the Pacific would raise other issues of conflict, these could be reconciled through patient study and mutual helpfulness. While Grew never minimized what he considered the constant struggle for control of the Japanese Government and foreign policy between the "moderate," or Western-oriented, civilian bureaucratic businessman elites and the more reckless military leaders and chauvinistic forces, in 1933 he was persuaded that the United States and Japan could make the coming Pacific era peaceful.

Equally significant for American diplomats was the condition of the Chinese Government and society. As Nelson Johnson, minister to Peking from 1929 to 1941, reported to the State Department in the fall of 1932, "the spectacle China presents abroad today is pathetic and humiliating." The central government, he said, had no effective authority and was incapable of bridging the rivalries between the semi-independent chieftains, while the military officers continued to be "a law unto themselves," using their private armies not to resist foreign invasion but to engage in "the sordid business of satisfying the thirst for territory and revenues of their commanders in China proper." In February 1933, he complained that the Chinese Government was factional rather than national, and that it had allowed affairs to drift. He insisted that Kuomintang prestige was at its lowest ebb, the people having lost all faith in their leaders. As for Chiang Kai-shek, Johnson said in May 1934, his modesty and patriotism notwithstanding, "he would be dictator of China"—and, in fact, there was no one on the horizon willing or able to replace him.

President Roosevelt's view of China's prospects was no more sanguine. His maternal grandfather, Warren Delano, had made a fortune in the nineteenth-century trade in tea, silks, and opium, and this undoubtedly inclined Franklin Roosevelt favorably toward China and the maintenance of American commercial opportunities there. It also probably led to his overestimating his own knowledge of Chinese affairs. But Roosevelt did understand, as he said with prescience in December 1934 to Treasury Secretary Morgenthau, that foreign finance had dominated China for the past century, and that neither the people nor the government had control—that is, sovereignty—over its own monetary or financial matters. "China has been the Mecca of the people whom I have called the 'money changers in the Temple.' They are still in absolute control. It will take many years and possibly several revolutions to eliminate them, because the new China cannot be built up in a day." Whether stated in sorrow, pity, contempt, or matter-of-factly, American diplomats in the 1930's doubted whether there was anything they could do to shore up the Chinese Government's authority or prestige and help it to save itself as well as its country from Japan.

Finally, there were the interrelated problems of Anglo-American and Anglo-Japanese relationships. Roosevelt and his aides, of course, distrusted the British, especially with regard to affairs in the Far East, where British investment was at least ten times greater than American investment and even more crucial to Great Britain's empire and security. American officials, including Roosevelt, tended to see most British leaders as old-fashioned imperialists, prepared to make a deal with Japan over spheres of influence in China or over naval ratios, provided British interests were safeguarded. If the British supported some form of collective action or sanctions against Japanese expansion or treaty violations, this was because they wished either to have their problems with Japan solved for them by the Americans or to maneuver the United States into the precarious position of being Japan's major antagonist. And for evidence many American diplomats pointed to Secretary of State Stimson's recent difficulties (their own disagreement with his policy notwithstanding) with the British during the Manchurian crisis.

Under the circumstances, then, the objects of United States foreign policy in the Far East during 1933–39 were to preserve traditional commercial and imperial interests, while avoiding direct conflict with Japan at virtually any cost, and to avoid involvement in China's myriad foreign and domestic problems—first, because there was little aid that China might be usefully afforded, and second, because the Japanese might regard such aid as having hostile intent toward them. American officials also wished to prevent the British from making any bilateral deals with their old Japanese allies and to maintain the rule of law and the treaty system—including the established naval ratios—in the Pacific.

Roosevelt's first "official" pronouncement on Far Eastern affairs came six weeks before his inauguration. On January 9, 1933, the President-elect and Secretary Stimson met at Hyde Park for a six-hour talk. The two patrician New Yorkers got on well, and Stimson's postwar memoirs emphasized their congenial meeting of minds and the general approval that Roosevelt gave to the Secretary's Far Eastern policies. On January 16, 1933, just as the League of Nations was reconvening to consider the Lytton report, Stimson informed that body, as well as the British and French, that they had "every reason to believe" that the new administration would maintain its predecessor's Far Eastern policy. At a press conference the next day, Roosevelt made a brief statement that American foreign policy had to "uphold the sanctity of international treaties," which some of Roosevelt's advisers—including Assistant Secretaries of State and Agriculture Raymond Moley and Rexford Tugwell, later detractors of the President—viewed as a disastrous endorsement of the Stimson doctrine that would lead ultimately to war with Japan. Such a view, however, clearly attributes too much meaning to Roosevelt's statement and ignores its context.

The day after his talk with Stimson, Roosevelt received a long message from his (and also Cordell Hull's) unofficial foreign-policy adviser, Norman Davis, stating that Americans working with the League Secretariat had informed him that the League Assembly's Committee of Nineteen, recently appointed to find some means of bringing the Sino-Japanese conflict to a conciliatory conclusion, had failed, and that there was great fear in Geneva that the fighting would be extended. There was also growing concern in Geneva over the fact that few assurances about American foreign policy had been forthcoming since before the November 1932 elections, and thus there was a desire, on the part of other nations, to synchronize their policies with those of the United States.

Roosevelt had little choice but to make some statement in mid-

January 1933. He inclined toward continuation of the nonrecognition doctrine, but he was aware that, if he reversed his predecessor's doctrine, he would provide the British and the French (reportedly wavering) with the opportunity to reverse themselves and the League attitude and lay the onus for this, if the need should arise, on the Americans. Without time or opportunity for the extended consultation with the British and French that Davis recommended, Roosevelt elected to issue an equivocal and innocuous statement with which any President—or contemporary foreign statesmen—could identify, and which he could hedge with qualifications. Indeed, historians have usually overlooked the fact that Roosevelt sought to qualify his own statement, for his opening remarks insisted that "any statement relating to any particular foreign situation [that is, the Manchurian crisis] must . . . come from the Secretary of State"—who, of course, was the as yet unnamed, and exceedingly cautious, Cordell Hull. Roosevelt had privately offered him the post the day before but had not yet received a reply. Although Roosevelt had approved the idea of nonrecognition, he avoided encouraging any hard line toward Japan, while leaving the way open to qualify or alter American foreign policy as the situation might demand.

When the League of Nations formally adopted the Committee of Nineteen's modified Lytton report on February 24, 1933, and the Japanese announced their departure from the League, the Roosevelt administration made no comment. In May 1933, the Chinese Minister of Finance, T. V. Soong, stopped in Washington en route to the London Economic Conference and urged Roosevelt to bring about an end to the fighting in North China. The President again limited himself to an innocuous joint statement on May 19, 1933, expressing the hope that both China and Japan would end their hostilities. When the Chinese shortly thereafter had to accept Japan's terms in the Tangku Truce of May 31, American officials declined official comment.

The administration's failure to deplore publicly Japan's action in Manchuria and now North China did not mean that it was unconcerned about the long-run implications of Japanese policy. In May and June 1933, Minister Johnson in Peking, who conceded Manchuria was a special preserve for the Japanese, worried that their expansion into North China threatened American interests in China and the Philippines and "must give us cause to wonder just what our position in the Pacific is to be"; and he advocated being "brutally frank" about America's intention to defend its legitimate interests. But he cautioned against any American intervention in Asia intended to solve China's problems with Japan or to preserve China's territorial integrity or administrative entity.

Ambassador Grew in Tokyo, who one year earlier thought Japan's control of Manchuria might bring order to the region and provide a buffer against Soviet expansion, now was upset over the prevalent "war psychology" and increasingly anti-American animus in Japan. He was convinced that neither moral, nor economic, nor military sanctions would deter the Japanese from consolidating their new position in China even at the risk of all-out war with the West. Stanley K. Hornbeck, the Chief of the Division of Far Eastern Affairs in the State Department, was enraged that the Japanese were making war an instrument of national policy, but in May 1933 he opposed any American initiative, because "we might reinvigorate Japanese animus" as well as bring about a "premature and inconclusive 'peace' " that would enable the Japanese to consolidate their position and prepare for expansion. Hornbeck also felt that any initiative had to come first from the British (or the Russians), who had more at stake than the United States; that Japan's logistical and political problems would become more complicated as its armies penetrated China; that Japanese advances ultimately would kindle responses of Chinese nationalism; and that, "in the long run, our interests would best be served by a complete exposure of Japan's program, her strength and/or weakness, and as complete as possible involvement of herself in the situation which she has created and is developing there: given time, the flood tide of her invasion will reach its height and the ebb will follow."

The policy of watchful waiting and hoping continued unabated into the autumn of 1933. Koki Hirota, a fierce nationalist and career diplomat, was appointed Foreign Minister, and Ambassador Grew reported that Hirota intended to live up to his pledge to him of making improved American-Japanese relations a cornerstone of his foreign policy. Secretary Hull urged Grew to maintain such close contacts with the Foreign Minister as would help to achieve that end, and by late autumn the outward form of Japanese-American relations appeared so good that British diplomats were speculating whether this *rapprochement* was not being achieved at the expense of their own commercial and political interests. Summarizing the previous year's developments on January 3, 1934, Ambassador Lindsay wrote from Washington that, while Roosevelt seemingly had endorsed the Stimson doctrine of nonrecognition, it was evident from the outset that there "was a change from idealist to realist conceptions of the Far Eastern situation. . . . There was no further lecturing of Japan. The Japanese delegates to the Economic Conference were received at the White House, and both economic and political discussions took place." The American view of Japan, Lindsay said, now was "empirical," and the United States desired to maintain a hands-off policy in the Far East.

A test of whether American officials intended to maintain such a policy was not long in coming. During 1933 and 1934, the League of Nations had provided the Chinese Government with a limited amount of technical assistance for civil construction and health projects, and the Reconstruction Finance Corporation had lent it $50 million to purchase American wheat and cotton—a good way, New Dealers thought, of disposing of farm produce and raising domestic prices. The Japanese opposed any aid to the Chinese, whom they suspected of using loans (or money acquired from reselling wheat and cotton at discounted prices) to buy war matériel. On April 17, 1934, Eiji Amau, a spokesman for the Japanese Foreign Office, stated at a press conference that, while Japan supported the Open Door policy and wished to see China unified and its territorial integrity maintained, this could be achieved only by the Chinese. "We oppose therefore," he said, "any attempt on the part of China to avail herself of the influence of any other country in order to resist Japan" and "any joint operations undertaken by foreign powers even in the name of technical or financial assistance" because these were "bound to acquire political significance."

On previous occasions, American diplomats had heard Japanese diplomats make similar, if less publicly stated, remarks, but in Tokyo in 1934 the Amau "doctrine" was widely interpreted as Japan's most historic statement in regard to China since the Twenty-one Demands of 1915. Amau's disclaimers about not violating China's sovereignty or the Open Door policy notwithstanding, the Japanese position contravened both China's sovereign right, guaranteed by the Nine-Power Treaty of 1922, to deal independently with other powers and the Open Door policy, which American diplomats revered. What remained to be clarified was whether Amau's statement constituted official policy, because he had spoken without formal text, and questions continued to be raised about the official or unofficial status of ensuing clarifying documents issued by the Foreign Ministry.

The American response throughout was low-keyed. For ten days, State Department officials refused comment, while Grew sought an interview with Hirota, who assured him that he had not sanctioned Amau's doctrine or "high-flown language," and that Japan would not take action in China that violated the rights of third powers or the Nine-Power Treaty. Grew nonetheless believed that the Amau doctrine marked the swinging of the pendulum in Japanese affairs in favor of the militarists, and that to remain in office Hirota would have to pursue, in one guise or another, their expansionist policies. The British, meanwhile, remained evasive in their contacts with American diplomats, and on April 26, 1934, they informed Washington that, while they would object to the language of the Amau doctrine and its challenge to the Nine-Power Treaty, they opposed concerted action and felt each nation should state its views independently.

The United States's formal response to the Amau doctrine was a bland aide-mémoire of April 29 that declared that the American Government and people adhered to the principle that their relations with, and interests in, China were governed by international law, which no third party could abrogate. At the same time, Hull cautioned American correspondents to refrain from statements antagonistic to Japan, while the Division of Far Eastern Affairs recommended discontinuing the Reconstruction Finance Corporation loans for wheat and cotton because the Chinese were not responsible debtors. The Division also recommended discontinuing all other economic assistance.

At precisely the time that the State Department was glossing over the Amau doctrine and proposing to wind down economic aid to China in order not to antagonize Japan, American domestic politics and economics were conspiring to compound China's economic problems. In response to agrarian inflationists and the special interests and influence of Western Democratic senators and their silver-mine-owner constituents, Congress passed the Silver Purchase Act of June 19, 1934, which authorized the Secretary of the Treasury to purchase silver—then selling at about $0.45 per ounce—at increasing prices until the metal constituted one-fourth of the entire monetary stock of the United States, or until its world market price reached $1.29 per ounce. Unfortunately, the Chinese were on a silver standard, and the more valuable silver became, the more China's private bankers and speculators (including the Soong family of Madame Chiang) exported it to build up their personal reserves in foreign currency. This led, by the end of 1934, to a serious drain on Chinese silver, monetary deflation, high interest rates, and hardship for those least able to afford it. When the Chinese Government requested that the United States halt its purchase of silver or stabilize its world price at $0.45 per ounce, Roosevelt and Morgenthau, conscious of domestic pressures, refused, and the President in fact took a hard line in December 1934, when he told Under Secretary of State William Phillips that the problem was "China's business and not ours; that they could stop the outflow of silver if they so desired and it was not up to us to alter our policy merely because the Chinese were unable to protect themselves." And again, when Fred I. Kent, governor of the Federal Reserve Bank of New York, wrote to Roosevelt in July 1935 that driving the price of silver up meant the business of the Chinese people was thrown into chaos, the President adamantly responded, "Silver is not the problem of the Chinese past, nor the Chinese present, nor the Chinese future. There are forces there which neither you nor I understand, but at least I know that they are almost incomprehensible to us Westerners. Do not let so-called figures or facts lead you to believe that any Western civilization's action can ever affect the people of China very deeply."

While Roosevelt could justify his policy through historical philoso-
phizing, the Chinese Government had no choice but to take over large
banks in Shanghai in May 1935. On November 2, it nationalized silver.
That is, it forced all private holdings to be redeemed for Chinese yuan
and hoped to sell a large amount of silver at a high price to the American Government, providing the yuan with a currency backing (dollars)
that would be more valuable than the real price of silver. The Chinese
nationalization of silver precipitated panic in the Chinese money markets
and also angered the Japanese, who presumed that the Chinese would
not have nationalized silver without guarantees of an American or
British loan.

The United States had continually balked at this because the State
Department wanted the silver-purchase policy ended, and it also insisted
that any loan agreement would have to be multinational so as not to
offend the Japanese (or the Amau doctrine). At the same time,
Morgenthau insisted that international politics could not impinge on the
American domestic problem (or politics) of silver purchases. He
opposed a loan, or purchase of a vast amount of Chinese silver at a
high price in dollars, because that would go beyond the monetary intent
or purposes of the Silver Purchase Act. Morgenthau believed that China
could best be helped by a reorganization of its currency that pegged it
at an official rate to the dollar, rather than, as was then done, to the
British pound, regardless (or perhaps because) of the political effect
such a move would have on England and Japan.

By mid-November 1935 the Chinese were in such dire economic
straits that Roosevelt instructed Morgenthau to purchase 50 million
ounces of Chinese silver for $20 million, provided the Chinese used the
dollars exclusively for stabilization and not for military purchases, and
provided they kept the agreement secret so as not to anger the Japanese.
Shortly thereafter, in 1936, Roosevelt and Morgenthau grew disen-
chanted with the domestic (or inflationary) aspects of their silver-
purchase program and cut purchases until the world price dropped back
to $0.45 per ounce, at the very time that the Chinese Government now
had huge quantities of the metal on its hands. After much further negotiation, in May 1936 the administration agreed to a dollar exchange (as
opposed to a loan) of $20 million in return for deposit of 20 million
ounces of Chinese silver. They also agreed to purchase outright, between
June 1936 and January 1937, 75 million ounces of Chinese silver at
current world-market prices, with the Chinese choosing payment in
dollars or gold. Once again, the Chinese were restricted to using the
new funds for stabilization only and to keeping the agreement secret.
The United States backed into a financial policy that helped the Chinese
Government stabilize and manage its currency and indirectly helped

it to resist Japanese pressures and encroachment on its affairs. But the British believed the Americans wished to encroach on their economic interests in the Pacific, and the at times irresponsible and contradictory American silver-purchase policy severely compounded China's difficult monetary and economic problems.

As the United States, Great Britain, and Japan maneuvered to defend or extend their interests in China, they had to deal with one another on naval policy. The Washington Naval Treaty of 1922 had established the 5:5:3 ratio on battleships and set a ten-year "holiday" on further construction. The London Naval Treaty of 1930 had extended the building holiday to 1936. It fixed the 10:10:7 ratio for cruisers and parity for destroyers and submarines, and it also provided another naval conference in 1935 in the event any nation exercised its option of giving two years' advance notice of intent to terminate the 1922 treaty that was due to expire in 1936. Whether the Japanese would do this was uncertain at the start of the Roosevelt administration, but their intense opposition and domestic strife over the "inferior" ratios of the 1920's was well known, and by the fall of 1933 indications were that Japan's Government had committed itself to achieving parity in all classes of ships.

President Roosevelt had a reputation for being a naval enthusiast in the tradition of Alfred Thayer Mahan and Theodore Roosevelt. During his tenure as Assistant Secretary of the Navy, he served as an emissary for militant admirals to his more skeptical superior, Secretary of the Navy Josephus Daniels, and as early as April 1914, at the time of the Veracruz crisis, he rashly declared that Congress should buy and build dreadnoughts "until our navy is comparable to any other in the world" —an expansive policy that not even the navy's General Board was prepared to endorse. In the fashion of big-navy men, Assistant Secretary Roosevelt trumpeted the size of the British and German fleets as yardsticks for American building to wrangle congressional appropriations and to avoid antagonizing the Japanese. With the "friendly" British controlling the Atlantic, Roosevelt reasoned, Japan was the only threat to American naval supremacy and security. The United States, therefore, needed not only a strong and undivided fleet in the Pacific but bases in its Western regions. Roosevelt wrote to his son James in January 1938 that defense of the American West Coast "lies not on the Coast, but three thousand miles from the Coast. Once the defense of the Coast is withdrawn to the Coast itself, no government can give adequate security to Portland or any other city within two hundred miles of the Pacific Ocean." Finally, from 1913 on through the later 1930's, Roosevelt was given to musing on the prospects, if the need arose, of blockading Japan into submission. Early in 1933, he issued an Executive Order allocating

$238 million in National Recovery Administration funds for naval construction, and in January 1934 he supported the Naval Parity Act, in which Congress authorized (but did not appropriate sufficient funds for) building up the navy to the limits of the 1922 and 1930 treaties.

There was, however, a much more dovish and realistic side to Roosevelt's naval policies and procedures for dealing with Japan. From the time he saw the costs and carnage of the First World War, he was distressed by "the terrible burden of armaments from which all nations are suffering," as he wrote in March 1921, and he declared himself out of sympathy with the view that the United States should maintain the largest navy in the world. Roosevelt was an early advocate of the idea that the Democratic party should push President Harding to call a conference to limit Anglo-American-Japanese naval spending. In 1923, in response to criticisms of the Washington Conference, he wrote an article, "Shall We Trust Japan?" that argued that the Japanese had been frightened by America's sudden entry into the Pacific in 1898 and concerned that the Open Door policy in China might cut them off from crucial outlets for their commerce and population. Both nations, he felt, had to stop naval threats and accustom themselves to the "deadlock of the present," and Americans had to alter their "old-fashioned habit of mind and recognize the greater necessity to Japan of the markets and the raw products of the Chinese mainland." In 1928, Roosevelt criticized the Coolidge administration for its expanded naval-building program, and while, as noted, the President-elect in 1933 supported Stimson's nonrecognition doctrine, he dropped the note-writing to Japan.

Roosevelt's thoughts about blockading Japan, as in the situation with Germany in the 1930's, were steps short of, or in place of, war, to be taken only after the other side committed aggression. As for the 1933 and 1934 naval appropriations, these were not provocative acts and perhaps suggested a touch of easy spending in an age of depression and unemployment.

Equally important, it was the British, in the process of reassessing their defense needs in view of Nazi Germany's challenge, who were seeking a large increase in their cruiser force (from fifty to seventy ships) and pressing to complete by 1937 their long-delayed fortifications in Singapore. For the most part, the British insisted on maintaining the present 5:5:3 ratio, although they seemed to waver on the issue, not because they thought the Japanese demand for parity was correct, but because they feared their Far Eastern possessions, Hong Kong especially, left no choice but to placate the Japanese.

American diplomats were unanimous in their view that the naval ratios had to be preserved. They agreed with Hornbeck, who argued vociferously in April 1934 that this was not a matter of politics but the highest consideration of national security. Even Ambassador Grew, who worked ceaselessly to avoid a clash in American-Japanese relations and was generally critical of any statement or act of his superior that he felt might pique Japanese nationalist sensibilities, wrote to Hull in February 1934 that the wise policy was to cultivate friendly relations with Japan and "build up our Navy to the limit." As he put it in December 1934, America's standing firm on the naval ratios and building up to its treaty limits was consistent with legitimate national interests and the good-neighbor policy. The Japanese, who were already appropriating nearly half of their budget to the army and navy, would be forced to seek a compromise.

Equally significant, in April 1934 Roosevelt told his roving ambassador and chief disarmament negotiator, Norman Davis, that he wanted a multilateral 20 per cent reduction of naval forces. As he later wrote to Prime Minister MacDonald, in June 1934, this view he put forward not as a bargaining position but out of conviction that any agreement had to keep the lid on naval strengths. But in talks in London in June and July 1934, Davis was unable to sell Roosevelt's view to the British: they considered it irreconcilable with their European-Asian defense needs and returned to their demand for increased cruiser strength. At the same time, the British began to ponder, on the basis of papers prepared for the Cabinet by the Imperial Defense Committee, the idea of a bilateral nonaggression pact with Japan. This, they felt, would reduce the threat to their Far Eastern interests and perhaps, by such political *rapprochement,* induce the Japanese to continue the 5:5:3 naval ratio.

Two ways of thinking, containing slight contradictions, inclined the British to consider this course. One view, expressed by Chancellor of the Exchequer Neville Chamberlain in a position paper drawn for the Cabinet in March 1934, argued that close Anglo-American cooperation or collaboration would make the Japanese feel more isolated, and that, since it was the Americans who were most threatened, he opposed "lining up" with them to preserve the naval ratio. "We must make clear to the Americans," he insisted, "that we could not pull the chestnuts out of the fire for them." The second British view, or fear, as Davis explained to Roosevelt, was that, in the event of another Manchurian-style crisis, the United States might again lead the British into a nonrecognition or moral condemnation policy and then withdraw from the Far East and leave them to suffer Japanese wrath. In addition, Davis said, the British Government was under pressure from its industrialists to reach agreement with Japan on a division of trade in China, which would keep the Japanese busy for years to come and away from British interests.

Roosevelt was disappointed that the British refused to consider naval reduction. Then, in early November 1934, amidst rumors about British interest in a bilateral nonaggression pact with Japan, he became enraged that Chamberlain, Foreign Secretary John Simon, and "a few other Tories" might be suspected of "preferring to play with Japan to playing with us," and he threatened to counter their policy by appealing over their heads to the public in Canada, Australia, and New Zealand and claiming that the Dominions' ultimate security was linked to that of the United States, not England. Further strife in Anglo-American relations was averted when political forces in England opposed to an agreement with Japan gained the initiative and forced the Cabinet to shelve its consideration. Next, the Japanese made known their unwillingness to agree to a British compromise whereby the ratio system, which the Japanese so despised, would have been scrapped in return for limits on the size of the vessels each nation could build (as usual, the Americans preferred larger but fewer ships, whereas the British and Japanese preferred smaller but more ships), and whereby each nation would have to announce its building plans for the next six years. On December 28, 1934, Japan formally denounced the Washington Naval Limitation Treaty of 1922, thus confirming the judgment of even the conciliatory Norman Davis that, whereas the Japanese Government of 1922 had had a "peace policy," the present regime had a "war policy."

The Americans, British, and Japanese made a final effort to resolve their differences at the London Naval Conference of December 1935–March 1936. The meetings, however, bogged down. The Japanese withdrew their delegation when the United States and Great Britain refused to agree to their demand that the size of the three navies be bound by a common upper limit, which, Davis pointed out, was another name for parity. The only agreement was an Anglo-American one limiting the size of battleships (35,000 tons, with 14-inch guns) and extending the construction holiday on heavy cruisers and battleships. Otherwise, every nation was free to build its navy to whatever extent it believed its national interest warranted.

The failure of the London Naval Conference of 1935–36 and the ensuing naval race was not nearly so much a cause of the Second World War as a barometer of the increasingly bad political climate and conflict of interests that virtually precluded agreement. The one positive feature of the London Conference that historians usually point to was the increasing Anglo-American accord and cooperation that later served both nations. To some extent, this is true. As Davis reported on December 8, 1935, the "pro-Japanese" group that favored a political agreement with Japan had been routed, and the appointment of Anthony Eden as Foreign Secretary at the end of the month (replacing Sir Samuel Hoare in the aftermath of the exploded Hoare-Laval plan) marked the coming to power of someone whom American diplomats liked, and who placed a high premium on Anglo-American cooperation. Indeed, when the Foreign Office, in January 1936, sent Eden a recapitulation of the dormant proposal for an Anglo-Japanese political agreement, he readily agreed with Davis's assessment of its drawbacks, especially as they related to Japan's infringement on China's sovereignty, concluding that the American view "must be decisive for us." But the years of naval negotiations and secret discussions and rumors concerning the proposed Anglo-Japanese accord had left a certain uneasiness, at least on the American side, and there remained in London and Washington a belief that each side was trying to maneuver the other into assuming the lead and cost of the approaching crisis in world politics. Notwithstanding the efforts of some individuals, it seemed that the worse the crisis became, the less could American and British statesmen agree on how to deal with it, as the Sino-Japanese conflict would soon show.

Between 1935 and mid-1937, American diplomats found few encouraging signs in Far Eastern foreign or domestic policies. In April 1935, Grew wrote that even the allegedly moderate Foreign Minister Hirota "aims at more or less the same goal for Japan [in China] as do the reactionaries," but that Hirota preferred to achieve that goal slowly and through international conciliation rather than by "force and the mailed fist." The important point in Grew's message was that the disagreement between Japan's moderates and extremists was over tactics, not policy, and that the current peace might end abruptly. Japanese forces continued to infiltrate Mongolia and North China and gain control of various local regimes, charging that the Chinese had violated the Tangku Truce of 1933 by not suppressing anti-Japanese activities. On June 10, 1935, Japan's General Yoshiro Umezu forced China's War Minister and head of the Peking Military Council, General Ho Ying-chin, to agree to banish Kuomintang party officials and Nationalist army men from Hopei province and to make the Chinese military commander in the Peking-Tientsin region employ Japanese advisers—all an infringement of the sovereignty of the Chinese Government, whose headquarters was farther south, in Nanking. Later that month, the Japanese forced the Chinese to accept a similar agreement expelling Nationalist forces from the province of Chahar, and by autumn the Tokyo government was thinking about severing from China its five northern provinces (Hopei, Chahar, Suiyuan, Shansi, and Shantung). These provinces would then he integrated into the Japanese economy and used as a buffer between Manchukuo and Nanking-controlled China.

At the end of October 1935, Foreign Minister Hirota, in an interview with the Chinese Ambassador in Tokyo, put forward his "Three Principles" for negotiations with China. These comprised, first, an alliance with Japan to suppress communism in Asia; second, abandonment of the policy of playing one "barbarian" (that is, foreign) nation against another; and third, *de facto* recognition of Manchukuo and establishment of economic cooperation between China and Japan. Innocuous as these points sounded, Ambassador Nelson Johnson (he became ambassador in 1935, and his legation was raised to embassy) wrote to the State Department, the first point meant that Japan would station troops throughout China, ostensibly to suppress Communist activities; the second point indicated that Japan would assume close supervision of China's foreign and financial policies; and the third point indicated that Japan would gain preference for continuation of its policies of extreme economic penetration and control of China. Johnson warned in November 1935 that acceptance of Hirota's three principles would "place China almost completely under Japanese control."

Hirota's points did raise some Chinese resistance to Japan, with the result that, while negotiations went on between Tokyo and Nanking, the Japanese for the time being had to limit their ambition in North China and content themselves with establishment in December 1935 of the Hopei-Chahar Political Council. Two of China's northern provinces became virtually autonomous—and subject to Japanese influence—although responsibility for their foreign and financial policies ostensibly remained with the Nanking government.

The explosive nature of Japanese politics, and its effect upon that nation's foreign policy, was a puzzling and menacing factor. In February 1936, the moderate Minseito party gained a parliamentary majority over the Seiyukai party, which was more receptive to the army's expansive policies in China, but on February 26, 1936, fifteen hundred young officers and soldiers of the First Division in Tokyo, inspired by ultra-nationalist writings and embittered over the removal of their idol, General Jinzaburo Mazaki, from the powerful post of Inspector General of Military Education, revolted against the government and seized the War Office, the Prime Minister's official residence, and the new Diet building. The Finance Minister, the Lord Keeper of the Privy Seal, and the new Inspector General of Military Education were murdered; Prime Minister Keisuke Okada escaped only because the rebels mistakenly killed his brother-in-law in his stead. The rebellion was put down within three days by the Emperor and loyal forces, and this led many, including Ambassador Grew, to conclude that perhaps moderate elements had triumphed.

Such was not really the case. In terms of intramilitary rivalries, the crushing of the February 1936 revolt marked the dominance of the so-called Control faction, composed of General Staff officers who believed that before Japan created a crisis it needed to mobilize and modernize the nation's resources and develop Manchukuo. This faction now took precedence over the Imperial Way faction, most influential during 1931–34, which had included General Mazaki, and which believed in a spiritual regeneration of the nation and in precipitating a crisis before 1936 with Russia. But the differences between the two groups were largely of means and timing, not of ends, insofar as Japan's ultimate domination of China and East Asia was concerned.

The military's control over the civil government and the contours of foreign policy were expanded when Koki Hirota, now Prime Minister, agreed that only active officers with the rank of lieutenant general or vice admiral could serve as Minister of War or Navy, giving the military extraordinary influence over the Cabinet through the threat of resignation. In August 1936, the Cabinet adopted its "Fundamental Principles of National Policy," which called for increasing military and economic integration of Japan, Manchukuo, and North China to strengthen the nation's defense against Russia. It also called for peaceful economic penetration ("footsteps," as the ministers said) of Southeast Asia to secure resources that would facilitate building a self-sufficient economy and a navy strong enough "to secure command of the Western Pacific" and to counterbalance the American Navy. Japanese officials determined to conciliate the Nanking regime and not to antagonize the United States, although they did not spell out the means whereby they could resolve contradictions between these goals and their new and sweeping "co-prosperity and co-existence" policy. In further efforts to gain leverage over China, in November 1936 Japan signed the Anti-Comintern Pact with Germany and promoted a military revolt for autonomy in Inner Mongolia, which was quashed by Chiang Kai-shek's Nationalist forces in Suiyuan.

After this, Japan's forward movement against China abated, while in Tokyo the civil-military struggle continued. The Hirota government was replaced in January 1937 by a more moderate one, and in April the Seiyukai and Minseito parties took a joint stand against militarism and gained a three-fourths majority in the Diet. But the new Cabinet, under Prime Minister Fumimaro Konoye and Foreign Minister Hirota, was composed chiefly of proarmy men, and responsibility for national policy-making was taken from the Cabinet and given to a Planning Board under Hirota. In the spring of 1937, Grew reported that all observers agreed that Japan intended to dominate the Far East south of Siberia, but it intended to do so through economic cooperation with China rather than through political means. This did not mean, however, that the Japanese were less ambitious. Certain that their hold on North China was now unbreakable, they simply preferred not to have to use force in seeking further concessions. Yet no one knew whether the past would repeat itself, with a wave of aggression replacing the current wave of moderation.

Reports from China were no more reassuring. The dark perspective of 1933–34 remained constant in 1935–36. Ambassador Johnson wrote disgustedly that, instead of galvanizing resistance to the Japanese, Chiang Kai-shek preferred to wage war against the Communists. "It would be funny if it were not so tragic," Johnson wrote in June 1935, and one month later, after the Japanese had imposed further restrictions on the Kuomintang in North China, he reported that the Nanking government had been reduced to "a jelly-like consistency." Even worse were reports of the American military attaché in Peking, Colonel Joseph W. Stilwell, who reiterated two essential grievances. First, he said, the Chinese Government was corrupt beyond redemption, and that, tragically, there was no alternative to Chiang—"a failing common to all dictatorships." Second, as Stilwell wrote in a report to Johnson and Secretary Hull in June 1936, despite the fact that Chiang spent 80 per cent of his revenue on the military, he made no effort to resist the Japanese— "no troop increase or even thought of it. No drilling or maneuvering," and no logistical system. Chiang either intended to continue doing nothing or was "utterly ignorant of what it means to get ready for a fight with a first-class power." And when, in July 1936, the Kuomintang made overtures for assistance, including a mixed Sino-American General Staff in Washington, Stilwell concluded that this was "another manifestation of the Chinese desire to get somebody else to do something they are afraid to do themselves."

The Nationalists' triumph in the Suiyuan campaign in November 1936 was one encouragement, and then came the Sian episode. In December, Chiang Kai-shek went to Sian, capital of the northwestern province of Shensi, to press Chang Hsüeh-liang and his troops (exiles from Manchuria since 1932) to undertake a sixth anti-Communist campaign. Chang Hsüeh-liang, however, astonished everyone by kidnapping Chiang and demanding more resistance to the Japanese, democratization procedures in the government, and coalition with the Communists. After delicate negotiations, which included assistance from the Soviet Union and Chinese Communists, Chang Hsüeh-liang released Chiang (and actually returned to Nanking as Chiang's prisoner!), and the Kuomintang agreed to end the anti-Communist campaign and negotiate a coalition to resist the Japanese. Western observers were impressed by this apparent unity, which had public support for Chiang as its symbol. Men such as Ambassador Johnson thought the Chinese might yet pull themselves together and throw off the Japanese yoke, although the acidic Stilwell insisted that the Chinese had "neither leaders, moral cohesion, munitions, nor coordinated training," and that the government waited only "to have their problems solved by someone else."

There matters stood on the night of July 7, 1937, when Japanese and Chinese soldiers clashed at the Marco Polo Bridge southwest of Peking. The causes of the clash remain obscure, but after four days of sporadic fighting the military commanders on both sides signed a truce. The Japanese Government wanted both to localize the conflict and to take a firm stand toward China. On July 11, the Cabinet approved mobilizing four divisions of troops. Prime Minister Konoye, blaming the Chinese for the fighting, demanded an apology and guarantees. He insisted that the government in Nanking neither obstruct a settlement nor participate in negotiating one, which had to be reached by July 27.

The Kuomintang, fearful for its prestige and of Japanese efforts to skewer North China, sent four divisions to areas of North China from which they had been excluded by the Ho-Umezu agreement of 1935, and on July 17 it demanded participation in a settlement that would surrender no more territory to the Japanese nor infringe on China's sovereignty. Both sides remained adamant; widespread fighting began after July 27, and by mid-August the Japanese controlled the entire Peking-Tientsin area. Seeking to recoup his prestige, Chiang sent his forces into the area bordering Shanghai that had been neutralized by the 1932 settlement, and on August 14 he attacked Japanese naval installations. The Japanese counterattacked, convinced they could win a quick victory and force a settlement for North China on their own terms. For the next three months, the devastating assault raged. Chiang, probably hoping to stir Western intervention, refused to order a retreat until too late.

Initial American diplomatic reaction to the Sino-Japanese conflict was to avoid any involvement. The rationale is easy to understand. The Japanese were strong and determined; the Chinese were weak and corrupt (the upswing of the past half-year notwithstanding), and the causes of the fighting murky. Hence, Ambassador Grew saw no reason to take action in the "Far Eastern mess," and said that it would be hard to see what the United States could do short of antagonizing Japan or participating in a settlement that would further impair China's integrity. Johnson thought America's main concern was not China's independence but "our independence of action in the Pacific both now and in the future." By September, he thought that the Chinese deserved some assistance for putting up a good fight against "a mad man that knows no pity," but in November 1937 he insisted "nothing makes me lose patience with my Chinese friends so quickly as when I hear them talk about the responsibility of America for failing to preserve the independence and integrity of China." Similarly, Assistant Secretary Hugh R. Wilson insisted that the United States had neither "a monopoly of the morality of the world [nor] a monopoly of obligation to enforce morality," and he "wished to God General Washington had heard of the Far East when he was still living and had warned our people against entanglements over the Pacific as well as the Atlantic."

Then there was American distrust of the British, which was compounded in the spring and summer of 1937 by the unhappy exchanges between Morgenthau, the State Department, and Roosevelt with the British over economic measures to preserve peace and a visit to the United States that Prime Minister Chamberlain rejected. There seemed no reason to cooperate with the British in the Far East, and Grew even relished the fact, as he wrote on July 27, 1937, that, in Japan's view, "the United States is still the fair-haired boy. I hope we can remain so and am making every effort to preserve that favorable position. What a change since 1931 and 1932!" The State Department's counselor, R. Walton Moore, reported that he was getting so many letters advising against "pulling the British chestnuts out of the fire" that he was getting sick of the phrase. Assistant Secretary Wilson thought that, in the event of conflict, the British could not offer substantial naval assistance, although they encouraged American involvement and were willing to run risks to ensure American help in the event they came under attack in Europe.

When British Foreign Secretary Eden made three inquiries in July 1937 about jointly urging moderation upon Tokyo and Anglo-American mediation of the conflict, the State Department approved only "parallel" representations about moderation and avoided responding directly to the question of mediation. On July 16, Secretary Hull issued a statement that reiterated America's commitment to international law and advocated self-restraint. In September, Eden, the one member of the British Cabinet willing to run serious risks in the Far East, pressed American officials about considering sanctions against Japan, but the State Department insisted that it would cooperate by "pacific methods" only.

President Roosevelt was of two minds. In mid-July, he apparently discussed the idea of sanctions with Under Secretary Welles but said nothing more. In Chicago, on October 5, 1937, he delivered his "quarantine" speech, noting that peace-loving nations had to make a concerted effort to uphold treaties. The statement was sharp but less so than one prepared by Norman Davis, and discarded by Roosevelt, which referred to America's willingness to fight for principles. Public response, including that in isolationist strongholds, was as favorable as not, and foreign reception of the speech was good. But when, the next day, a reporter asked Roosevelt whether he meant to imply sanctions, the President said these were "out of the window," and Under Secretary Welles conveyed the same message to the British in two interviews on October 12 and 14. It was at this time that Roosevelt was approving Welles's aborted Armistice Day scheme, the purpose of which was economic and political appeasement.

From autumn 1937, Roosevelt began to see Japanese action not only as a threat to American interests but as a challenge of global dimensions. So he wrote to Ambassador Anthony Biddle in Warsaw in November 1937: "There is no question that the German-Italian-Japanese combination is being amazingly successful—bluff, power, accomplishment, or whatever it may be." Roosevelt's letters to friends were filled with comment about his need to battle public psychology and the "peace at any price" mentality. Evidently, Roosevelt intended his "quarantine" speech to be not a call to action but a means to educate the public to ultimate dangers. As he wrote at the time to his former headmaster at Groton, Endicott Peabody, the "most peaceful" thing to do to the Japanese was to "quarantine" them for "this is more Christian, as well as more practical, than that the world should go to war with them."

Roosevelt continued his cautious line in mid-October, when he instructed Norman Davis, who headed the American delegation to the League of Nations–sponsored Brussels Conference to consider the Sino-Japanese conflict, that "there is such a thing as public opinion in the United States," and that under no circumstance was America to be "pushed out in front as the leader in, or suggestor of, future action," nor could it be made to appear to be "a tail to the British kite." If the Japanese refused conciliation, other nations might "ostracize Japan, break off relations," but only if this had the overwhelming support of world opinion—an unlikely possibility.

Meanwhile, the British Cabinet, urged on by Eden but restrained by Chamberlain, informed American officials that it viewed deferred action or moral condemnation as worthless, but that widely supported economic sanctions might be effective. The State Department replied that the question of sanctions could not arise at a conference to solve the conflict by agreement, a position that opened the way for Chamberlain to instruct his Cabinet that thereafter all parliamentary statements should present the purpose of the conference as appeasement.

The Brussels Conference opened on November 3, 1937, with all the 1922 Nine-Power signatories present except the Japanese, who refused two invitations. The Italians took the Japanese side and Mussolini hoped his signing the Anti-Comintern Pact would wreck the meeting and discredit the British. The French had already cut off rail shipments to the

Chinese through Indochina, and, fearing a Japanese reprisal against their colonies, would not reopen the line without a guarantee of support, which was not forthcoming. The smaller nations feared that sanctions against Japan would damage their trade and lead to reprisals on their possessions—and this left the initiative to the Americans and British.

Trying to make both his own and the American Government act more firmly, Eden spent the first week emphasizing to Davis the increasing lawlessness in Europe and Asia and England's willingness to take as much direct action as the United States. Davis stuck by his instructions and said only that the United States might stop purchasing Japanese goods. Eden said that Britain would consider real sanctions—which meant risking war—if it could get appropriate guarantees. But when the Foreign Secretary returned to London on November 9, Chamberlain said, "On no account will I impose a sanction!"—although Eden forced him to back off having this repeated to Davis.

Davis's patience with conciliation was wearing thin, and the next day he proposed to the State Department steps to "startle and worry Japan," which included repealing the 1937 Neutrality Act and supplying military aid to China. Hull ruled these proposals unacceptable, and Welles informed the British that Davis had exceeded his instructions, and that there was no legislation allowing Roosevelt to undertake sanctions. On November 15, the Brussels delegates declared their intention of considering a common attitude toward Japan's violation of the Nine-Power Treaty but went no further and adjourned *sine die* on November 24. That day, the Japanese seized British customs vessels at Tientsin and Shanghai, and at Eden's behest Ambassador Lindsay inquired about the possibility of an "overwhelming display of naval force." Welles retorted in the clearest terms that this meant an "unmistakable display of United States naval forces" before Hull formally refused on the grounds that the Japanese did not seem to be "running wild."

That perspective altered on December 12, 1937, when Japanese aviators, opening their country's brutal assault on Nanking, sank the gunboat *Panay* and damaged several other American and British ships. Roosevelt and Hull were enraged and demanded full apologies and compensation. And they lodged their protest quickly, so as not to have to act in concert with the disappointed British. The Japanese immediately apologized for their "grave blunder," but as information trickled in suggesting the attack was not accidental, the President became more bitter and told Cabinet aides he thought the Japanese had assaulted American ships to intimidate the Chinese and as a prelude to driving Westerners out of China. Between December 14 and December 18, Roosevelt talked about an embargo on oil and cotton and an Anglo-American blockade of Japan. He expressed interest in a plan proposed by Morgenthau—

who thought it time for the United States to go to war against Japan—
to declare a national emergency and invoke the Trading with the Enemy
Act to seize Japanese assets, and he let Morgenthau sound out the
British over the telephone. Throughout these discussions, Roosevelt kept
insisting, especially when Secretary of the Navy Claude Swanson demanded war, that the purpose of his efforts was to modify Japan's behavior without war. In an interview with Ambassador Lindsay on
December 16, Roosevelt ruled out a British request for naval movements, and by December 21, when the British said they felt Morgenthau's economic sanctions were insufficient, Roosevelt had lost interest
in retaliation. Indeed, the naval emissary he now dispatched to London,
Captain Royal E. Ingersoll, was instructed to limit his talks to technical
matters only, with the insistence that any joint action was possible only
after some future Japanese transgression. The Americans were clearly
pleased when on December 24 the Japanese offered a formal apology for
the *Panay* incident and agreed to an indemnity.

American officials maintained their aloofness toward the Sino-
Japanese war, refusing to participate in mediation because they feared
any settlement acceptable to the Japanese would infringe China's guarantees under the Nine-Power Treaty. The initiative fell to the Germans,
who were then enjoying strong commercial ties with China and growing
political amity with Japan. Hitler, seeking to avoid a choice between
traditional diplomats and military men who favored China and the
more adventurous Nazis, such as Ribbentrop, who favored Japan, agreed
to allow German officials to serve as a conduit for Sino-Japanese exchanges. In November 1937, the Japanese demanded that the Chinese
recognize Manchukuo *de facto,* grant Inner Mongolia autonomy, cease
all anti-Japanese activities, and join a common front against communism. Chiang refused to comply, insisting that the terms would topple
his government; he hoped the Brussels Conference would secure a better
agreement. When that did not materialize, he offered to negotiate on the
basis of the November terms. But the expansionist clamor in Japan was
rising, and the government had authorized the seige of Nanking, early
in December, to beat the Chinese into submission.

The Konoye-Hirota government increased its terms, and at the end of
December, after Nanking had fallen and Japanese forces had engaged in
an appalling orgy of destruction, murder, and rape against the city and
its inhabitants, it demanded not only close economic cooperation with
China and the end of all anti-Japanese, anti-Manchukuo policies but an
indemnity (an admission of Chinese war guilt) and the right to establish
special regimes in China wherever they deemed necessary. Even the
Germans transmitting the terms warned that they were unacceptable,
and Roosevelt told Hull on January 4, 1938, that they were "utterly

impossible." When the Chinese made a final appeal for assistance, the President had the State Department reply only that the United States was interested in a peaceful settlement, and Hull refused a Chinese request for a $500-million loan by saying that Congress probably would not appropriate the funds.

On January 14, 1938, the Japanese, noting China's failure to secure foreign aid, termed its reply to their demands "too broad," and two days later the Konoye-Hirota regime ended negotiations and broke diplomatic relations with China, a major step that committed Japan to mobilization of its resources for a war of annihilation against the Kuomintang government. The Roosevelt administration, disturbed by Japan's unyielding and increasingly brutal military and diplomatic tactics, considered simultaneous American and British fleet movements in the Pacific but chose to launch the Roosevelt-Welles plan for European appeasement that, it hoped, would entice Japan to settle with China on terms consistent with the Nine-Power Treaty. The Roosevelt-Welles plan never got off the ground, as was noted earlier, but it intensified the Chamberlain-Eden dispute and precipitated the Foreign Secretary's resignation on February 20, 1938. That same day, Hitler recognized Japan's conquest of Manchukuo and shortly thereafter signed a friendship treaty aimed at securing economic concessions (which never materialized). In the spring, he terminated military aid to China and recalled his military advisers working with the Kuomintang.

Throughout 1938, the Japanese continued their relentless undeclared war in search of the final military victory that they believed would bring about China's capitulation. By June, Japanese forces controlled every important rail and seaboard communication from northern Manchuria to the Yangtze River in Central China, and in October they launched a successful million-man offensive against Hankow and Canton (upriver from Hong Kong) in the south of China. The Japanese established puppet governments in North and Central China, and through their Reserve Bank in China they pursued an aggressive currency policy to devalue the Chinese yuan against all foreign currencies except the Japanese yen to such an extent that the Chinese could afford to buy only Japanese goods. The Japanese set up Development Companies in North and Central China to assume control of all basic industries. Then, on November 3, 1938, partly to justify the enormous military and economic ventures that had grown beyond anything originally contemplated, Premier Konoye proclaimed "a New Order" in East Asia that envisioned coordinating the political, economic, and cultural lives of Japan, Manchukuo, and China and declared the Kuomintang a local regime only. Peace would come only after a reformed China accepted the New

Order, legally recognized Manchukuo, allowed Japanese troops in China at specified areas, accepted Inner Mongolia as a special anti-Communist area, and afforded the Japanese freedom of movement and access to facilities to achieve their purposes. Third powers would be welcome in China, but only if they accepted the New Order and Japan's special position. The Kuomintang government refused these terms and, in December 1938, retreated to Chungking in Southwest China, cut off from supply routes, including the 650-mile Burma Road.

Not only did American officials in 1938 take a dim view of Japan's activities in China, but their perspective on the Sino-Japanese war began to alter. The conflict could no longer be seen as bilateral but had to be viewed in terms of long-run implications for American national interests and the balance of world politics. State Department officials worried that the Japanese had got Germany to remove its military advisers from China and grant Japan tactical freedom in the Pacific in return for support of Germany's European ambitions. Ambassador Johnson saw a link between German and Japanese maneuvers, and on June 9, 1937, he wrote to Stanley Hornbeck—who agreed—that America would never realize its "heritage as the hope of a war-weary world unless we are prepared to stand at Armageddon with the powers of righteousness and the rule of law against [the] gangsterdom that is raising the banner of might, force, and international bad faith." Even the patient Grew was aghast at Japan's proclaimed New Order: "So much for international agreements," he said, never before having "experienced quite that sort of thing."

If ever so cautiously, American policy-makers began to think about measures that might slow down Japan's aggression. In the spring of 1938, the Chinese, for the first time, were allowed to use proceeds from the sale of silver to the United States for military supplies rather than currency stabilization. Secretary Hull announced in June that the government would discourage the sale of airplanes to regions where they were used to bomb civilians—thus inaugurating a virtual embargo on planes and parts to Japan.

Hope persisted that Japan might assume a more moderate course. In October 1938, Grew presented to the Japanese a long message complaining that Japan's restrictive political and economic policies in China were clearly infringing American treaty and trade rights and requesting, in effect, that Japan reaffirm the Open Door policy. In succeeding weeks, Grew could get only equivocal responses from the Japanese, who captured Canton at the end of October and then proclaimed their New Order. Finally, on November 19, 1938, the new Foreign Minister, Hachiro Arita, told the counselor of the American Embassy in Tokyo, Eugene Dooman, that world conditions demanded that Japan guarantee its markets and access to raw materials. Japan could no longer give assurances about the Open Door as the Americans understood it, although foreign economic activities would be tolerated in China, provided that they did not impinge upon "Japanese economic defense plans."

Japan's stiffening attitude provided Morgenthau with opportunity to press for assistance to China. In June, he and Secretary of Agriculture Henry Wallace had tried to arrange a huge loan for the Chinese to purchase American wheat and flour, but Hull insisted this was feasible only if the Japanese had the same option. During September and October, the Munich crisis and the Japanese advances alarmed Morgenthau, who was persuaded that, unless the United States resisted fascist aggression, "we might just as well recognize that the democratic form of Government in my life time is finished." Interior Secretary Ickes recorded on September 30, 1938, that the entire Cabinet "would like to help China if we only knew how, of course again without running the risk of our own involvement in war." Consequently, Morgenthau and his Treasury aides proposed a scheme whereby the Chinese Government would sell, over five years, $50-million worth of tung oil (valuable in making paints) to its own private Universal Trading Corporation, which would sell the tung oil to a syndicate of American purchasers and then use the funds to buy supplies for the Chinese Government. To allow the Chinese to benefit at once from the arrangement, the Export-Import Bank would lend the Chinese Government $25 million, half the amount of the projected tung-oil sales. Roosevelt agreed but insisted that the plan be cleared with Hull, who balked at the almost purely political aspect of the agreement. State Department officials such as Hornbeck felt that the tung-oil loan would be provocative but insufficient without a comprehensive retaliatory economic program and fleet maneuvers that would show Japan "we 'mean business.' "

Morgenthau thus could not get Roosevelt's approval until November 30—after Japan had announced its New Order and proscribed the Open Door, and after assurances were forthcoming that Chiang's government would survive in Chungking. Under Secretary of State Welles, still determined on appeasement, effected delay, but Roosevelt gave approval on December 13, and two days later the tung-oil deal and $25-million loan were made public. The Chinese, Ambassador Johnson reported, were elated, and their morale was never higher; on the basis of the loan, they were able to secure another $75 million in British and American credits. Foreign Minister Arita publicly denounced the tung-oil loan as a regrettable act and reiterated Japan's resolve to strengthen its New Order in East Asia.

During December 1938, the State Department considered trade or credit reprisals against Japan for its failure to respect American rights and interests in China, but as might have been surmised from its opposition to the tung-oil loan, it concluded that neither American interests in the Far East nor general world interests at the time warranted the risk of armed conflict. Nor did the State Department believe that the British would afford the required whole-hearted cooperation. The State Department restricted itself to a long note, dated December 30, 1938, informing the Japanese that it denied their right to prescribe the terms and conditions of any New Order in territory not under their sovereignty. The United States would continue to reserve its rights in China.

Tensions between the United States and Japan increased during the next twelve months, despite efforts to find ground for accommodation. In January 1939, Premier Konoye resigned in favor of Baron Kiichiro Hiranuma, which led to speculation that Japanese society was becoming increasingly totalitarian, even if it was, as Grew said, "totalitarianism *sui generis.*" The significance for world politics, the ambassador added in his diary, was that "the totalitarian states on the one hand and the democracies on the other are rapidly lining up in battle array for what may well become another Armageddon."

The Japanese in February defied the French and occupied Hainan Island in the Gulf of Tonkin between the southern coast of China and Indochina. Also, ostensibly for economic purposes, they extended their jurisdiction over the Spratly Islands and 100,000 square miles within the China Sea region, from which they could threaten the main shipping routes around Indochina, the Dutch East Indies, and the Philippines. Ambassador Johnson, visiting in Washington, wrote to Roosevelt that the Japanese intended to seize everything west of the 180th meridian, and that, while time was on the side of rejuvenating China in its conflict with Japan, "time is with the totalitarian states in their relations with the democracies." The United States, he insisted, had to play its proper role in world affairs and "to show our teeth" by cutting off all financial assistance to Japan, without which it could not sustain its war against China. "It is not a question of saving British chestnuts," he concluded, for "our own chestnuts are involved."

During the first half of 1939, there were rumors that Germany was pressing Japan to expand the Anti-Comintern Pact to a Rome-Berlin-Tokyo general military alliance. Hitler had been persuaded by his Foreign Minister, Ribbentrop, that such an agreement would intimidate the British and Americans in the Pacific and tip the balance in Europe in Germany's favor. Japanese diplomats thought an agreement with Germany would strengthen their hand with China; Japanese Army officials thought it would protect them from Soviet assault; and Japanese Navy officials thought a pact aimed also at the United States would increase their share of the budget. The sticking point in negotiations was Japan's unwillingness to commit itself without reservation to intervening in a European war, whereas, from Hitler's standpoint, an unqualified and highly publicized commitment was vital to his strategy of intimidating, or bluffing, the Western powers into inaction.

Grew believed a German-Japanese alliance would be aimed at the Soviet Union, but he nonetheless spent his energies during the spring of 1939 trying to persuade every influential Japanese he met, including Prince Chichibhu, Emperor Hirohito's brother, that the alliance would have a calamitous effect on American public opinion and United States relations with Japan. State Department officials disliked the idea of German-Japanese collaboration but downplayed its importance. As Hornbeck argued, Germany and Italy had already betrayed China and were affording the Japanese all the aid they could. Japan had little to gain by the alliance except American enmity. If war came to Europe, Germany and Italy would have to shut off their arms and ammunition flow to the Japanese, who would not want to enter a European war because the British and French would prevail by virtue of controlling more of the world's resources and having greater reinforcements. Hornbeck divined that the Japanese would string out negotiations for purposes of diplomatic leverage and advised that the United States should pursue its policy and purposes without regard to their alleged effect upon a possible German-Japanese alliance.

Roosevelt had no desire to threaten the Japanese, and in March 1939 even agreed to send a special cruiser to Japan to return the remains of the late Japanese Ambassador to the United States, Hirosi Saito, a gesture that produced such an outpouring of gratitude in Tokyo that Grew was instructed to tone down the significance of the act. The President's primary concern was Europe, and it was Germany's occupation of truncated Czechoslovakia that led him to seek repeal of the arms embargo embedded in the 1937 Neutrality Act. Similarly, Roosevelt's speech on April 15 asking Germany and Italy for nonaggression guarantees and his ordering the fleet to return six weeks early from Caribbean maneuvers in order to report to San Diego and take some pressure off the British in the Pacific were responses to fear of war in Europe.

American officials wished to protest to the Japanese, as a way of showing concern over recent developments. This desire was heightened in June, when the Japanese, charging the British and French in Tientsin with harboring the murderers of a man who had collaborated with the Japanese, seized the British and French concessions and subjected all foreigners to searches and seizure in violation of treaty rights. On July 6 and 7, Japanese planes bombed Chungking, damaging an American church and narrowly missing an American gunboat and the residence of Ambassador Johnson. During the first six months of the year, the State Department had reviewed and rejected proposals for economic sanctions against Japan. In the spring, during the drive for revision of the neutrality law, the Department rejected Senator Pittman's proposal for an arms embargo against any nation violating the Nine-Power Treaty as a measure aimed too specifically at Japan. Now, after the rumors about a German-Japanese alliance and the Tientsin and Chungking episodes, officials determined on what they regarded as a mild measure, but one that would encourage the British not to compromise over Tientsin and the Chinese not to feel abandoned, and which would be understood in Tokyo without provoking retaliation. On July 26, 1939, Secretary Hull informed the Japanese that the United States was giving its six-month notice of abrogation of its 1911 Treaty of Commerce and Navigation, which formed the legal basis for trade between the two countries.

The reaction in Tokyo was "strong," Counselor Dooman reported, but the Japanese were aware of the United States's determination to assert its treaty rights, and they "had been prepared for the shock." Moreover, Dooman said, "American stock is still higher than any other" in Japan. In August, there were renewed negotiations concerning a German-Japanese alliance, but they floundered on Japan's insistence on determining exactly when it would enter a European war. With the Polish crisis heating up, Hitler could wait no longer, and to the astonishment of everyone he signed his nonaggression pact with the Soviet Union. For the Japanese, this was a telling diplomatic shock. In July of 1938, their troops had clashed with Soviet forces in a disputed region around Lake Khasan, where the Manchurian, Korean, and Siberian borders join. Between May and September 1939, the Kwantung Army and Soviet forces clashed on the border between northern Manchuria and Soviet-controlled Outer Mongolia, which led to 50,000 Japanese casualties before reaching a cease-fire and diplomatic settlement. For many Japanese, especially the army, Russia was their primary enemy in the Pacific, and the Nazi-Soviet Pact on August 22 had left them isolated. German-Japanese talks were suspended, and all eyes were focused on the war in Europe, which began in September.

At this juncture, Roosevelt and the State Department determined that Ambassador Grew should make a signal effort to improve American-Japanese relations. Reasons for a détente were varied, but the conclusion was the same. Grew had opposed abrogating the commercial treaty because he believed such pressures were ineffective and only increased the likelihood of war, which the American people opposed, and which American interests in China did not justify. State Department officials felt much more keenly about American interests in China and feared that the European war would force the British and French to withdraw from the Pacific and give the Japanese free reign. On July 20, 1939, Admiral Harry Yarnell, commander of the Asiatic Fleet, drew up a long report on conditions in the Far East that Hornbeck sent to Hull, with a highly approving memorandum, on September 16. The Yarnell-Hornbeck thesis argued that maintenance of a "free, stable, and democratic government" in China was "essential to the peace of eastern Asia and our own welfare," and that the United States had to support the Chinese "even if it results as a last resort in armed intervention." If Chiang's government fell, Hornbeck warned, "chaos will rule in China."

"Chaos" had a specific as well as a general meaning. Most American officials believed Chiang and the Kuomintang now would resist Japan and, if American support were not forthcoming, would draw closer to the Soviet Union, which, Ambassador Laurence Steinhardt reported on September 22, 1939, had already given China $500 million in aid, more than the combined total of all other nations. One month later, Grew reported that the British, too, feared that Chiang Kai-shek was moving closer to the Soviet Union, while the Japanese were pushing Wang Ching-wei, a former associate and rival of Chiang, as a national nucleus and head of an alternative government. In this struggle, with the Kuomintang and the Soviets on one side and the Japanese and Wang Ching-wei's regime on the other, Western interests in the Pacific would suffer. The obvious course, whether seen from Grew's perspective, which placed the highest premium on American-Japanese relations, or from that of Hornbeck, who was more concerned with the fate of China and American interests in China, was to persuade the Japanese to improve relations with the United States by respecting American treaty rights and interests in China.

In Tokyo on October 19, Grew delivered a speech before the Japan-America Society, composed of Western-oriented businessmen and diplomatic and Court officials, the gist of which had been worked out with officials in Washington. Emphasizing that he was affording information "straight from the horse's mouth," he insisted that he was not presenting the Japanese with a "bill of particulars," that he understood there were "two sides to every picture," and that the American people accepted the "new order in East Asia" if the Japanese meant by that, as they had said, "security, stability, and progress." The Japanese had to understand that the American insistence on the Open Door policy in China was not a "legalistic" maneuver but a firm conviction that nations had to refrain from even thinking of using force to solve disputes, and that the highly complicated world economy rested on the ability of nations to buy and sell under conditions of free competition that could not exist in areas where pre-emptive rights were claimed on behalf of nationals of one country. Grew said that the American people were convinced that Japan's New Order deprived them of their long-established rights in China, and they regarded Japan's widespread bombing as inhumane, a threat to American interests and the correlated principles of national sovereignty and equality of economic opportunity. He insisted that many of the injurious acts perpetrated by Japanese agencies were *"wholly needless,"* and he concluded that it was possible to establish real security and stability in the Far East without running counter to American rights.

Grew's speech, applauded in Washington, met a mixed but hopeful response in Tokyo, and between November 4 and December 22, 1939, he met three times with Admiral Kichisaburo Nomura—the new Foreign Minister, known for his friendly attitude toward the United States— seeking to improve American-Japanese relations. Grew's strategy was to persuade the Japanese that the bombings and indignities inflicted on foreigners in China had to end; at the same time, the United States would negotiate a new trade agreement with the Japanese, who would guarantee freedom of navigation and commerce along the Yangtze. Grew believed that this was the most that the United States could achieve, because nothing was more "mathematically certain" than that the Japanese would not give up their grip on Manchukuo, North China, or Inner Mongolia. In short, they would not respect the territorial integrity or administrative entity allegedly guaranteed by the Nine-Power Treaty of 1922.

Nomura told Grew that the bombings and indignities against foreigners would cease, which they did, but he said that he could not give assurances about trade and travel on the Yangtze until after Wang Ching-wei's semi-autonomous regime was established in Nanking. The State Department would make no concessions regarding Wang's regime, or, as Welles said, there would be no more "Manchukuoizing" of China. Nor was a trade agreement conceivable before the Japanese guaranteed full rights on the Yangtze.

Grew attempted to gain a compromise: negotiation of a new trade agreement that would not be carried out until the Japanese opened the Yangtze. The State Department insisted that such an arrangement implicitly recognized Japan's right to control the Yangtze, while the Japanese insisted that they would always have to maintain restrictions on foreigners on the river. Negotiations finally foundered. The State Department promised that it would do all it could to facilitate trade without a new treaty, while it also extended its moral embargo to include aluminum and molybdenum (important in war-matériel manufactures) and technical information on the production of high-octane fuel. On January 14, 1940, the embittered Nomura had to step aside as his Cabinet was reorganized, while twelve days later the 1911 commercial treaty between the United States and Japan expired. Grew blamed the failure to achieve an American-Japanese *rapprochement* on "the fire-eaters on both sides of the fence," a view more sympathetic, or resigned, to Japanese political and economic hegemony over China than that of virtually any other American diplomat in 1940. The Japanese now began to search for some new means to extricate themselves from their ever widening but inconclusive war, while American officials shifted their focus to Europe, seeking to determine whether there might not be some way to appease the belligerents before their war overflowed the Continent and assumed world-wide proportions.

7

The Price of Freedom

In September 1939, the Western world learned the meaning of *Blitzkrieg*. German forces swept through Poland and within two weeks wiped out all resistance except that in Modlin and Warsaw. If Hitler had had his way, the Soviet Union, which had gained Germany's recognition of its sphere of interest over eastern Poland in their nonaggression pact of August 22, 1939, would have crumbled Polish defenses even faster by a simultaneous invasion. But the Russians, alarmed and surprised as everyone else at the rapidity of the German advance, held back until September 17, when they unleashed their armies on the pretext of protecting "kindred" and "defenseless" Ukrainians and White Russians in Poland, as Foreign Minister Molotov stated. Within ten days, the Poles were routed, their government fleeing to London. German and Russian forces converged in the town of Brest-Litovsk. In Moscow, on September 28, Germany and the Soviet Union formally partitioned Poland out of existence, with the demarcation line between occupied areas approximating the Curzon line of 1919. In return for a larger slice of Poland, the Germans ceded to the Russians their claim to a sphere of interest in Lithuania, and as had been done in 1918, the Germans and Russians shortly worked out agreements for extensive economic collaboration, with the Russians supplying grain, barley, cotton, and a million tons of petroleum products annually, and the Germans reciprocating with machinery, armor plating, and naval equipment.

In early October, the Russians successfully pushed their claims to establish military bases in Estonia and Latvia and then forced Lithuania to accede to bases and a mutual-assistance pact. Seeking to consolidate their defenses from the Arctic to Leningrad, the Russians pressed Finland for bases (in northern Finland and the Gulf of Finland) and a mutual-assistance pact. The Finns balked, determined to preserve their neutrality and their own defense line, which fronted on the Soviet Union. On November 30, the Russians attacked.

Hitler, meanwhile, declared to the Reichstag on October 6 that Germany had no claims against England or France, and that it was futile to seek to restore Poland when Germany and the Soviet Union had guaranteed that "the Poland of the Treaty of Versailles will never rise again." He offered peace on the basis of Western recognition of the new *status quo* or the alternative of a fight to the finish. Three days later, he drew a memorandum for his military commanders that set Germany's aim as the "destruction of our Western enemies," and at the end of the month he drew up plans for an attack on Belgium and Holland to commence on November 12. Bad weather and resistance from the General Staff caused the date of the attack to be postponed, first to late November and then to January 1940—and yet again for another couple of months when a German Air Force officer had to make a forced landing in Belgium, where authorities recovered some of the operational plans he was carrying. Hitler now became interested in a plan to invade Norway and Denmark in order to cut off British sea routes prior to an assault on Belgium and Holland.

Throughout this period, the French and British maintained a stiff diplomatic front toward Germany. Premier Édouard Daladier rejected Hitler's peace offer, insisting on October 10 that the French had taken up arms against aggression and would not lay them down without guarantees of security that "cannot be called in question every six months." Two days later, Prime Minister Chamberlain told Parliament that Hitler's peace offer was unacceptable, based on "recognition of his conquests and of his right to do what he pleases with the conquered." The barrier to peace, he insisted, was "the German Government and the German Government alone," whose burden it now was to give convincing proof of its desire for peace by definite acts and effective guarantees.

The British and French were not prepared to alter the current situation militarily. They had no operational plans to aid Poland, which they believed could be reconstituted only after a settlement with Germany. The British sent an expeditionary force to France (it saw only limited action), strengthened Franco-Belgian defense lines, and, as their most forward step, instituted a naval blockade of Germany that, however, could be effective only in the long run. After Russia attacked Finland, the British and French gave the Finns modest supplies and considered plans (which appealed to the French Right and British Conservatives) to move troops into Norway and Sweden, joining the war against Russia and perhaps depriving Germany of Swedish iron ore. The rationale, though, for fighting a war against both Germany and the Soviet Union remained dim and the chances of surviving such a contest even more so. In January 1940, Norway and Sweden refused the proposal put forth by the British and French, and by the time the latter decided to act, Finland, on March 12, 1940, had acceded to Russian demands for cession of about a sixth of its eastern territory, including the Arctic port city of Petsamo and the Karelian Isthmus. The Germans would beat the British to the punch in assaulting Norway in April 1940.

For the most part, the major Anglo-French efforts during this so-called phoney war from September 1939 to April 1940 were devoted to economic and military mobilization, drawing up favorable war-trade agreements with Norway, Sweden, Holland, Belgium, Iceland, Denmark, Greece, and Spain. It was hoped that these measures would persuade Hitler that he could not retain at the negotiating table what he had won by bluster or on the battlefield during 1938–39; or, if this were not possible, it was hoped that the German people (or General Staff) could be induced to replace Hitler with someone else, perhaps Air Marshal Hermann Goering, who would negotiate a reasonable and guaranteed peace. As Chamberlain wrote to Roosevelt on October 4, 1939, the British did not think they could win "by a complete and spectacular victory, which is unlikely under modern conditions, but by convincing the Germans that they cannot win. Once they have arrived at that conclusion, I do not believe they can stand our relentless pressure, for they have not started this war with the enthusiasm or confidence of 1914." In the meantime, he said, the Americans could render invaluable assistance by lifting the embargo on arms and munitions, which would have a "devastating" effect on German morale.

In the autumn of 1939, the Roosevelt administration sympathized with the British as opposed to the Germans, or at least the Hitler regime. In his fireside address of September 3, Roosevelt had said that conscience would not allow neutrality in thought, even if Americans had to be neutral in act. Two days later, he issued a Wilsonian pronouncement, warning against illegal aid to the belligerents and travel on foreign ships, and proclaimed in effect the Neutrality Act, with its arms embargo. But on September 11, he wrote to Chamberlain that he intended to seek the law's repeal, and that the Prime Minister should feel free to write to him "personally and outside of diplomatic procedure" about any problems. Roosevelt also wrote similarly to Winston Churchill, who had just joined the Cabinet as First Lord of the Admiralty, and whose determined opposition to the Hitler regime was well known.

Acting more decisively than at any time since 1933, Roosevelt, on September 19, told Hull that the Neutrality Law was "miscalled" because it "puts us on the side of the offenders." He proposed revising it to place all goods on a cash-and-carry basis, while prohibiting credits for belligerents and entry of American ships into combat zones. This was done in order to avoid the problems of 1914–17—problems involving entangling financial arrangements with the British or allowing American ships to travel where they would risk attack by German submarines. The next day, the President met with Democratic and Republican congressional leaders, as well as with Alf Landon, his 1936 presidential opponent, and Frank Knox, who was the Republican publisher of the *Chicago Daily News* (and an outspoken advocate of preparedness and opponent of the Hitler regime). On this occasion, Roosevelt insisted that the Neutrality Act was unfair because "we are handing a navy to Germany." Roosevelt discussed strategy to seek the law's revision by courting dissident Democrats (frequently conservative anti–New Dealers in domestic affairs) and by enlisting support of people like Henry Stimson, the Republican newspaperman William Allen White, and the presidents of Harvard and MIT. Before a special session of Congress, on September 21, Roosevelt recapitulated the collapse of the structure of peace since 1931. Setting out the most agreeable argument, which he largely believed himself, he insisted that "by repeal of the embargo the United States will more probably remain at peace than if the law remains as it stands." The President alluded to his belief that the United States was the joint heir of European culture and that "fate now compels us to assume the task of helping to maintain in the Western world a citadel wherein that civilization may be kept alive."

Roosevelt's campaign for neutrality revision met resistance from Senators Borah, La Follette, and Nye, from pacifist and socialist groups, and from Charles Lindbergh, who had been to Germany in 1938 and was overawed by its air power. The President was aided politically by conservative Democrats such as Senators James F. Byrnes of South Carolina and Tom Connally of Texas, and his proposals were supported by influential bankers, businessmen, and international lawyers, as well as labor for the most part. On October 27, the Senate, by a vote of 63–30, repealed the arms embargo and placed all goods on a cash-and-carry basis. American ships were prohibited from traveling to the war zone (North Atlantic) but were permitted, in deference to business interests, to sail to the belligerents' imperial ports, that is, to the British and French empires in Asia, Africa, and the Middle East. The House approved the legislation by 243–172, with 110 of 118 Southern congressmen providing administration support, and Roosevelt signed the measure into law on November 4. The British were delighted but held off on large-scale purchases in America in order to preserve their dollar reserves.

American officials viewed sympathetically Finland's resistance to Soviet encroachments in 1939. In October, Roosevelt wrote to Presidium President Mikhail Kalinin that he hoped the Soviet Government would not make demands on Finland inconsistent with maintaining peaceful relations. Administration officials skirted Finnish requests for diplomatic assistance by saying that the United States could not project itself into a political controversy between sovereign states. Privately, Roosevelt referred to the Russian attack as "this dreadful rape of Finland," and Under Secretary Welles urged breaking relations with the Soviet Union, which he said might have a deterrent effect on Germany and Japan. Hull was skeptical and feared that, after the high tide of pro-Finnish, anti-Soviet sentiment receded, the United States woud be left "holding the bag." The Neutrality Act was not invoked because the Soviets did not declare war, claiming to be aiding a newly announced Finnish "People's Government," under the Communist Otto Kuusinen, against the "illegal" regular Finnish Government. The most American officials would do was declare a moral embargo on war matériel to the Soviet Union. And when Treasury Secretary Morgenthau said that he could not prevent the sale of aluminum and molybdenum, Roosevelt included these items in the embargo.

Roosevelt inclined toward honoring Finland's request for a $60-million loan, but again Hull's caution and fear of congressional ire caused the President to retreat. On January 16, 1940, he sent a tepid message to Congress, saying it could authorize loans for nonmilitary manufactures and agricultural surplus. Congress approved a $20-million loan through the Export-Import Bank on February 28, by which time, however, the war was virtually over.

Roosevelt at first approved selling war matériel to Finland. Hull was opposed and resisted Roosevelt's alternative solution of selling arms to neutral Sweden for export to Finland. In mid-February, Hull acquiesced in the latter scheme, but by the time negotiations were concluded, the Russo-Finnish war had ended, with the Finns having won only a lot of sympathy, which, their Foreign Minister bitterly noted, "nearly suffocated us."

The sentiments and cautious diplomacy of the Roosevelt administration in the fall of 1939 are clear. The President and his aides were pleased with diplomatic reports that the British and French were serious about resisting German demands. When, on September 30, Ambassador Kennedy lamented that it was the British public that prevented its government from making peace, and that the British did not have a "Chinaman's chance" against the emerging Russo-German combine, Roosevelt testily remarked that "Kennedy has been an appeaser and always will be an appeaser. . . . If Germany or Italy made a good peace offer tomorrow, he would start working on the King and his friend, the Queen, and from there on down to get everybody to accept it. . . . He's just a pain in the neck to me."

Roosevelt did not share either of Kennedy's twin anxieties—that war with Germany would bring political, economic, or social ruin to England, or that, if Hitler were eliminated, Germany might go Communist—although he conceded that Germany might "blow up and have chaos for a while." But by mid-December 1939, Roosevelt, as he wrote to William Allen White, was worried that, if the Germans and Russians were able to force a peace favorable to them, "the situation of your civilization and mine is indeed in peril. Our world trade would be at the mercy of the combine and our increasingly better relations with our twenty neighbors to the south would end—unless we were willing to go to war in their behalf against a German-Russian dominated Europe." He confessed that he did not know how to avoid this dilemma, for he did not think he could do much to achieve lasting world peace, and he did not wish "to take part in a patched-up temporizing peace which would blow up in our faces in a year or two." Nonetheless, at about this time the President concluded that he would make one final effort to discern whether there existed some basis for an enduring peace, and he entrusted this assignment to his closest diplomatic aide, Under Secretary Welles.

It is difficult to know how long a peace mission had been in Roosevelt's mind, or what were his precise intentions. Throughout the 1930's, peace. The President was noncommittal but apparently indicated he assented to Welles's 1937 Armistice Day scheme, which became the basis for the approach to Chamberlain in January 1938. On September 11, 1939, Kennedy had urged that, since the British Government could not afford to propose peace to Hitler, the President might emerge as the "savior" of the world by putting forward a peace plan. The administration, however, replied that it was unthinkable to support any effort that might consolidate a regime of force and aggression.

A few days later, Roosevelt received William Rhodes Davis, an oil promoter with strong economic ties to Germany, who said associates there told him that Goering might be receptive to a Roosevelt-mediated peace. The President was noncommital but apparently indicated he might mediate if the belligerents requested mediation. Davis was given a special passport to travel to Berlin, where on October 1–3 Goering suggested that Roosevelt might arrange a conference that would liquidate Versailles forever and create a "new order" that might include new, if smaller, Polish and Czechoslovak states. Davis returned to Washington just as the British and French were rejecting Hitler's October 6 peace offer, and the President refused to see him, perhaps because it would have been impolitic or because Davis's German connections and affinities made him suspect. State Department officials concluded on October 7 that "the time was not ripe for mediation, although it might be ripe for setting forth certain broad principles on which ultimate peaceful relationships would have to be built." Hull insisted that any mediation would fail, embarrass the British and French, and "embroil us in Europe." A few days later Assistant Secretaries Adolf A. Berle and J. Pierrepont Moffat met with Davis, who insisted that only Roosevelt could prevent the war that would "devastate and exhaust Europe and destroy international capitalism." The President, he said, could "write the ticket" for peace. Berle and Moffat were skeptical and upbraided Davis for having distorted, for benefit of German ears, Roosevelt's thoughts about British and French war motives and his willingness to mediate.

The mediation idea died hard and received occasional encouragement from neutral sources in Europe. Then came the Russo-Finnish war and the specter of Europe divided and dominated by Germany and the Soviet Union. By January 1940, Roosevelt was prepared to dispatch Welles to Europe. No one else was consulted. The British received only notice of the mission. Chamberlain protested that no settlement was possible unless Germany first restored Poland and gave guarantees against future aggression—unlikely developments so long as Germany remained organized "on the present lines and is under her present rulers." He insisted that it was best to propose conditions that Hitler would reject but that would appeal to "considerable elements" in Germany. Moreover, he felt, Welles's mission might arouse false hopes in the democracies that the Germans could exploit.

Roosevelt brushed aside these objections and on February 9, 1940, announced that Welles would go to Europe solely for the purpose of advising him and Secretary Hull on current conditions. Welles's letter of introduction to the heads of state stated that the President hoped the exchange of views would help achieve a peace that "is neither inconclusive nor precarious." At the same time, Roosevelt insisted to Assistant Secretary of State Breckinridge Long that his real purpose was to "get the low-down on Hitler and get Mussolini's point of view" and perhaps split the Axis alliance or delay a suspected German spring offensive. Roosevelt also said that he was not at cross purposes with the British, but that Welles had to travel to London and Paris for "window dressing," to give the appearance of neutrality.

Roosevelt was more disposed to a negotiated settlement than he would admit, and this was even truer of Welles, who probably inspired the mission. Welles was the author of the 1937 and 1938 "peace" schemes and was antagonistic toward the British and bitterly anti-Soviet (Moscow was not on his itinerary). He had always favored appeasing Germany (without being pro-Nazi) and wooing Mussolini and recognizing his conquest of Ethiopia. Welles may also have been prepared to press some ideas the implications of which Roosevelt did not grasp.

Welles reached Rome on March 1. On his arrival, he emphasized that the United States and Italy were two great neutrals whose cooperation might help construct a lasting peace. He presented a letter from Roosevelt in which the President said that he hoped to meet with Mussolini one day, and that recognition of Italy's conquest of Ethiopia, owing to the Manchukuo problem, would come only as part of a general world settlement. Foreign Minister Galeazzo Ciano, who was bitter about both German and Russian rapaciousness, said that in the autumn of 1939 Hitler probably would have made peace on the basis of Germany's retaining Austria, the Sudetenland (Bohemia-Moravia and Slovakia would be independent German protectorates), and Danzig and the Polish Corridor (with Russia retaining eastern Poland); but whether this would suffice now was unknown. Mussolini insisted that Hitler would negotiate on this basis, and the men agreed that Welles would return to Italy at the end of his trip.

Welles traveled to Berlin, where, on February 29, Hitler had issued a directive to all officials forbidding the discussion of concrete political matters of interest in a peace settlement. He insisted that Germany must impress everyone with its determination to break the British and French desire to "annihilate" the Reich. Welles met first with Foreign Minister Ribbentrop, whom he found "aggressive" and having a "completely closed" and "very stupid mind." Welles hewed to the American position that, if the basis for political negotiations could be established, the United States would participate in parallel talks on arms reduction and international trade and economics. Ribbentrop bristled that the British had rejected Hitler's peace offers, and that Germany was economically and militarily invincible. Despite this truculence, Welles, following the lead of his talks in Italy, inquired whether German war aims (meaning clearly defined and militarily respected spheres of interest for the Great Powers and room for small countries that had shown "historical proof" of an independent national life) might be achieved before Germany resorted to all-out war. Ribbentrop replied that a "rational consolidation of Europe could be achieved only through a German victory."

In his talk with Hitler, Goering, and other officials, Welles tried a carrot-and-stick approach. He insisted that a massive war would have strong effects on the social, economic, financial, and commercial life of every nation, including especially the United States, which could not remain passive in that event. Welles emphasized that Mussolini believed a negotiated settlement possible. He said it was unfortunate that Hitler's efforts at arms reduction "had not been generously examined and put into effect," and he listened sympathetically to the Chancellor's exposition of the historical memories and political and economic interests that had brought about German unification, interests that the Allies had destroyed in 1919, but which he had restored in the last seven years. Now, Hitler said, his task was to organize and make viable the "Central European *Lebensraum* of the German people." To this Welles replied that the greatest guarantee of peace was a "unified, contented, and prosperous Germany." When Goering defined German needs as including not only means to supply its economy, colonies, and international respectability and acceptance but absolute security for the German nation "united in a Greater Reich" (meaning retention of the territory it had gained during 1938–39), Welles said that these points had to be taken into account in any settlement.

In Paris, Welles offended the French by praising Mussolini and contending that Italy would play a "singularly strategic" role in any settlement. Welles was also more emphatic that Austria would have to remain part of the German Reich than was Premier Édouard Daladier, who believed that Germany's ultimate ambition was to dominate all Europe. Nonetheless, Daladier said he would negotiate with Germany if France got guarantees of physical security, to which Welles responded that the United States could not assume any responsibility in that regard.

Welles's conversations in London during March 11–13 were only slightly productive. Indeed, it was not until the eve of Welles's arrival that Kennedy was able to convince Chamberlain that the trip was not solely for "putting over a peace plan." Privately the British disliked Welles as an "international danger" and a "stooge" sent to "shake hands with the authors of Polish atrocities." They remained convinced that Roosevelt hoped to impose a peace plan, even against British wishes, in order to bolster his election campaign. In his initial talks with Chamberlain and Foreign Minister Halifax, Welles agreed that the German regime was untrustworthy but insisted that the Germans believed that the British sought to annihilate them. He suggested peace might be achieved if the Germans were persuaded to withdraw from Poland and Bohemia, after which the belligerents would adhere to a plan of progressive disarmament and economic reconstruction that would provide Europe with confidence and security and lead to permanent peace.

Chamberlain denied British intent to annihilate the Germans but spoke with "white-hot anger" about their determination not to deal with the Hitler regime. He insisted that freedom and independence for Poland and "Czechia" were conditions for any negotiations. In succeeding talks at social functions, British officials argued that peace was possible only after "Hitlerism has been overthrown," as Anthony Eden said, while Welles reiterated that no nation could be taught a lesson or have peace imposed on it.

Welles's final talk with Chamberlain and Halifax was on March 13, the day after the end of the Russo-Finnish war, which the Prime Minister happily concluded would lessen Russia's need to be responsive to German demands. Chamberlain said he would offer a public pledge to the United States that England and France would not attack Germany, but he still refused to deal with Hitler. Welles asked if Chamberlain would negotiate with Hitler, provided that satisfactory terms for restoring and maintaining Poland, Bohemia, and Moravia could first be worked out, along with disarmament-security proposals. Chamberlain and Halifax assented, provided the settlement were understood to signify the failure of Hitler's aggressive policies. Welles then posited that there was "one chance in ten thousand" that agreement could be reached and that Mussolini was of like mind.

Welles now returned to Italy. In the interim, his travels had inspired Hitler to dispatch Ribbentrop to Rome on March 10 with a letter for Mussolini. In January, Mussolini had written to Hitler that the Italians favored peace, the independence of Finland, and the reconstitution of Poland, and that they were angry over Germany's dealings with the Bolsheviks when its *Lebensraum* was in Russia and its mission was "to defend Europe against Asia." Hitler's letter now declared that the fates of both Germany and Italy were linked by the war, and that when the ultimate clash came "your place will then more than ever be at our side, just as mine will be at yours." To this Mussolini replied that "at the given moment" Italy would enter the war. Now, on March 16, Welles tried to persuade the Italians that the British and French were not intransigent about peace terms, to which Ciano replied that the Germans thought only of imposing their *Diktat* and would soon launch their invasion. Welles told Mussolini that peace might be achieved along the lines they had spoken of earlier, to which Mussolini replied that he was meeting Hitler at the Brenner Pass on March 18, and that he could not hope to get Hitler to postpone his offensive without offering him something. Welles said he would call Roosevelt. In his phone conversation, the Under Secretary told the President that he considered it unwise for the United States to associate itself with proposals for territorial readjustments and setting political bases for peace. Roosevelt agreed.

Welles waited in Rome while Mussolini met Hitler on March 18 and was overwhelmed by his talk of war preparations. Mussolini pledged Italian intervention "at the decisive hour." The next day, Ciano told Welles only that the Germans had made no peace proposals, that he would do his best to keep Italy neutral, and that he would be in touch if Hitler became receptive to negotiations.

Welles now judged that Mussolini's "obsession" was to re-create the Roman Empire, and that Italy would go to war if Germany occupied

Belgium and Holland. The Germans, he felt, were living in another world of lies and deception, where evil was good and aggression was self-defense, but were united behind Hitler because "they sincerely fear their own safety is at stake." Europe would never achieve peace until it recognized that its primary problems were not political and territorial readjustment but "the problem of security, inseparably linked to the problem of disarmament." No one in Europe, which lacked statesmanship of "vision, courage and daring," could launch a peace initiative, Welles concluded, but if the United States "felt it possible to move, I am confident that both the Vatican and Mussolini would support such an initiative."

Welles's mission to Europe proved to be counterproductive: The British and French were aggrieved by his insistence that Europe's problems were security and disarmament rather than territorial and political readjustment, and they were upset by the United States's effort to move Europe toward accepting the solution it proposed without involving itself in the process. Hitler was inspired to consolidate his "alliance" with Mussolini. Whatever Welles's hope, therefore, his report to Roosevelt left the President little choice but to declare, on March 29, that there was "scant immediate prospect" for establishing a just and lasting peace in Europe.

Peace negotiations became academic after April 9, 1940, when German forces occupied Norway and Denmark. On May 10, Hitler unleashed his assault on the West through Holland and Belgium, stunning everyone by sending five armored (tank) divisions through the supposedly impenetrable Ardennes Forest in southeastern Belgium. The Dutch surrendered on May 15, and Hitler surprised everyone again by sending tanks and dive bombers not toward Paris but north toward Abbéville and the English Channel, trapping British and French forces in a vise. On May 24, Hitler halted his tank assault for two days just south of Dunkirk, partly because he wanted to preserve his armor for attacking Paris and partly because Goering insisted that his Luftwaffe be allowed to finish off the British. This momentous hesitation allowed the British miraculously to evacuate 350,000 troops across the English Channel between May 28, when Belgium stopped fighting, and June 4. This escape probably preserved England, if not France.

Mussolini now sensed his share of the victors' spoils and declared war on France on June 10. The French agreed to an armistice on June 20, signed in the Forest of Compiègne, northeast of Paris, where Marshal Foch had dictated Germany's surrender in 1918. Hitler was less concerned with destroying the French than with persuading the British to make peace, and to show his reasonableness, he rebuffed Italy's claims to Nice, Corsica, French Somaliland, and Tunisia, and merely partitioned France. The Germans occupied the northern three-fifths of the country and a nominally independent government at Vichy, headed by Marshal Henri Pétain and Pierre Laval, was left in control of the southern sector and French North Africa.

Master of Western Europe, Hitler for the first time faced the question of how to defeat Great Britain. He concluded that air assaults had to precede an invasion. As part of this operation, named "Sea-Lion," from mid-August through September German planes attacked first Royal Air Force bases, and then London and other cities, in an effort to break British morale. At the end of the "Battle of Britain," however, the RAF still controlled the skies. Hitler now sought to press the British through other means. According to his Chief of Staff, General Franz Halder, he said on July 31, 1940, that "Britain's hope lies in Russia and the U.S.A. If Russia drops out of the picture, America too is lost, because the elimination of Russia would greatly increase Japan's power in the Far East." The logic of this position implied the "destruction" of Russia and the diplomatic immobilization of the United States by making Japan the German "dagger" against it.

Hitler, furious that the Soviet Union had used the occasion of the war in the West to annex Latvia, Lithuania, and Estonia in the summer of 1940, now entrenched Germany in the Balkans by forcing Rumania to cede southern Dobruja to Hungary. This brought about a new and subservient government in Rumania, which joined the Axis Alliance on September 23 and then summoned German troops to preserve its defense. Next, Hitler achieved the diplomatic alliance that he hoped would immobilize the United States.

Hitler's position toward the United States often reflected his crazy patchwork of superficial, spurious, and contradictory racial and sociopolitical ideas. In the bitter aftermath of 1919, Hitler said that 2 million Jews controlled New York's banks, press, and industry and had impelled America to war against Germany solely for financial gain. In *Mein Kampf,* written during 1923–24 while he was imprisoned after the Munich putsch, he attributed the "unheard-of internal strength" of the American "Colossus" to its "enormous wealth of virgin soil," which, he indicated, demonstrated Germany's need for new European territory. In 1928, in a book that remained undiscovered until after the Second World War and unpublished until 1961, Hitler argued that America's entry into the First World War had made it a decisive power in international politics. He also argued that American financial, productive, and technical capacities—he noted specifically the automobile's invasion of Europe—had made it a first-rank imperial nation capable of challenging England, if not all Europe, for markets and materials. He considered the Americans a "young, racially select people," composed of Europe's best emigrants. The United States could be contested economically, and prevented from achieving world domination, only by an Anglo-German entente.

Contrarily, in 1925 Hitler declined a friend's suggestion that he visit the United States, insisting that it could play no role in European or Asian conflicts: "You would only have to blow up the Panama Canal and they would not be able to exert pressure either way." He made no effort in 1933 to learn anything about American conditions from Ambassador von Prittwitz, who had resigned and returned from Washington. Later, Hitler remarked that the United States consisted only of "millionaires, beauty queens, stupid records, and Hollywood," that America's chance for greatness had vanished when the South lost the Civil War. The country was now "in the last death rattle of a corrupt and outworn system" and could be saved only by its "immigrants of German stock." Throughout the rest of the decade, Hitler held to his view that America was racially inferior and politically and economically effete, brushing aside more realistic assessments from career diplomats, whom he scorned as a class.

Hitler never abandoned this view. In January 1942, he denigrated the United States as a "half-Judaized and the other half Negrified" country of no consequence. Only when the Third Reich faced its *Götterdämmerung* in 1945 did he lament that this "madman" Roosevelt had tricked "this Jew-ridden, half-American drunkard" Churchill into opposing Germany, which was only seeking to ward off the "Bolshevist peril." By placing its material resources at the disposal of the Russians —"these Asiatic barbarians"—the United States demonstrated both its lack of international wisdom and its decadence, which not even German émigrés could correct. "Transplant a German to Kiev," Hitler raged in January 1945, "and he remains a perfect German. But transplant him to Miami and you make a degenerate of him—in other words, an American."

Whatever the inconsistency in Hitler's views of America, he had interested himself in 1938 and 1939 in Ribbentrop's efforts to achieve a German-Japanese alliance directed at the United States. He told Mussolini first in March 1940 that Japan was a "necessary counterweight" to the United States, and then in mid-September he said that such an agreement was "the best way to keep America entirely out or render her entry into the war ineffective."

Thus, Hitler and Ribbentrop were delighted when, after much diplomatic pressure, they were able to secure Japan's signature on the Tripartite Pact of September 27, 1940. This pact pledged Germany, Japan, and Italy to a New Order in Asia and Europe, and it promised cooperation and assistance "with all political, economic, and military means" if any signatory were attacked by a power not then involved in the European or Sino-Japanese wars. That the pact was directed against the United States is clear from the fact that the Soviet Union was excluded from its terms, or, as Ribbentrop explained to the German Ambassador in Moscow, "The alliance is exclusively directed against the American warmongers. Its exclusive purpose is to bring the element pressing for America's entry into the war to their senses."

The Tripartite Pact was less than the automatic, straightforward military instrument Hitler and Ribbentrop had sought, for the Japanese, in their exchange of diplomatic notes with the Germans and in their Cabinet deliberations, were steadfast about determining independently when their political, military, and economic commitments became operational. From the German perspective, the purpose of the pact was not to provoke the United States into war but to intimidate it into not aiding the British, while the Japanese hoped, of course, that the United States would refrain from aiding China.

Hitler next met with Spain's Francisco Franco at Hendaye on October 23, 1940, and, in exchange for Gibraltar, tried to lure him into war against England. But Franco, who was interested earlier in acquiring part of French North Africa, would not commit himself to anything less than sure victory. He remained evasive, insisting that the British would continue the war from North America, and he demanded enormous quantities of military and economic support from Germany. Hitler left Hendaye frustrated and furious and proceeded to Montoire, where he exchanged guarantees about France's imperial status after the war for an agreement from Marshal Pétain that France would collaborate in defeating Great Britain. But as Pétain said, "It will take six months to discuss this program and another six months to forget it."

In talks with Molotov in Berlin on November 12–13, the Germans tried to persuade the Soviet Union to join the Tripartite Pact with the lure of participating in the distribution of the "bankrupt British Empire," as Hitler put it, while Ribbentrop insisted that American involvement in the war would be of "no importance at all," and that "Germany and Italy would never again allow an Anglo-Saxon to land on the European Continent." The Russians were angry over German troop movements in Finland and Rumania, and they suspected that the Germans encouraged them to move south toward the Indian Ocean in an effort to bring them into conflict with Great Britain. At the end of the month, the Russians put forward demands, including a mutual-assistance pact with Bulgaria and bases in Turkey on the Bosporus and Dardanelles, to which Hitler did not respond.

Meanwhile, the Italians had invaded Egypt through Libya on September 13, but their attack slowed after sixty miles at Sidi Barani, while the British mobilized their forces from elsewhere in Africa. Hitler, who had been persuaded of the need to shut the Suez Canal in order to choke England, refrained from aiding the Italians, whose prestige required a victory gained alone. Mussolini became infuriated by Hitler's march on Rumania, and contrary to his pledge, sent Italian troops into Greece on October 28. Once again, the resistance proved stronger than the Italians had anticipated. The British, meanwhile, turned the Mediterranean naval balance in their favor by occupying Crete and destroying half the Italian fleet at Taranto. They then launched a counteroffensive in Egypt. As 1940 ended, Hitler increasingly turned his attention toward aiding his blundering ally and, above all, to planning other than diplomatic means for dealing with the Soviet Union.

From April through June 1940, the Roosevelt administration moved cautiously. Roosevelt denounced Germany's invasion of Denmark and Norway, and on April 15 deplored that "old dreams of universal empire are again rampant." He warned that what happened "in the Old World directly and powerfully affects the peace and well-being of the New." The administration froze $267 million in Danish and Norwegian funds in the United States to prevent them from falling into German hands, and it extended the combat zones under the Neutrality Act to the entire Norwegian and Finnish coasts and to Murmansk in the Soviet Union.

The administration's chief concern was to see that no belligerent claimed the Danish possessions of Greenland (which had cryolite mines, a source of aluminum) or Iceland. American officials warned that they would not tolerate British or Canadian occupation of Greenland, and they assumed responsibility for its defense under the Monroe Doctrine. The British were permitted to take responsibility for Iceland, which is geographically and economically European, but only after pledging that occupation was temporary. The Americans quickly established a consulate there as evidence of future interest.

As the Germans assaulted Belgium and Holland, Churchill replaced Chamberlain as Prime Minister on May 10, dramatically declaring that he could offer only "blood, toil, tears, and sweat" and pledging England to "victory—victory at all costs." On May 15, the Prime Minister asked Roosevelt for all aid short of armed forces, including forty or fifty destroyers. He said that, although the British would pay dollars as long as they could, "I should like to feel reasonably sure that when we can pay no more, you will give us the stuff all the same." On May 28, the start of the evacuation from Dunkirk, Churchill pledged the British to fight on the beaches, landing grounds, fields, and streets, or from abroad if the British Isles were overrun, "until, in God's good time, the New World, with its power and might, steps forth to the rescue and liberation of the Old."

By now Roosevelt believed that Great Britain's survival marked the first line of American defense against Germany's global aims, and he was pleased by Churchill's accession to power. The personal chemistry between the President and the Former Naval Person was exceptional, if marked by egoistic rivalry, and Roosevelt admired Churchill's wartime leadership and eloquence. The President also considered Churchill "a real old Tory," "mid-Victorian," and always enjoyed twitting him about imperial preferences, India, Hong Kong, and British holdings in Africa and the Middle East. Roosevelt also had to keep a watchful eye on domestic politics in a presidential election year.

On May 16, Roosevelt told Churchill that he could not supply the requested destroyers, and he was evasive about Britain's financial troubles. However, he allowed Morgenthau to press him, the War Department, and Chief of Staff General George C. Marshall (distressed over the frightfully unprepared state of American forces and supplies) into selling the British $37 million in "surplus" planes, guns, and ammunition. In May, Roosevelt requested $1.5 billion for defense and money to produce 50,000 planes annually. As the Germans gained ground, he secured, by year's end, another $8.5 billion for defense. By Congress and Executive Order, the regular army was also raised from 225,000 to 280,000 troops, the legal limit.

In a more conservative vein, Roosevelt tried to keep Italy out of the war by writing (at British and French prompting) to Mussolini on May 26 and offering to communicate Italy's "legitimate aspirations" to England and France, which would welcome Italy as an equal at any future peace conference. Roosevelt said he could not involve himself with bargaining over terms, but his letter was an unmistakable effort to appease Mussolini, with the United States an implicit guarantor of an Anglo-French-Italian settlement. Mussolini was not interested, for, as Ciano then noted, "what he wants is war, and even if he were to obtain by peaceful means double what he claims, he would refuse." Roosevelt still was prepared to renew his offer as late as June 3, but Hull dissuaded him.

Speaking at commencement at the University of Virginia in Charlottesville on June 10, Roosevelt denounced Italy's declaration of war against France: "The hand that held the dagger has struck it into the back of its neighbor." He pledged to provide "the opponents of force the material resources of the nation" while building American defenses to deal with any crisis. The next day, Churchill renewed his request for destroyers to be enlisted "in what we may now indeed call the Common Cause." As Paris was being evacuated, Premier Paul Reynaud, pledging to fight if necessary from North Africa or North America, pleaded for every means of American support "short of an expeditionary force." The administration's reply was to have Hull lecture Ambassador Lord

Lothian that "any friend of Great Britain . . . would expect her to fight to the last dollar, to the last man, and to the last ship," to warn against allowing the British Fleet to fall to the Germans, and to dismiss the need for Anglo-American staff talks. Roosevelt, meanwhile, told Reynaud that the United States was already providing all the aid it could. And when Churchill tried to view this statement of support as a further American commitment, the President instructed that his message to Reynaud was not to be published "under any circumstances," and he had Churchill reminded that only Congress could authorize participation in the war.

The fall of France prompted Roosevelt to act more forcefully, even if by indirection. He had long been dissatisfied with the administrative performances of Navy Secretary Charles Edison and Secretary of War Harry Woodring, the latter a virtual isolationist whose Department, Colonel Joseph Stilwell remarked in 1940, functioned "just like the alimentary canal. You feed it at one end, and nothing comes out at the other but crap." Roosevelt had been considering for at least a year the idea of creating a "coalition" Cabinet to cope with a world crisis. In May 1940, he had Edison enticed to run for governor of New Jersey, and on June 19 he demanded Woodring's resignation. The next day, the President named Republicans Frank Knox, publisher of the *Chicago Daily News,* and Henry Stimson to head the Navy and War departments.

Knox was a former Rough Rider who modeled himself after Theodore Roosevelt. He had helped garner support for revision of the Neutrality Act in 1939 and had been under consideration for the Navy job since then. Stimson's credentials as Secretary of War under Taft and Secretary of State under Hoover were well known, as was his nonrecognition policy toward Japan in Manchuria. Stimson took the same position toward Italy's conquest of Ethiopia. Both men were proponents of increased aid to Great Britain. Both were prepared to see the United States intervene directly against Germany, and both could also rally anti–New Deal Republicans—corporate officials, bankers, and international lawyers—to the administration's side on foreign policy. In his Senate confirmation testimony, Stimson was evasive about his policy-making influence. He insisted that repairing British ships in American ports was an act of self-defense rather than war, said it would be unwise to "sit down and wait for the enemy to attack our shores," and was relieved that Senator Robert A. Taft did not follow up his rhetorical statement that "you are in favor of joining the war just as soon as you figure that the British no longer have a chance." Roosevelt, however, appointed Knox and Stimson not because he wanted them to edge the United States to war, but rather because, in his mind, from an administrative and domestic political point of view, they would help him fulfill his pledge, given at Charlottesville on June 10, to strengthen American defenses to meet any emergency.

This was especially the case with conscription. Increased defense spending made little sense without an expanded army, but the administra-tion feared involving itself too directly in the effort to inaugurate the nation's first peacetime draft. Selective service was fostered by private preparedness groups, while responsibility for introducing legislation on June 21, 1940, fell to Senator Edward R. Burke of Nebraska, an anti-New Deal Democrat, and Republican Representative James Wadsworth of New York. Stimson took on the yeoman tasks, first, of persuading General Marshall to support a conscripted army over a smaller volunteer force, and then of persuading Congress to enact the legislation. Roose-velt avoided public endorsement until August 2, which brought a strong reaction from Senators Norris, Vandenberg, and Wheeler. But on Au-gust 17 Wendell Willkie, Republican nominee for President, strongly supported selective service, and on August 28 the Senate approved it by 69–16. In the House, Republican Representative Hamilton Fish of New York amended the bill to delay registration until after the election. Willkie deplored this, however, and both houses finally passed the Burke-Wadsworth bill on September 14. Roosevelt signed it two days later.

Roosevelt was even more cautious with regard to the stickier subject of destroyers for Great Britain, especially since Congress, on June 28, 1940, had amended the naval-appropriations bill to prohibit sale of military equipment unless it was deemed essential for the national defense. The next day, Roosevelt insisted to William Allen White that legal and political problems barred his selling the destroyers, and he kept to that view despite the urgings of Interior Secretary Ickes that "by hook or by crook we ought to accede to England's request." The job of stirring public support in behalf of providing the British with destroyers fell to White's Committee to Defend America by Aiding the Allies, formed in May 1940, and the committee's own Century Group, com-posed of influential businessmen, lawyers, and journalists. In July, the Century Group determined that the United States might justify trading the destroyers for bases in British possessions in North America as a Hemispheric defense measure. They discussed this possibility with the British Ambassador, Lord Lothian, who had already proposed it to his government. The British Cabinet expressed its approval on July 29, and Churchill cabled Roosevelt that "in the long history of the world this is a thing to do *now*." On August 1, the Century Group formally pre-sented Roosevelt with the destroyers-for-bases proposal, and on August 2, Ickes, using the metaphor Roosevelt would adopt later, pleaded "that we Americans are like the householder who refuses to lend or sell his fire extinguisher to help put out the fire in the house that is next door, although that house is all ablaze and the wind is blowing from that direction."

In a Cabinet meeting that day, Secretary Knox took the lead in recounting how desperate the British were for the destroyers, and everyone agreed that the exchange had to be made, although Roosevelt noted that if he proposed legislation it would meet "defeat or interminable delay." Nonetheless, he asked that White secure Willkie's approval. Willkie, though lukewarm, pledged not to attack the deal. White's Committee to Defend America rallied public support, including a significantly ringing endorsement on August 4 from General John J. Pershing, the aging and ill former commander of the American Expeditionary Force in the First World War, who insisted that "today may be the last time when, by measures short of war, we can still prevent war." One week later, several prominent lawyers from the Century Group, including Dean Acheson (who had quit the Treasury Department in 1933 over New Deal gold policy), published a long letter in the *New York Times* insisting that the sale of the destroyers could be legally justified under the June 28, 1940, legislation. Speed, they said, required the President to act without congressional authority.

Roosevelt himself seems to have become impressed with both the gravity of the British military situation and British resistance in the Battle of Britain. He did not express himself decisively on the destroyer deal until he met with Morgenthau, Stimson, Knox, and Welles on August 14, when the consensus was that "he should do it first and tell Congress afterwards"—meaning by executive agreement. Two days later, Attorney General Robert H. Jackson ruled that the deal would be legal if the Chief of Naval Operations certified that exchange of the destroyers for military bases would "strengthen rather than impair the total defense of the United States." By August 20, the State Department had prepared a draft agreement. Still, at his press conference on August 16, Roosevelt, admitting that the United States was negotiating for bases, denied their connection to the transference of destroyers to Great Britain.

Such a deal, however, was in the works. On August 8, Roosevelt wrote to Churchill that the United States would contract to provide fifty destroyers, various torpedo and PBY-4 "flying" boats, and rifles and ammunition in exchange for ninety-nine-year leases on military bases in Newfoundland, Bermuda, the Bahamas, Jamaica, St. Lucia, Trinidad, and British Guiana and for a pledge that the British Fleet would never be turned over to the Germans. Churchill was amenable to providing Roosevelt with the bargain he would need for domestic political purposes. In Parliament on August 20, he said that his government was considering leasing North American bases, and he affirmed that thereafter the United States and Great Britain "will have to be somewhat mixed up together in some of their affairs for mutual and general advantage," a process he welcomed. Two days later, fearing that his public would not approve a contractual agreement weighted so heavily on the American side, he proposed that the destroyers and bases be exchanged independently and gratuitously—"two friends in danger helping each other as far as we can." Typically, Hull felt that the British were "crawfishing," while Roosevelt feared "giving" the destroyers outright. A compromise was reached, however, when Green Hackworth, State Department legal adviser, proposed that the British make a gift of the leases for bases in Newfoundland and Bermuda, and that the Caribbean bases be exchanged for the destroyers. On September 2, 1940, the deal was completed. Quite unbelievably, in the hasty redrafting of the agreement, nothing was said of the planes, boats, guns, and munitions that the Americans had also promised, and while Roosevelt and Stimson preferred to admit the oversight to the public and to make good on it, Hull insisted that that would lead to further charges of secret dealings. The British therefore had to content themselves with the destroyers and some rifles later certified for release.

At a press conference on September 2, Roosevelt said that his action was a *fait accompli,* and he likened it in style and substance to Jefferson's purchase of the Louisiana Territory in 1803, when Britain and France were almost at war. Roosevelt's precedent-invocation notwithstanding, his administration probably overstepped executive authority in ignoring Congress and violated the spirit, if not the letter, of the June 28, 1940, prohibition on the sale of defense supplies. The destroyer deal was clearly an unneutral act (as Churchill confessed, with delight) and a violation of the Hague Convention of 1907 prohibition on the sale of supplies to any belligerent power. The administration brushed off this charge, however, on the ground that the Convention was inapplicable, in that neither England nor Italy had signed it.

More important from the administration's point of view was the fact that the anticipated storm of public criticism never materialized, although a predictable number of politicians and newspapers denounced the deal, international-law scholars challenged its legality, and the fiercely anti-interventionist America First Committee was formed two days after the deal was completed. For the most part, as Willkie's running mate, Senator Charles McNary, had tipped the White House in August, congressmen in an election year were grateful that Roosevelt's executive action had spared them a roll-call vote on a controversial issue, and Willkie was content to rebuke the secrecy shrouding the deal.

Caution was Roosevelt's watchword during the 1940 election campaign. He had no intention or desire to go further than the destroyer deal and willingly accepted the plank in the Democratic platform pledging that American forces would not participate in "foreign wars" in "foreign lands" except in case of attack. Roosevelt tried to avoid discussing foreign policy and between July 19 and the end of October spoke only twice on that issue. He reiterated on September 11 the Democratic pledge to avoid war, and he emphasized Hemispheric defense on October 12, while warning that "no combination of dictator countries in Europe and Asia will stop the help we are giving to almost the last free people now fighting to hold them at bay."

Fortunately for Roosevelt, his opponent, Willkie, a corporation lawyer and utilities official, and a registered Democrat until 1938, was a strong proponent of providing aid to "the opponents of force," as he said in his acceptance speech of August 17. Willkie insisted that his election would mean that the United States would "outdistance Hitler in any contest he chooses in 1940 or after." He favored conscription and the destroyer deal, and in campaigning in September 1940, he scored Roosevelt for having "telephoned to Hitler and Mussolini and urged them to sell Czechoslovakia down the river" and for having "appeased the democratic world into destruction."

With his campaign faltering, Willkie shifted his emphasis to the Democrats as the war party. On October 22, he said that if Roosevelt were elected American boys were sure to be sent to war, that if Roosevelt's pledge "to keep our boys out of foreign wars is no better than his promise to balance the budget . . . they're almost on transports." On October 30, he claimed, on the basis of Roosevelt's broken promises, that his re-election would mean war in six months. Willkie was aided by CIO President John L. Lewis, who was bitterly at odds with Roosevelt's foreign policy, and who pledged to resign if Roosevelt were re-elected.

Roosevelt affirmed on October 23 that there was no secret treaty or obligation that would directly or indirectly involve the United States in any war. However, he had grown increasingly upset over demands made upon him for absolute assurances and over Willkie's charges and gains in the polls. In Boston on October 30, he offered "one more assurance. I have said this before, but I will say it again and again: Your boys are not going to be sent into any foreign wars." Two days later, he insisted that "this country is not going to war."

These assurances were too categorical, though less so than later critics charged, for he always assumed that everyone understood American forces would not go to war "except in case of attack," and it was this phrase, part of the Democratic platform, that he had not repeated in his Boston speech. More to the point, Willkie's late campaign charges were excessive, and Roosevelt, as he sought re-election, was unsettled by them and overresponsive. In the end, Willkie, Roosevelt, and probably the vast majority of the American public believed, and hoped, that it would be sufficient to provide the British with enough military supplies to withstand the Germans until Hitler was persuaded to abandon his ambitions and was removed from power. They all hoped that other alternatives would not have to be faced.

Roosevelt was delighted with his re-election; so were the British (who regarded Willkie as an acceptable alternative). Churchill promptly wrote that he had prayed for and was thankful for the President's success. More to the point, as Lothian told reporters in a "calculated indiscretion" on November 25, Great Britain "was beginning to come to the end of her financial resources." Then, on December 8, Churchill put the case to Roosevelt at length and with characteristic directness. The British were forming fifty to sixty divisions to defend the home islands, Africa, and South Asia and were otherwise doing well enough. But they had lost 400,000 tons of shipping at sea in October alone; German submarines and bombers were increasing their attacking range, and the possible defection of the Vichy French Fleet to the Germans would menace British communications between the North and South Atlantic. The British wanted the United States to reassert its policy of freedom of the seas and to protect its ships lawfully trading with England. Failing this, Britain wanted "the gift, loan, or supply" of "a large number of American vessels of war, above all destroyers," plus 2,000 planes (especially bombers), every month, as well as machine tools, guns, and ammunition for fifty divisions in 1941 and another ten divisions in 1942. Insofar as financing was concerned, "the moment approaches when we shall no longer be able to pay cash for shipping and other supplies." The British people, however, were prepared "to suffer and sacrifice to the utmost for the Cause," and "the rest we leave with confidence to you and your people, being sure that ways and means will be found which future generations on both sides of the Atlantic will approve and admire."

Roosevelt's aides were aware of Britain's financial dilemma but wanted the British to liquidate their New World assets, variously estimated at $9–$18 billion, before claiming their inability to pay. The Americans had concluded, by December 1940, that the time had come to get congressional approval for providing the British with military aid. The extent to which Churchill's letter of December 8, delivered to Roosevelt while he was on a postelection cruise, affected the President's thinking cannot be determined, but, when he returned to Washington on December 16, he asked for details of the British supply needs and finances and the next day laid out his thoughts to reporters. He dismissed as "banal" the idea of repealing the Johnson Debt Default Act of 1934, or the Neutrality Act, to allow loans, and he insisted that it would be best for selfish and national-security reasons to build production facilities and then either lend, lease, or sell the materials, subject to mortgage. Above all, it was necessary to "get rid of the silly, foolish old dollar sign," to substitute "a gentlemen's obligation to repay in kind." The President then reiterated Ickes's July analogy about a neighbor and a fire hose.

Roosevelt elaborated on his intentions in a fireside chat on December 29, insisting that he was speaking about national security, which affected "you now, your children later, and your grandchildren much later." American civilization faced the greatest challenge in its history. The "Nazi masters of Germany" intended "to enslave the whole of Europe" and then "the rest of the world," and there could be no peace with them except "at the price of total surrender." If Great Britain fell, the Nazis would be tempted to assault the Western Hemisphere. The United States had to "take risks now for peace in the future" and afford the British arms and munitions in the fight "for their liberty and our security." America "must be the great arsenal of democracy."

Secretary Stimson would have preferred even more, insisting that the solution to the British problem was not to build ships for them but for American ships "forcibly to stop the German submarines." Roosevelt replied he was not ready for that. Instead, he "went as far as he could at the present time" and gave his ringing address, which produced a highly positive public response, as a satisfied Stimson noted.

The focus of the Roosevelt administration in 1940 was on Europe, but events there cast a shadow on Great Power diplomacy in Asia and influenced it significantly. The American effort in the fall of 1939 to reach accommodation with Japan prior to the expiration in January 1940 of their Commercial Treaty had failed, and this contributed to the collapse of the moderate Abe government. The new regime under Prime Minister (and Admiral) Mitsumasa Yonai and Foreign Minister Hachiro Arita, a career diplomat, seemed reasonable. In January 1940, Ambassador Grew, while not disputing that certain problems could not be resolved through orderly processes, wrote reassuringly that the Japanese showed no inclination to ally themselves with Germany or the Soviet Union, and that shrewd Western diplomacy could circumscribe the influence of Japan's Army or extremist elements.

Grew's assessment was accurate enough, although Arita's public reference on February 29 to his country's "Holy War with China," and Japan's establishment on March 30 of Wang Ching-wei's regime in Nanking as a rival government to Chiang Kai-shek's Kuomintang in Chungking, was evidence of Japan's increasingly hard position on the "China Incident." On February 2, the Japanese insisted, not unreasonably, that the Dutch Government remove its restrictions on the flow of exports from the East Indies to Japan, and that Japanese businessmen have freer access to trade there. Following Germany's invasion of Denmark and Norway on April 9, and Britain's occupation of Danish Iceland, the Japanese felt compelled to reiterate their economic interest in the Dutch East Indies, and on April 15 Arita warned against a change in their *status quo* (that is, British or French occupation) as a consequence of the European conflict.

The American response was a mixture of admonitions and ambiguous half-steps. Hull denounced Japan's support of Wang as an effort to impose its will on China by force. But Washington officials felt that little could be done to bolster Chiang's government, although in March they acceded to a $20-million loan through the Export-Import Bank in exchange for Chinese tin. Further loans were ruled out, and the Soviet Union remained China's primary source of funds. Moreover, the War Department felt that it could spare little, and by the end of 1940 it had released only $9 million in military aid to the Kuomintang. As for the Japanese concern over the Dutch East Indies, on April 11 Hull warned that interference there would upset the balance of peace and stability in the Pacific.

Hull's unusually sharp statement reflected American anger at Japan's support of Wang but, even more, an excessive fear that a wider European war would provide the Japanese, by aggressive design or in self-defense, with the occasion to invade the Dutch East Indies. Hence, when Germany attacked Holland on May 10, and when, the next day, the British and French occupied the Dutch Caribbean Islands of Aruba and Curaçao, American officials moved to secure British and French pledges not to occupy the East Indies. The Dutch declared that they did not need foreign assistance and then on June 6 acceded to Japan's request for increased trade.

Amidst these developments, Roosevelt had to decide what to do with the U.S. Fleet, which had gone to Hawaii in April for maneuvers and remained there during the German offensive against the Low Countries. Fleet Commander Admiral James O. Richardson felt that training could best be facilitated at the home port of San Diego, but Roosevelt's Liaison Committee of Welles, General Marshall, and Chief of Naval Operations Admiral Harold Stark was uncertain, and on May 27 Stark told Richardson that they believed Germany and Italy had given Japan a "free hand" in the Pacific, and "you are there because of the deterrent effect which it is thought your presence may have on the Japs going into the East Indies." Further discussion about the fleet was inconclusive. "When I don't know how to move, I stay put," Roosevelt told Stark, and on June 24 he postponed any decision to remove the fleet from Pearl Harbor.

The governing attitude in Washington at this juncture accorded largely with the advice given in late May by Stanley Hornbeck, now Hull's adviser on Far Eastern Affairs: "The situation in Europe being what it is, the situation in the Far East being what it is, and the limitations upon possible courses of this country being . . . what they are, the most advisable course for this country to pursue for the present with regard to the Far East and the Pacific is to 'sit tight': make no new diplomatic move of major import, make no change in the disposal of the United States Battle Fleet, maintain the positions which we have taken, neither suggest nor assent to compromises, keep our hands free and our eyes and ears open."

Hull authorized Grew to open talks with Foreign Minister Arita, with the aim of achieving an American-Japanese understanding and minimizing the adverse effects of the European war. Grew was instructed to remind the Japanese that American military capacity would vastly improve shortly, that the United States was ready "to ward off any aggression which may be undertaken against it," and that the talks did not signify that the United States had "modified or will modify its position of opposition to policies and courses, whether of Japan or any other nation, which involved the use of force." In his initial talk on June 10, Grew insisted that American-Japanese relations could not move into "fundamentally happier channels" until Japan stopped using force and interfering with American rights in China, and he suggested that Japan align with the United States and espouse a liberal trade program. Arita implied that the American Fleet in Hawaii threatened Japan, which Grew disputed. Arita also hinted at the use of America's good offices to settle the Sino-Japanese conflict, which idea Grew rejected, and suggested a commercial *modus vivendi,* which Grew insisted was already operative. Despite this diplomatic impasse, Grew believed that the Japanese were ready to take a fresh look at the "long haul," but his conversations with Arita over the next four weeks failed to break the deadlock between the American insistence on a commitment to principles prior to concessions and the Japanese insistence on concessions before any general agreement. By July 2, even the determined Grew was convinced that "the vicious circle is complete, and how to break it is a puzzle which taxes imagination." Nine days later, the talks were suspended, Grew reported, because of this dilemma, and because Germany's rapid conquest of France and threat to England was leading the Japanese into the temptation of a *rapprochement* with the Axis powers and hegemony in the Pacific.

Indeed, the Japanese were using the European conflict to achieve their ends in the Pacific. Seeking to shut off supplies to the Nationalists in China, they put troops on the Indochina frontier, maneuvered ships in the Gulf of Tonkin, and demanded that the French close supply routes through Indochina and the British shut the Burma Road and Hong Kong frontiers and remove their troops from Indochina. The French, being routed by the Germans, could not refuse, although their military commander in Indochina wanted to resist. When the French inquired, on June 19, about the American view and prospect of aid, Hornbeck and Welles were emphatic that the United States could take no part and implied that the French had better yield.

At this time, the British made inquiries and suggestions the intent of which remains murky, although they were most likely intended to force officials to choose between outright resistance and appeasement. On June 19–20, British Embassy officials told Hornbeck that it would be helpful if the American Government stated publicly that "any attempt to change the status quo in the Far East or Pacific will not be tolerated." Hornbeck said only that he would talk to his superiors, but the next day, when the French capitulation to Germany left the British fighting alone in Europe, their Chiefs of Staff felt that they could not defend their Asian empire north of Malaya. On June 26, the Australian Ambassador, Richard Casey, speaking as well for the British, told Hornbeck that they had to reach an agreement with the Japanese that would give them "not merely a shoestring but something substantial, something according the Japanese what they want in China," and he advised the United States to do likewise.

In an aide-mémoire, the British said that alone they could not oppose aggression in both Europe and the Far East. The United States would either have to force Japan to respect the *status quo* by imposing a full embargo or sending troops to Singapore (steps that might provoke war), or would have to "wean Japan from aggression by a concrete offer," which meant assisting jointly in settling the China war and affording the Japanese "all financial and economic assistance" immediately and in the postwar period, in return for Japanese neutrality in the European war and maintaining the Far Eastern *status quo*.

American officials refused a decisive commitment. Hornbeck said that he saw "no virtues in appeasement" in Europe in 1938 and in Asia in 1940, and that it would weaken Chinese resistance and encourage the Japanese to attack South Asia and aid Germany. He insisted there was "at present going on in the world one war, in two theaters," and he strongly implied that resistance in both realms was all that prevented them from being joined. Concerning American action, Hull replied, on June 28, that moving the fleet to Singapore would only leave the Atlantic vulnerable to European threats, and that the United States had been exerting economic pressure on Japan for over a year and was "doing everything possible short of a serious risk of actual military hostilities" to stabilize the Japanese. France's surrender, however, had encouraged Japan's militarists to move "in the direction of Hitler and Hitlerism with all that that means in making aggravated application of their doctrine of the new order in eastern Asia." While the United States did not object to searching for accommodation with Japan, the principles underlying the Japanese new order in Eastern Asia required "negativing or at least serious modifying," and no settlement was acceptable that made peace at the expense of either China or the principles that the United States had been enunciating with regard to the Sino-Japanese conflict since the summer of 1937.

Lothian made a final effort to encourage the United States into a settlement with Japan by stating, on July 1, that Great Britain was ready "to throw some material contributions into the pot herself," that the Australians and Dutch were ready to offer economic concessions in return for a Japanese pledge not to seize the East Indies or British colonies, and that this would allow asking Chiang Kai-shek with "better grace" to make concessions to Japan. Welles remained skeptical and noncommittal, although he said that he did not object to a settlement that did not impair China's integrity or American national security. Two weeks later, the British Government announced that it was closing the Burma Road and Hong Kong frontiers for three months, while a search was made for a "just and equitable" peace acceptable to both China and Japan. Without American support, the British felt they could do neither more nor less than this—the oncoming rainy season eliminated travel over the Burma Road anyway—but Hull sanctimoniously deplored this blow to China and closing of an artery of "international commerce."

While the State Department hewed to its policy of objecting in principle to meeting Japanese demands but running no risks, Cabinet officers were more disposed to action. At a dinner on July 18 at the British Embassy, Secretary Stimson reproached his hosts for closing the Burma Road. Lothian replied that there was no choice so long as the United States refused aid and shipped aviation fuel to Japan. Secretary Morgenthau rejoined that no one had asked that aviation fuel be cut off, to which Lothian responded that, if this were done, the British would blow up the oil wells in Dutch East Indies to prevent the Japanese from seizing them.

Morgenthau and Stimson were excited, and the former enlisted Interior Secretary Ickes to support an oil embargo that could be justified on the basis of domestic fuel needs and carried out under the July 2, 1940, National Defense Act allowing the President to restrict export of materials vital to national defense. Roosevelt was "tremendously interested," Morgenthau noted, and Stimson "gave his usual argument, that the only way to treat Japan is not to retreat." Welles objected vehemently, giving a "beautiful Chamberlain talk." Roosevelt hesitated, while Morgenthau encouraged Ickes to advocate an oil embargo and got Edward R. Stettinius, Jr., former chairman of U.S. Steel and now head of the new National Defense Advisory Board, to assert that scrap steel reserves were below the safety level. Roosevelt held back until July 24, when he learned from reports through Stimson that the Japanese were virtually cornering the market on American oil exports for 1940. On July 25, the President embargoed iron, scrap steel, and oil products. Again, Welles objected, and at Roosevelt's insistence a compromise was achieved the next day that limited the embargo to aviation fuel and the highest grades of iron and scrap steel—a significant if incomplete victory for the Morgenthau-Stimson faction.

The tendency toward a harder line was now encouraged as well by Grew's reports on events in Japan. On July 22, the Yonai government gave way to that of Premier Fumimaro Konoye and Foreign Minister Yosuke Matsuoka. Domestically their regime established a "New Structure," which evolved in October into the Imperial Rule Assistance Association, that dissolved all political parties and labor organizations for the ostensible purpose of eliminating fanaticism and factionalism and allowing the national government to direct a unified political and economic policy. But as Grew wrote to Hull on September 5, differences between Japanese and European traditions notwithstanding, the "impelling force" behind the New Structure "is the same as that which brought into being Fascism and Nazism." Industry, finance, politics, and national defense, he reported, "are becoming inextricably interwoven in the totalitarian pattern."

In foreign policy, the Konoye government's Liaison Conference meeting of July 27, 1940, composed of the Prime Minister, Foreign Minister, War and Navy ministers, and chiefs of the Army and Navy, formally decided that, while Japan would try to avoid a clash with a third power, it would use any means to settle the China Incident (including eradication of third-power aid to China), and, if foreign and domestic circumstances permitted, it would use force to gain its ends in Southeast Asia. Between August 30 and September 22, the Japanese extracted from the Vichy regime in France the right to station troops in northern Indochina, from where they could operate against the Nationalist Chinese in Chungking.

Grew was not privy to the Liaison Conference decision, and he still thought Konoye would be able to control the "wild men." But by August 1, he was convinced that the government was moving "hell-bent toward the Axis and the establishment of the New Order in East Asia," and that it would ride "roughshod" over American and British policies, principles, and interests. In sum, the demise of the French, the vulnerability of the British, American unwillingness to fight Japan while Hitler boasted of conquering the Western Hemisphere, and Germany's military success, which had gone to the Japanese head "like strong wine," was persuading most Japanese that they now had a "golden opportunity" to achieve their expansionist goals.

The seeming convergence of totalitarian tactics in Japan's foreign and domestic politics led Grew to conclude, by the end of August, that the United States would have to protect the *status quo* in the Pacific even at the risk of war. Then, on September 12, 1940, he sent the State Department his "Green Light" dispatch, which he considered his most important one to date. Reiterating his pessimistic view of recent events, Grew lumped Japan among the "predatory powers" with Germany, Italy, and Soviet Russia, which menaced the "way of life" of the "great group of English-speaking nations" that America and England professed to lead. Japan's southward expansion was a threat to American interests in the Pacific, and American security was linked to the British Fleet. Thus, it was emphatically in America's national interest "to support the British Empire in this hour of travail" by preserving the Pacific *status quo* until the European war was won or lost. The Japanese would have to be convinced that the United States was prepared to use its power to defend its interests. Only "a show of force, together with a determination to employ it "if need be," could bring about a "complete regeneration" of Japanese thought and an equitable Far Eastern settlement.

Ten days later, Japanese forces began to enter northern Indochina, and Grew reported that the Japanese were about to sign the Tripartite Pact. Goaded by these developments, and the reports and arguments of Grew, Morgenthau, and Stimson, among others, Roosevelt on September 26 imposed a complete embargo on export to Japan of all grades of iron and scrap steel. This step, most historians have agreed, marked crossing the bridge from words to deeds. Morgenthau, however, believed it brought too little pressure too late.

The following day, September 27, 1940, Japan, Germany, and Italy signed the Tripartite Pact. Although Secretary of the Navy Knox publicly denounced it as the greatest threat ever posed to the American way of life, most American officials regarded the agreement as making formal the existing situation; or, as even the usually bellicose Stimson put it, substantively the pact meant "making a bad face at us." Neither the Germans nor the Japanese were believed to have the military capacity to assist one another in the event of war with the United States.

From the American perspective the purpose of the Tripartite Pact was to intimidate the United States into cutting off aid to Great Britain, thus allowing Germany and Japan to settle in Europe and Asia on favorable terms. These were indeed German and Japanese intentions, but the pact had the opposite effect; for, as Stimson noted in his diary on September 27, "clamors are being made for an alliance with Great Britain already." More important, it aroused Roosevelt's animus toward a German-Japanese effort to "checkmate" the United States, as Stimson noted on October 4 after a Cabinet meeting. The ever cautious Grew was persuaded by November that "the precise problem facing our Government, as I see it, is to determine not *whether* we are going to act, but at just what point in the Japanese advance we are going to act." Much as he had worked over the past eight years to minimize the possibility of war, he wrote, "our unwillingness to contemplate war might well lead to a future catastrophe of far greater proportions." Alas, he noted, " 'peace in our time' " was a temporarily soothing but highly dangerous formula, "and in the Far East we should profit by Mr. Chamberlain's bitter experience in Europe." Japan, he asserted, cannot be trusted any more than Germany and must be treated "as part and parcel of that system which, if allowed to develop unchecked, will assuredly destroy everything that America stands for."

By autumn 1940, American officials were virtually unanimous in viewing Japan as part of a system that challenged American interests in Asia and might ultimately threaten the American way of life. Just as certain is the fact that Roosevelt, amidst his presidential campaign, and cautioned by his military advisers about American unpreparedness, was not ready to take any action likely to provoke Japan. In October, he shrugged off suggestions from both Ickes and Stimson for a full embargo on oil, and when, one week after his re-election, his wife, Eleanor, wrote "Now we've stopped scrap iron, what about oil?" the President replied that the "real" (and private) answer was that such action might cause the Japanese to attack the Dutch East Indies.

Roosevelt ignored Stimson's suggestions of moving a "flying squadron of our own" to the Dutch East Indies, and he was extremely cautious about providing the British with even the most oblique show of support in the Far East. The State Department advised against any joint Anglo-American program of economic pressure on Japan, and Roosevelt, supported by Hull, Welles, and General Marshall, refused Stimson's proposal, following upon a British invitation, to move part of the American Fleet across the Pacific to Singapore by "a non-provocative route." The administration remained completely evasive in responding to British inquiries into what it would do if the Japanese assaulted England's Asian colonies.

The furthest the Americans would go by way of deferring to the British was to agree, in principle, in mid-October to Churchill's oft-repeated request for naval staff talks, which Welles insisted to the British would imply no American commitments of any kind. After the

November election, the date for talks was set for January 1941. Then, in early December 1940, in an effort to bolster Chiang Kai-shek's regime against the Japanese, who on November 30 had granted formal diplomatic recognition to Wang Ching-wei's rival regime in Nanking, the Roosevelt administration afforded the Kuomintang $100 million in credits. Next came Churchill's long letter of December 8, 1940, outlining the military-industrial supplies the British would require, and on December 14 Ambassador Grew sent Roosevelt a "Dear Frank" letter insisting that, "sooner or later, unless we are prepared . . . to withdraw bag and baggage from the entire sphere of 'Greater East Asia including the South Seas' (which God forbid), we are bound eventually to come to a head-on clash with Japan." Only a "progressively firm policy" showing that "we mean to fight" would make preliminary measures successful and dissuade the Japanese from steps that would lead to war.

Roosevelt's public response was his "arsenal of democracy" talk on December 29, 1940, which not only attacked German ruthlessness and insisted that " a nation can have peace with the Nazis only at the price of surrender" but assailed the entire New Order of the Axis powers as "an unholy alliance" seeking "to dominate and enslave the human race." Roosevelt declared that Great Britain and the British Empire were the "spearhead of resistance to world conquest."

Grew listened with ecstasy to the talk on the radio, had copies of it printed in *Japan News Week,* which circulated among influential government and business figures, and read Roosevelt's words so many times himself that he had them virtually memorized. Roosevelt's declaration, he then believed, truly constituted a turning point in a war that, for most American officials, had now assumed global proportions. Or, as the President wrote to Grew on January 21, 1941, in direct response to the ambassador's letter of the previous December 14, "I believe that the fundamental proposition is that we must recognize that the hostilities in Europe, in Africa, and in Asia are all parts of a single world conflict. We must, consequently, recognize that our interests are menaced both in Europe and in the Far East. We are engaged in the task of defending our way of life and our vital national interests wherever they are seriously endangered. Our strategy of self-defense must be a global strategy."

8

A World Without Doubt

By January 1941, President Roosevelt's conception of the world crisis and the part the United States had to play in it was firm. For months, he had argued publicly as well as privately that the Axis Alliance was a global threat to freedom with which there could be neither peace nor compromise. He had committed the United States as the arsenal of democracy to sustaining the British war effort, partly because he believed that an Anglo-American community of ideas was larger than Anglo-American differences, and partly because he believed that England was the first line of America's defense. Roosevelt did not yet contemplate full belligerency for the United States, but as he wrote on New Year's Eve to his High Commissioner in the Philippines, "for practical purposes there is going on a world conflict, in which there are aligned on one side Japan, Germany, and Italy, and on the other side China, Great Britain, and the United States. This country is not involved in the hostilities, but there is no doubt where we stand as regards the issues." America's responsibility was to supply the British and keep open their sources of communication and supply around the globe. Roosevelt said he had no intention of getting "sucked into" a war with Germany and Japan and added, with perhaps more resignation than his present plans justified, that "whether there will come to us war with either or both of those countries will depend far more upon what they do than upon what we refrain from doing."

A week later, Roosevelt dispatched Harry Hopkins, formerly his Relief Administrator, then Secretary of Commerce, and now his Special Assistant, to England on an information mission, although Hopkins confided to CBS correspondent Edward R. Murrow that his real purpose was to "try to be a catalytic agent between two prima donnas." After six weeks of surveying and talks with officials, Hopkins was enormously impressed with British resistance and with the damages suffered, as well as with Churchill's "amazing hold on the British people

194

of all classes." Hopkins's consistent message was that "this island needs our help now, Mr. President, with everything we can give them," and there followed lists of destroyers, bombers, guns, and munitions.

In a spontaneous after-dinner speech, he reassured his obliging hosts that upon return to America his position would be: "Whither thou goest I will go; and where thou lodgest I will lodge; thy people shall be my people, and thy God my God. Even to the end." Churchill was so moved he cried, one observer noted, but when this censored speech leaked throughout England, Hopkins was embarrassed that it suggested more than he intended. And when Anthony Eden, newly reappointed Foreign Secretary, pressed him about American intentions in case the Japanese followed Hitler's and Ribbentrop's urgings and attacked Singapore or the Dutch East Indies (believed highly likely by the British), Hopkins reverted to the standard evasion that only Congress could declare war, and that this was unlikely in that circumstance.

Roosevelt could be equally sentimental about what he now viewed as the Anglo-American cause, and, as he dispatched Wendell Willkie on a fact-finding mission in mid-January, he scrawled a few lines from Longfellow, for Churchill:

> Sail on, O Ship of State!
> Sail on, O Union, strong and great!
> Humanity with all its fears,
> With all the hopes of future years,
> Is hanging breathless on thy fate!

Like his aides, Roosevelt eschewed any consideration of direct American involvement in the World War and devoted himself to finding the means of fulfilling America's task as the arsenal of democracy.

To carry out his design, Roosevelt turned to Morgenthau and Treasury aides who during the first week of January 1941 drafted the Lend-Lease bill. Their proposed legislation authorized the President to have manufactured in American arsenals, factories, or shipyards any defense article for any country whose defense he deemed vital to American security and "to sell, transfer title to, exchange, lease [or] lend" these materials to any government. At Justice Frankfurter's advice, the President's powers, and the countries eligible for aid, were unspecified, and the bill was entitled "An Act to Promote the Defense of the United States, and for Other Purposes."

The most difficult question was that of repayment for Lend-Lease goods, and proposed answers reflected differing views about the Anglo-American "cause" and the British Empire. Morgenthau and Stimson estimated total British foreign assets at about $9 billion, with only $3 billion readily realizable. British assets in the United States were figured at $1.5 billion, with only $1 billion easily liquidated, not even enough to pay for goods on order. Morgenthau's financial and political strategy was to insist that the British step up selling their American assets (from $2 million to $10 million weekly) and provide a full accounting of 1941 receipts and expenditures, as well as dollar assets and long-term investments in the United States and elsewhere, and a comparison of British and American taxes. Morgenthau's purpose was not to force the British to dismantle their empire; but by insisting that they bare their economic souls in unprecedented fashion, the United States would gain commercial advantage, and the administration could tell Congress that the British were doing all they could in the war. Morgenthau insisted that the President set repayment terms for Lend-Lease, which meant not only that the American people "would just have to trust Mr. Roosevelt" but that the British would, too.

Secretary Hull and Secretary of the Navy Knox estimated British foreign assets at $18 billion and wanted $2–$3 billion worth turned over to the United States as collateral for Lend-Lease, a position that reflected their suspicion of hidden British resources as much as it refuted charges that the United States was supporting a "busted" Great Britain. Morgenthau countered that the collateral scheme gave the appearance of the United States's becoming a receiver for the bankrupt "Birmingham crowd," a phrase that revealed his contempt for the Neville Chamberlain elements in British society. Roosevelt sided with Morgenthau's lower $9-billion estimate of British assets, while inclining toward taking colonies such as Bermuda or the West Indies as collateral. But he concluded to Hull that "if we can get our naval bases . . . why should we buy them with two million headaches"—namely, the people who "would be a definite economic drag on this country, and would stir up questions of racial stocks." The administration opted for Morgenthau's financial and political strategy for Lend-Lease, while the British obediently and hopefully liquidated their American holdings and provided all requisite financial information.

Roosevelt still feared congressional opposition and wanted to send the bill to either the Appropriations or the Military Affairs Committee to evade the more critical House and Senate Foreign Affairs committees. But the administration decided to face these hurdles with the unprecedented procedure of having the bill—numbered H.R. 1776—introduced not by the committee chairmen but by the House and Senate majority leaders, John W. McCormack and Alben Barkley.

Testifying before the House Committee, Hull, whose enthusiasm had waned after he lost his financial argument to Morgenthau, nonetheless put forward a strong contention that the main object was to prevent the high seas from falling into the hands of powers bent upon unlimited conquest. He refuted charges of the bill's unneutrality by arguing that Germany and Italy had flaunted international law and neutrality. At Roosevelt's instruction, Morgenthau was evasive about the funds to be expended, but he forthrightly laid out England's financial plight. Stimson argued that allowing the administration to order war matériel instead of awaiting foreign requests would systematize ordering and guarantee that goods would be manufactured to meet American military specifications. Knox insisted that the purpose of Lend-Lease was strictly to promote American security, what Stimson termed the "last call for lunch on that kind of procedure."

Republicans Hamilton Fish of New York and George Tinkam of Massachusetts argued that the bill gave Roosevelt dictatorial powers and would involve the United States in Britain's wars. Diverse witnesses such as Charles Lindbergh, Norman Thomas, and former Ambassador Joseph Kennedy warned against foreign entanglements. None denied German rapaciousness, although, when asked which side he hoped would win the war, Lindbergh replied "neither." Still, he proposed to build a "fortress America," and Kennedy paradoxically opposed Lend-Lease yet favored aiding the British in their struggle against a power that, he warned, menaced reason, religion, conscience, and family. The issue was not passage of Lend-Lease but what limits or safeguards to attach. The House Committee approved the bill by 17–8 and amended it to prohibit convoys, to allow Congress to terminate Lend-Lease before its statutory end, and to limit current transfer of foreign military aid to $1.3 billion, while not imposing limits on future congressional appropriations. After nine days of discussion, the House, with overwhelming Democratic support, passed the bill on February 8 by a vote of 260–165, including 24 Republican votes that came primarily from the Northeast.

Fierce opposition was expected in the Senate, where men like Burton K. Wheeler of Montana had proclaimed that Lend-Lease was the New Deal's "triple-A foreign policy; it will plough under every fourth American boy"—a statement Roosevelt denounced as the "rottenest" of his lifetime. Administration witnesses reiterated the House arguments and were helped by the strong endorsement of Wendell Willkie, who had just returned from England. Senators Nye, Johnson, La Follette, Vandenberg of Michigan, and Clark of Missouri led a spirited opposition, but again the issue was only what form Lend-Lease would take. The senatorial objection was conservative and bipartisan: Republican Robert Taft of Ohio and Democrats Harry Byrd of Virginia and James Byrnes of South Carolina felt that the President had too much authority to dispose of army and navy supplies, and that he would be unrestrained financially because Congress would have no choice but to vote new funds for replacement materials. The Senate satisfied itself with a Treasury-inspired compromise allowing Congress, if it chose, to restrict the disposition of Lend-Lease goods. The bill passed the Foreign Relations Committee by 15–8, and the whole Senate on March 8 by 60–31, again with overwhelming Democratic, and some Republican, support. The House repassed the amended measure on March 11; Roosevelt signed it immediately; and the next day Congress appropriated $7 billion of an ultimate $50-billion Lend-Lease commitment. On March 15, Roosevelt, restrained from an attack on Lend-Lease opponents, proclaimed, "Let not the dictators of Europe or Asia doubt our unanimity now." Democracy made decisions slowly, he said, but "the world is no longer left in doubt."

Churchill promptly cabled his blessings for Lend-Lease, which he told Parliament was the "most unsordid" act in the history of any nation. Perhaps it was, but Morgenthau's insistence that the British divest themselves of their gold, dollars, and American stocks and bonds (although he never forced compliance with regard to the last) and Stimson's forcing the British to take weapons of American specification showed that Lend-Lease was not the most innocent act. Senator Vandenberg agonized in his diary that Lend-Lease reversed a hundred fifty years of neutrality and threw the United States "squarely into the power politics and power wars of Europe, Asia, and Africa," wed the nation to spending *"billions upon billions"* to the verge of bankruptcy, and was tantamount to telling the President *"You are monarch of all you survey."* Vandenberg's idea of America's world role, at least since 1917, was naïve, if not myopic, and Congress retained control over the tenure and appropriations for Lend-Lease as long as it chose to exercise its prerogatives.

General Marshall's admission in 1957 that Lend-Lease made American involvement in the war on the British side "a probability rather than a possibility" would seem accurate, but it overlooks two matters: that the purpose of the law was to sustain the British, and that the United States was propelled into the war by events unrelated to the consequences of Lend-Lease and in defense of principles, wisely conceived or not, that most Lend-Lease opponents approved. Although it was a partisan act, Lend-Lease reflected the American consensus of all aid short of war to the British and provided a lever for the State Department to press the British to relax their imperial preference system as part of the *quid pro quo* repayment.

American officials pressed the British for just such an understanding from March 1941 until February 1942, when they signed the Master Lend-Lease Agreement, which pledged both parties to eliminate "all

forms of discriminatory treatment in international commerce" and to reduce "tariffs and other trade barriers." The British viewed this as a
vague commitment in return for aid, but the Americans insisted that it
implied abandoning imperial preferences and opening the British Empire
to American commerce in accordance with the Open Door principles
that Democrats and Republicans had been advocating since 1900. Or,
as Hoover wrote to Hull in March 1941, while "Lend Lease obviously
involves us deeply in the consequences of the war . . . it also gives our
government a measure of responsibility to see that the policies pursued
by the British are in the interest of both winning the war and winning a
peace, and in the interests of the United States."

In like manner, the Anglo-American military staff talks held in Washington during January 29–March 27, 1941, reflected American partisanship and national interest. The Americans had agreed to the talks in the
fall of 1940 to assuage the British, but Roosevelt, wary of commitment,
took no part. He never formally received the British delegates (who
came in civilian garb, as much to underscore the purely technical nature
of the discussion as to avoid domestic political criticism), and he emended
Admiral Stark's proposed basis of any understanding as being not one
between "allies" but "associates."

The joint conclusions of the "ABC-1 Staff Agreement" provided that,
if the United States became involved in a war with Germany or Japan,
or both, the primary American military involvement would be in
Europe; that the United States would increase its forces in the Atlantic
and the Mediterranean to release British Commonwealth forces to
defend their Far Eastern holdings; and that the American Pacific Fleet
would defend Hawaii, the Philippines, Guam, and Wake. This Europe-
first strategy accorded with an American military strategy drawn up in
the 1920's, when U.S. military planners determined that, in the event
the United States, with a one-ocean navy, faced enemies in two oceans,
it would be necessary, first, to fight the stronger power in the Atlantic
and, then, do battle in the Pacific. The army and navy jointly had
reasserted their Europe-first war strategy in a planning report in December 1940. Both General Marshall and the War Department planners
were conservative men who believed that the United States had naïvely
and too liberally provided the man power for a British victory in the
First World War without sufficiently promoting American national
interests; they were always suspicious of the political implications of
British military strategy. Moreover, while the British regarded the defense of Singapore as central to the defense of their Asian empire, including Australia and New Zealand, the Americans refused to allocate
any portion of their Pacific Fleet for that purpose. At a subsequent
American–British Dominion conference in Singapore in April 1941,

military strategists agreed on the separate (that is, not joint or jointly commanded) disposition of forces and command, with the security of sea communications and the Singapore naval base declared to be "most important interests" for the "associated" powers. They also tentatively defined a line in Southeast Asia beyond which Japanese penetration would become a cause for war. Marshall and Admiral Stark rejected this agreement as excessively political.

The Anglo-American staff talks provided for a significant exchange of technical information and an unprecedented peacetime and moral commitment to the British. Strategic and tactical plans were consistent with long-defined American military planning and civil definition of national interests, and they became operative only in the event Germany or Japan brought war upon the United States. As if to underscore to the British the theoretical aspects of the planning, Roosevelt in June 1941 withheld formal approval of the ABC-1 Agreement and accompanying military plans.

Although officials of the administration frequently disagreed on how to aid the British, they shared the President's belief that America's involvement would be determined less by what they did than by the European war's unforeseeable turns and the consequences these would have on the world balance of power and American interests. In this respect, German political and military strategies, those long contemplated and those improvised, tended to heighten the worst of American fears.

Hitler's effort to use the Tripartite Pact to intimidate the United States into not aiding the British had failed. On January 8, 1941, he put forward to his admirals the strategy that would predominate throughout the year. The Japanese, he said, had to be encouraged to expand, "even if the U.S.A. is then forced to take drastic steps." Shortly thereafter, he insisted to Admiral Erich Raeder, Chief of the Naval Command, that America was no threat, "even if she did come in." In February, Ribbentrop urged the Japanese to attack Singapore to achieve three objects: The Japanese would secure immediately everything they sought after the war; the British would be dealt a death blow; and the United States would be kept out of the war. Even if the United States entered the war, its fleet, divided between the Atlantic and the Pacific, would be weak and easily defeated.

When Foreign Minister Yosuke Matsuoka visited Berlin in late March–early April, Ribbentrop reiterated his views and dismissed American war supplies as "junk." Hitler gave the Japanese a virtual diplomatic blank check by telling their emissary that Germany "would immediately take the consequences if Japan should get involved with the

United States." When Matsuoka said that the Japanese were considering a first strike because they believed war with America was inevitable, Hitler approved.

The Germans hoped to use Japanese aggressiveness to preclude American involvement in the war in Europe, where Hitler was expanding his operations partly by design and partly because he was determined to assist the Italians, whose operations in the fall of 1940 in North Africa and Greece had proved disastrous. Between December 1940 and February 1941, the British had swept back through Egypt and Libya, retaking Bardia, Tobruk, and Benghasi, and they had driven into Italian East Africa (Ethiopia). The Greek Army had repulsed the Italians and overrun a quarter of Italian-occupied Albania. In March 1941, the British moved a 60,000-man expeditionary force into Greece.

Hitler wanted to redress the military balance in the eastern Mediterranean–North African region not only out of loyalty to Mussolini. Hitler's plan was to bring the British closer to defeat by driving them from Greece while protecting his hold over Rumania's oil wells. He also wanted to consolidate his grip on the Balkans before invading the Soviet Union. In December 1940 he sent a reinforcement of 50,000 men to the beleaguered Italians in Greece, and in February 1941 he ordered General Erwin Rommel to prepare a North African offensive. Later that month, Hitler forced Bulgaria to join the Tripartite Pact, and on March 25 Yugoslavia had to accede, although this touched off a *coup d'état* in Yugoslavia by the military, which replaced Prince Regent Paul with young King Peter II and announced a policy of neutrality. At the same time, Hitler extended the war zone in the Atlantic from Iceland west to Greenland (the thirtieth meridian), although he instructed his navy to avoid incidents with American ships. On March 31, Rommel's Afrika Korps attacked the British in Libya, and on April 6 Germany invaded Yugoslavia and Greece.

German victories came fast. Within weeks Rommel's Afrika Korps had retaken Libya, except for Tobruk, and prepared to assault Egypt. Yugoslavia capitulated on April 17, and Hitler promptly partitioned the country out of existence, although partisan forces continued to resist. Greece agreed to an armistice on April 23, with King George II fleeing to Crete. The British, suffering domestic political strife as well as military defeat because their commitment to Greece had weakened the North African defenses, evacuated their expeditionary force to Crete, leaving 12,000 casualties and prisoners and much military equipment. At the end of May, German parachutists captured Crete, and the British fled to Cyprus and Egypt. The Vichy regime in France appeared to be moving toward outright alliance with Germany and war against England by affording trucks to Rommel's Afrika Korps and oil to the Italian Navy and by negotiating, in late May, the Paris Protocols (which remained unratified) promising the Germans bases in Syria, Lebanon, Tunisia, and West Africa.

The United States made oblique efforts to counter Germany. Late in January 1941, Roosevelt had sent Colonel William J. Donovan, a prominent Republican and Wall Street lawyer, to the Balkans and Middle East to encourage resistance to German advances. Donovan could offer only the prospect of Germany's ultimate defeat, which could not dissuade Bulgaria from signing the Tripartite Pact or permitting Hitler to mass troops there before his April invasions. The most Roosevelt could do was force the Navy Department to release thirty new fighter planes to Greece, but by then the armistice had been signed.

American officials were slightly more successful in dealing with the Vichy regime, which they had recognized in 1940 partly because they hoped to influence its policy and partly because they took a jaundiced view of the French nation, its future, and General de Gaulle, whom they instinctively disliked, and who they often believed was an instrument of British policy. The administration supplied Vichy France with foodstuffs, and in March 1941 the diplomat Robert D. Murphy and General Maxim Weygand, who ruled North Africa for Vichy, agreed that the United States would supply North Africa economically in return for stationing observers in ports and on transit lines. These "technical assistants" provided some valuable information on political and military developments in North Africa, and, by maintaining diplomatic relations with the Vichy regime, the Roosevelt administration was able to dissuade Vichy from sending the battleship *Dunkerque* for repairs from Algeria to Toulon in southern France, where the Germans might have seized it. It is doubtful, however, that the Roosevelt administration gained any meaningful long-term political or military benefits from diplomatic ties with the Vichy French.

The British grew increasingly angry at America's Vichy policy in 1941 because they now wanted to bring down Marshal Pétain's collaborationist government by intensifying their blockade of unoccupied France. The British were enraged at America's dealings with General Weygand, a leading advocate of capitulation in June 1940, who, in 1941, refused British overtures to bring North Africa into the war against Germany, and who also sought to eliminate every vestige of support for de Gaulle and Free France.

The most successful direct aid, other than Lend-Lease, that the United States gave England in the spring of 1941 was naval aid. At the start of the year, German submarines were sinking 115,000 tons a month of British shipping and by expanding the war zone to Greenland were able to triple their havoc. As the Battle of the Atlantic heated, Roosevelt acted within Lend-Lease provisions and, on April 2, happily told Churchill that he had made arrangements for repairing British merchant ships "and your larger friends" in American shipyards, and that he had allotted funds for two hundred new ships. At the Treasury's behest, the administration seized thirty German and Italian ships interned in American ports, along with thirty-five Danish ships, and shortly afterward got Congress to approve American use of them.

The administration also announced, on April 10, that Greenland was being incorporated into the American Hemispheric defense system in return for the right to build military bases. The agreement, negotiated in secret with the Danish Ambassador in Washington, embarrassed the government in German-occupied Copenhagen and angered the Canadians by their exclusion. But a new American commitment to a Hemispheric Joint Defense Board assuaged the latter, while Roosevelt told the Danes that Greenland was being held in trust for them. Actually, the American takeover was prompted not by fear of German invasion but because of Greenland's potential use as a facility to keep German warships well east of the mid-Atlantic.

Had Roosevelt followed his own inclination or the urgings of Secretaries Morgenthau, Knox, and Stimson, he also would have agreed to convoy supply ships to Iceland. But Lend-Lease prohibited convoys, and the President, as he told the journalist John Gunther on April 7, did not feel the public was ready for convoys—yet. Three days later, Roosevelt proposed to announce that American ships would patrol the waters to the mid-Atlantic (Iceland was soon included) and alert British ships to German submarines, but instead he issued the orders to the navy quietly on April 15. Two weeks later, he made this news public, rationalizing that the patrols were "reconnaissance" and reporting to Washington. Stimson believed the procedure a "hostile act to the Germans" and wanted Roosevelt to be "honest with himself"—and with the public, he might have added.

Secretary Ickes believed that the patrols were intended to provoke a hostile German act that would become the pretext for convoys. Throughout April, however, Roosevelt resisted his advisers' pressure for convoys —as well as Knox's insistence that, "if the Navy were turned loose, they would clean up the Atlantic in thirty days"—with the rejoinder that the United States could only help but not insure the delivery of goods to Britain. Early in May, the President agreed to transfer a quarter of the Pacific Fleet to the Atlantic to cover the enlarged region of patrol and allow the British to concentrate on waters nearest to them.

Roosevelt's real feelings were as ambiguous as his policies. Replying to criticism of his recent moves, he wrote to Norman Thomas on May 14 that he regretted that times had changed so much that they could no longer live out their lives under conditions "at least somewhat similar to the past." A few days later, on May 19, he told isolationist Congressman James O'Connor that he would soon have to decide whether "to keep your country unshackled by taking even more definite steps to do so—even firing shots—or . . . submitting to be shackled for the sake of not losing one American life." Roosevelt also warned that it was time for Anglophobic Irishmen to get over their "ancient hatreds"; for, "if England goes down, Ireland goes down too." When, on May 17, Morgenthau told Roosevelt that it was time for the United States to enter the war, Roosevelt replied, "I am waiting to be pushed into this situation."

German advances in Greece and North Africa provided an impetus, along with news on May 21 that the American freighter *Robin Moor* had been sunk in mid-Atlantic. In a nationwide broadcast on May 27, Roosevelt, insisting that the delivery of supplies to the British can, must, and will be made, emphasized the more essential point that the European war had "developed, as the Nazis always intended it should develop, into a world war for world domination." The Nazis, he said, intended "to treat the Latin American nations as they are now treating the Balkans" and planned to strangle the United States and Canada. "Our Bunker Hill of tomorrow may be several thousand miles from Boston," he warned, and since it was stupid to allow an enemy to gain a foothold for invasion, the American people would decide whether, when, and where their security or interests were threatened. For that reason, he would not hesitate to use American troops that were now being stationed in "strategic military positions." Finally, he declared an "unlimited national emergency."

Roosevelt's speech was "calculated to scare the daylights out of everyone," as Assistant Secretary Berle noted, but to the regret of his entire Cabinet, except Hull, the President proposed no new action. At a press conference the next day, he admitted that he had no proposals for the unlimited national emergency. Privately he agreed to send occupying forces to the Azores or Cape Verde Islands if Hitler invaded Spain or Portugal. This measure, however, was couched in Hemispheric-defense language. It assumed Brazilian cooperation and hinged on an invitation from the Portuguese Government, which was not forthcoming. On June 11, word came from survivors of the *Robin Moor* about the unprovoked German torpedoing far from the war zone. Roosevelt was infuriated, and Hopkins advised that the navy be allowed to take whatever steps it deemed necessary to secure freedom of the seas. Roosevelt vacillated and decided only to impound German and Italian assets in the United States and to order German and Italian consular staffs to leave. On June 20, he announced that the Germans had sunk the *Robin Moor* to warn everyone "not to resist the Nazi movement of world conquest." The United States, he said, would never yield to this threat.

The administration moved ahead with its plans to occupy Iceland. The British had undertaken this in April 1940 but wanted to release their forces for duty elsewhere. At the end of May 1941, they asked the Americans to assume their obligation, and Knox, Stimson, and Hopkins pressed for occupation. Roosevelt was his usual cautious self, and while he agreed on June 5 to ready Marines for the task, he insisted upon an invitation from the reluctant Icelandic Government. The British acted as forceful intermediaries. The necessity of Icelandic defense was heightened when Germany extended its blockade to Iceland and, on June 22, 1941, attacked the Soviet Union. The government in Reykjavik agreed to American occupation forces, with the proviso that they would leave at the war's end, and that Iceland's independence and sovereignty would be respected. On July 7, Roosevelt announced the dispatch of 4,000 Marines, and, as in the Greenland case, he used the rubric of Hemispheric defense and the need to preclude German invasion of Iceland. Stimson and Knox wanted Roosevelt to announce the convoying of all shipping between the United States and Iceland, and on July 19 Roosevelt issued orders for the navy to convoy all American and Icelandic ships and the "shipping of any nationality which may join such convoys." But before these orders went into effect on July 25, the President restricted convoys to American and Icelandic ships, which led a distressed Stimson to liken the situation to the days before the Civil War, when there was considerable "pulling back and forth, trying to make the Confederates fire the first shot."

While the administration stepped up its North Atlantic activities, it had to deal with the political and military implications of the German invasion of the Soviet Union. Rumors of the impending attack had been widespread in 1941, and in January Under Secretary Welles passed along to the Russians military intelligence indicating Germany's intent. As recently as June 15, Churchill cabled Roosevelt that, if an attack occurred, the British would give the Russians all possible aid, "following the principle Hitler is the foe we have to beat." Roosevelt responded that he would support any announcement Churchill made welcoming Russia as an ally.

After the German attack, Churchill proclaimed that England's "one aim, and one single, irrevocable purpose," was to destroy Hitler's regime, and that any nation that "fights on against Nazidom will have our aid." Hitler's attack, he said, would not cause any divergence of American and British aims or cause them to slacken their struggle against Germany. On July 12, Great Britain and Russia signed an agreement for mutual aid, which also precluded a separate peace with Germany.

American reaction to the Russo-German war was more mixed. Outright isolationists agreed with the *Chicago Tribune* argument that "the heat is off" for American involvement in Europe, because it would be senseless to go to war to make the world safe for communism. Or, as Herbert Hoover said, it would be a "gargantuan jest" to conceive of preserving democracy by aiding Russia to fight Germany. Even New Dealers like Senator Harry S. Truman said that, "if we see that Germany is winning we ought to help Russia and if Russia is winning we ought to help Germany and that way let them kill as many as possible." He added, though, that Hitler should never be allowed to win.

The inherent conservatism of State Department officials, especially Hull and Welles, inclined them to be anti-Soviet. Their feelings were reinforced by their belief that the Russians had not honored the pledges they made in 1933, when American-Soviet diplomatic relations were established, pledges concerning freedom of religion and increased trade and debt payments. William C. Bullitt, the first ambassador to the Soviet Union during 1933–36, had become bitterly disillusioned with life in Moscow and with Soviet diplomacy; and American diplomats were highly suspicious of Russian collective security efforts during 1935–38, considering the Nazi-Soviet Nonaggression Pact and the Russo-Finnish war of 1939–40 more indicative of the sinister side of Soviet diplomacy. American military officials were also anti-Soviet, and their conventional wisdom, subscribed to by Marshall and Knox, argued that military aid for the Russians was pointless, because the Russians could not resist the Germans for more than a few weeks or months. The administration's first statement on June 23, drafted by Welles and edited by Roosevelt, condemned both German and Russian domestic dictatorship but said that American foreign policy would be formulated on the premise that "Hitler's armies are today the chief danger." Welles sidestepped the question of aid by saying it had not been requested.

Roosevelt's approach to aiding the Russians was cautious but intuitively optimistic. He distrusted them but did not think that they, in contrast to the Germans, intended to conquer Europe. It was his thought that they would resist the German assault longer than anyone anticipated, which would help the British and perhaps preclude America's involvement. At first, he cagily said that he favored aid but did not know what was needed, but he lifted a recent freeze on $40 million in Russian assets in America and did not invoke the Neutrality Act so that Vladivostok would be open to American shipping.

Roosevelt's optimism about Russian resistance was reinforced by Morgenthau and the former ambassador to the Soviet Union (1937–39),

Joseph E. Davies, who insisted that Hitler could occupy but never govern that vast country, and that he would meet relentless guerrilla warfare. Later in July, Harry Hopkins went to Russia and reported that dealing with Stalin "assures you that Russia will stand against the on-slaught of the German Army. He takes it for granted that you have no doubts either."

Initial Russian aid requests on June 30 included anti-aircraft and large machine guns, planes, aviation fuel, and military-industrial machinery, but questions about American and British priorities and Russian finances slowed assistance in July. Morgenthau advanced as much money as possible against Treasury purchases of Russian gold, and at a Cabinet meeting on August 1 Roosevelt, primarily admonishing Stimson, de-manded that more planes and other war matériel be shipped "with a bang next week," including matériel from American and British orders. The Russians, meanwhile, for their own peculiar reasons, insisted that planes then available but already in England not be delivered via Archangel but shipped back across the United States and via the Pacific to Vladivostok. General Marshall, anxious to hoard supplies for American forces, remained convinced, then and years later, that the Russians would complain bitterly no matter what they were afforded.

Lend-Lease held the only solution to the problem of supplies and finances for the Russians, but Roosevelt feared to include them in that arrangement because of the possibility of a public outcry, especially among Catholics. The original $7 billion appropriation for Lend-Lease had been expended by September 1941, and there was thus concern that congressional renewal could be jeopardized. The administration's caution was increased later that month when Pope Pius XII responded coolly to Roosevelt's personal message that it was necessary to distin-guish between Germany's effort to spread its system by force of arms and the Russians' reliance on propaganda. Nonetheless, Roosevelt sent Averell Harriman to Moscow to work out with British representatives a temporary military-aid program, and in October both the House and the Senate rejected amendments to the new Lend-Lease appropriation that would have prohibited including the Soviet Union. Roosevelt made the most of this negative endorsement and on October 30 approved $1 billion in aid for the Russians, to be repaid in ten years, interest free. Stalin accepted on November 4, and three days later Roosevelt made the decision public with a letter to Lend-Lease Administrator Edward R. Stettinius, appropriately declaring the defense of 'the Soviet Union "vital to the defense of the United States."

The Russians were pleased, but with the Germans advancing on Leningrad and Moscow, they were insistent as ever that the British open a second front in France or the Balkans or send troops through Iran, which the Russians and British had jointly divided and occupied in August in order to preclude German influence there. Churchill, however, was equally insistent that the British lacked the forces for a second front. He, Stalin, and Roosevelt understood that there was yet no agreement on war or peace aims.

The latter were a subject of discussion at the famous meeting between Roosevelt and Churchill and their diplomatic aides and chiefs of staff at Placentia Bay, Newfoundland, during August 9–12. Once again, however, an agreement of American and British minds and interests was difficult. Churchill had wanted a highly publicized conference and dramatic demonstration of Anglo-American solidarity; Roosevelt, on the other hand, kept the meeting shrouded in secrecy, partly for reasons of personal and diplomatic security, but also because he intended only to feel out Churchill and move toward a working relationship rather than reach significant agreements. Technically speaking, the Americans and British agreed on matters relating to Icelandic defense and occupation of the Azores, and the Canary and Cape Verde islands, if necessary—all of which demonstrated considerable American commitment. Aid to Russia was agreed upon, although the British feared that their defense orders thus might be shortchanged. The Americans felt that the British were not coordinating their orders, that they were ignorant "of how far the cupboard was bare" as regards producing and training American forces, as Stimson said afterward.

Disagreement over supply allocation reflected disagreement over how to fight the war, and when, if not whether, the United States would enter the war. On the first night, Churchill gave a brilliant after-dinner exposition on the world crisis and emphasized resolving it through blockades and strategic bombing in Europe and peripheral assaults on Hitler's forces in the Middle East. President Roosevelt's son Elliott, who was present at the meeting, has recorded that the Prime Minister pleaded for immediate American involvement: "The Americans must come in at our side! You must come in if you are to survive." It is extremely unlikely that Churchill was so politically unsubtle, but the military tactics he advocated were conveniently British and calculated to imply or entice American involvement at a relatively low cost in casualties.

Roosevelt, and to some extent the navy, liked Churchill's tactics, but the army insisted that the war could be won only by building a huge land army and assaulting Hitler's forces in Europe. For reasons of strategy as well as availability, they resented the British demand for "great big 4-engine bombers." The army's War Plans Division paper, submitted to the British in September 1941, refuted their approach and insisted that it was "an almost invariable rule that wars cannot be finally won without the use of land forces." This approach implied that direct

American involvement was some time off and was in accord with Roosevelt's political thinking about actual American belligerency, even though he mused about Churchill's more glamorous naval and air tactics. The British correctly concluded that, psychologically and militarily, the Americans did not intend to enter the war soon, and that the debate over military tactics would continue through the war years.

Discussions at Placentia Bay about the Far East also revealed differing views about American belligerency. The British (and the Australians) wanted a pledge or warning that the United States would go to war if Japan struck at Malaya or the Dutch East Indies, but Under Secretary Welles, in a talk on the first day with his Foreign Office counterpart, Sir Alexander Cadogan, insisted that the Americans were determined "to put off a show-down (if such was inevitable) until such time that such a show-down was from our standpoint more propitious," and he also said that Roosevelt wished it understood that even Japan's occupation of Thailand should not be made a *casus belli* by Great Britain. The next day, the British proposed parallel American-British notes warning Japan that further encroachment in the Southwest Pacific would compel countermeasures, "even though these might lead to war between the United States and Japan" (and likewise Great Britain and Japan). Churchill told Welles, and then Roosevelt, that these warnings were crucial to restraining Japan and saving Great Britain. Welles revised the British draft notes to read that further Japanese military domination in the Pacific would force the United States to take all steps "in its own security," even if these "may result in conflict between the two countries." Then, in Washington, Secretary Hull and his aides resisted even this moderate statement, rewriting it to say only that the United States would ensure the safety of its citizens and interests and omitting reference to a possible American-Japanese conflict. Roosevelt was unaware of these changes until he presented the note to the Japanese Ambassador in Washington on August 17. The President was relieved at the absence of a military threat or commitment and not troubled by having reneged on his pledge to the British to deliver a warning to the Japanese. Churchill could only tell himself that the Americans had lived up to their word.

The most enduring, if unheeded, agreement to emerge from the Newfoundland meeting was the Atlantic Charter. Since 1939, State Department officials had been toying with principles or blueprints for the postwar world, and there was a general feeling that the imperial British and Soviets should not enter into any agreement that might tarnish the purity of the struggle against German and Japanese aggression—or American liberal trade principles. Welles drove these points home in his first talk with Cadogan on August 9. Roosevelt was amenable to trying to draft an outline for the postwar era, although he believed that the key for world security was the "elimination of costly armaments," as he had told Assistant Secretary Berle. The British had said little about war aims, except for Foreign Secretary Eden's statement on May 29, 1941, that postwar Europe would be economically disorganized and distraught and require pooling of resources.

Churchill accepted Roosevelt's proposal for a joint declaration, recognizing that this was the most common commitment he could get from the United States. The President, fearing that his diplomatic aides might use the occasion for an exaggerated attack on British colonialism and imperial preferences, suggested that the British provide the working draft. Agreement on the first three principles came easily: no territorial aggrandizement; no territorial changes without the consent of the concerned peoples; the restoration of self-government to those nations forcibly deprived of it. The fourth British point proposed a fair and equitable distribution of essential produce within and among the nations of the world, but Welles insisted this meant "precisely nothing," and he and Roosevelt revised it to call for commitment for all nations to have "access, on equal terms, to the trade and to the raw materials of the world." The British, believing that this was an attack on their commitment to the Dominions and imperial preferences, qualified the American statement about providing equal access to trade and materials with the phrase "with due respect for their existing obligations." Hull was angry and demanded a public "clarifying statement" from the British, but he was dissuaded from this by the argument that this would bring sharp criticism from those Englishmen who felt that the United States was presumptuous in making such demands upon England while remaining uncommitted in the war. This, in turn, would rouse American anti-interventionists.

After agreeing on three more vaguely stated principles concerning economic collaboration, freedom from fear and want, and freedom of the seas, the Americans and British struggled over the eighth and final point concerning postwar security. The United States avoided a commitment. The British wanted an "effective international organization" to guarantee world security, but Roosevelt, ever mindful of Wilson's debacle over the League of Nations and thinking that an Anglo-American world police force might be a better temporary expedient, insisted that the statement be limited to disarming the aggressor nations, "pending the establishment of a wider and permanent system of general security."

The Atlantic Charter was issued on August 14, bringing forth charges from the likes of Senators Hiram Johnson and Robert Taft that Roosevelt had entered into a secret alliance that presaged sending an expeditionary force to Europe. There were, however, paeans of praise from stalwart Democrats and from men like Justice Felix Frankfurter, who favored more American commitment. Frankfurter said that "it wasn't what was said or done that defined the scope of the achievement. It's always the forces—the impalpable, the spiritual forces, the hopes, the purposes, and the endeavors—that are released that matter."

Both sides missed the mark. Roosevelt and Churchill (the "two prima donnas," in Hopkins's words) had "broken the ice," as Roosevelt noted, learned more about each other's political attitudes and problems, and established a working relationship. Each had relieved himself of subtle insecurities about his ability to impress the other. The Americans viewed these as achievements. Roosevelt's very act of conferring with Churchill indicated where American sympathy lay in the current world conflict. From the perspective of the British Minister of Supply, Lord Beaver-brook, what mattered was not spirituality or appearances but, he told Cabinet colleagues, the fact that "there isn't the slightest chance of the U.S. entering the war until compelled to by a direct attack on its territory, and it seems that this could not happen until Britain and Russia have been defeated." This assessment was realistic enough in the grim summer of 1941 to depress even the optimistic Churchill. The British had been thrown off the Continent and had their backs to the wall in Egypt, and the Russians were in desperate straits as the Germans advanced on three fronts from the Baltic to the Ukraine. And not long thereafter, in December 1941, Stalin, anxious to secure commitments from the British about Russia's postwar territorial claims from the Baltic to the Black Sea, but meeting with temporizing inspired largely by American officials, would say, "I thought that the Atlantic Charter was directed against those people who were trying to establish world dominion. It now looks as if the Charter was directed against the U.S.S.R." Clearly, for all its good fellowship and noble expression, the Atlantic Conference and Charter covered over but did not resolve the differences that had plagued Anglo-American relations in the past two decades. They demonstrated the Roosevelt administration's unwillingness or inability to act decisively in the world crisis that, it recognized, was worsening daily.

In the summer of 1941, a problem arose over renewing the draft. The 1940 Selective Service Act fixed service at one year, although it allowed the President to extend it if Congress declared the national interest imperiled. The administration preferred that Congress renew conscription for an unlimited duration. Many congressmen felt obligated to the original one-year commitment and feared their constituents', and the soldiers', wrath if they reneged; other congressmen opposed conscription on isolationist or noninterventionist grounds; and others still simply did not trust Roosevelt. For the last reason lobbying was left to the military, but General Marshall did not do a good job. The Senate approved extension of the draft for one year on August 7, but opposition in the House was much stiffer, and the Democratic leadership had too long been overconfident. It communicated poorly and failed to keep tabs on those who were doubtful supporters. Numerous congressmen would vote against renewal, thinking that the bill would pass anyway, while they would retain their constituents' favor. The result was a cliff-hanger 203–202 vote in favor of passage on August 12, which gave the impression that the administration was on the verge of congressional re-pudiation, despite the fact that actual sentiment was closer to the Lend-Lease majorities of March. The vote came as a "bombshell" to the assemblage at the Atlantic Conference. It left many Britons wondering how the United States could seek to guarantee world freedom one day and propose to disband its army the next.

Roosevelt was not alarmed by the draft vote, but it probably con-firmed his cautious approach toward American commitments or belli-gerence in the world war and heightened his tendency toward expedient, or even devious, means to achieve his ends or rouse the public. At the Atlantic Conference, he had agreed to extend American convoys to British ships traveling between the United States and Iceland, and while the system was virtually effected by late August, he did not make this public or issue formal orders. Then, on September 4, a German sub-marine fired two torpedoes at the destroyer *Greer,* 175 miles southwest of Iceland, which was within both the proclaimed American defense zone and the German war zone. The *Greer* had been tracking the sub-marine for a British plane that was trying to sink it, finally causing the submarine to fire at the *Greer,* which in turn dropped eight depth charges.

The circumstances were irrelevant, or perhaps useful, for Roosevelt. He insisted, without evidence, at a press conference the next day that the German attack was deliberate. On a nationwide broadcast on September 11, he branded the action "piracy legally and morally" and proof of Germany's determination to dominate the seas, the United States, and the Western Hemisphere—"one determined step toward creating a permanent world system based on force, on terror, and on murder." Likening the submarine to a "rattlesnake poised to strike," he said that American ships would no longer await attack but assume an "active defense," implying but not stating clearly a policy of shoot on sight. He also announced that British ships would be convoyed within waters deemed vital to America's defense—a vast zone even larger, Churchill noted, than the public understood. Orders were issued promptly, and as Admiral Stark, Chief of Naval Operations, wrote on September 22 re-garding the Atlantic war, "We are all but, if not actually, in it."

Roosevelt was not prepared to accept the realities or political consequences of his administration's actions. He resisted the urgings of men like Stimson to press Congress to repeal the 1939 Neutrality Act, which forbade arming merchant ships or their entry into combat zones (waters between Iceland and Great Britain). On October 9, Roosevelt asked Congress to repeal the ban on arming merchant ships and implied that he would like the other restriction lifted. While the House debated, word came on October 16 that a German submarine had torpedoed the destroyer *Kearny,* which had gone to aid a convoy under attack four hundred miles south of Iceland. The next day, the House repealed the ban on arming merchant ships by the wide margin of 259–138.

Democratic leaders in the Senate were encouraged to press for repeal of the whole neutrality legislation, and on October 27 Roosevelt delivered a scathing Navy Day speech in which he pulled forth what he insisted was "a secret map made in Germany by Hitler's Government." This map purported to show how Nazi planners intended to reorganize Central and South America into vassal states. Roosevelt then said that the American Government possessed another secret document detailing the Nazis' intent to dominate the world, abolish all religions, liquidate the clergy, and replace the God of Love and Mercy with the God of Blood. He was confident, he said, that Americans would meet this challenge as they had met all others, that "we Americans have cleared our decks and taken our battle stations" and stand ready "in the defense of our Nation and in the faith of our fathers to do what God has given us the power to see as our full duty."

The Senate was not swayed, and news on October 31 that the Germans had sunk the destroyer *Reuben James* six hundred miles west of Iceland seemed to intensify opposition to neutrality revision. The administration finally mustered enough votes on November 7 to secure, by 50–37, repeal of the ban on arming merchant ships and on entering war zones, and the House repassed the bill on November 17. All that remained of the 1939 Neutrality Act were its prohibitions on travel on belligerent ships and loans to belligerents, and these minor details were superseded by convoying and Lend-Lease.

In a legal or technical sense, the law of the land had finally caught up with administration policy, but the question of when the undeclared shooting war in the Atlantic would become a formal one between the United States and Germany remained unresolved. Almost all the President's Cabinet and military advisers, except Secretary Hull and General Marshall, were prepared and even eager for a declaration of war against Germany. But Roosevelt retained the final decision. Although he clung to a faint belief that American objectives might be achieved without war, he felt certain that neither Congress nor the public would accept a war unless it was thrust upon them.

This the German admiralty would have done, for throughout the summer and fall of 1941 they pressed for the right to expand operations in the Atlantic, insisting that American and British ships were one and the same, and that they were ready to accept the consequences of full-scale war. Hitler restrained his admiralty and ordered that incidents with American ships be avoided, not because he feared American power but because he neither understood nor cared much about naval maters and was engrossed in his Russian campaign. He insisted to his military throughout 1941 that Germany first had to achieve its "blockade-proof *Lebensraum*" in the East, and then there would be time to "fight the naval war against the Anglo-Saxons to the end." He also continued to urge a stiffer diplomatic course upon the Japanese. This would contribute to bringing East and West into conflict sooner than anyone imagined.

9

The Coming of
Global War

President Roosevelt had written to Ambassador Grew in January 1941 that the hostilities in Europe, Africa, and Asia were part of a single world conflict that menaced American interests everywhere and necessitated a defense policy based on a global strategy. Throughout the year, the European situation remained the administration's chief concern, but the Far Eastern crisis was viewed with increasing alarm. Japan's war against China appeared even more ominous now with Japan's expansion into Southeast Asia and the threat it posed to the Southwest Pacific. There was also the dual problem of China, involving not only its ability or willingness to defend itself, but whether Chiang Kai-shek's beleaguered and corrupted regime would be able to remain in power.

These problems were significant singly or in concert, and they assumed transcendent importance as they might, and did, affect the European war. While the American way of responding to Far Eastern problems remained bound by a Europe-first strategy, there is little doubt that, for almost all officials of the Roosevelt administration, the issue remained how and when the European and Far Eastern wars would be joined.

The problems most easily dealt with were those that held little hope of solution, but for which, the administration hoped, superficial treatment might buy time, if not give the appearance of decisive action. After lending the Kuomintang $20 million in the spring of 1940, the Roosevelt administration decided against further loans. The pressure for additional funds from China's lobbyists was relentless, and Ambassador Nelson Johnson insisted that money was necessary not only to sustain China's war effort but to offset Soviet aid and influence in China. He argued throughout the latter half of 1940 that the Kuomintang and the Chinese Communists "must eventually come to grips in a military struggle for military and political supremacy," and he feared that lack of aid "may in the end result in Communist ascendancy."

Johnson, who in 1938 had blamed Kuomintang corruption for the success of the Chinese Communists, now insisted that Chiang was not a military dictator but a leader who worked for his nation's improvement. The ambassador's turnabout had to do less with reality than with the fact that since 1938 he had been isolated in Chungking and consorted with Kuomintang officials, while—somewhat paradoxically—he feared that failure to provide them aid would lead, first, to their compromising with, or capitulating before, the Japanese and, then, to America's exclusion from China.

Washington officials did not delude themselves about the Kuomintang but felt that it had to be propped up and by November 1940 Roosevelt was urging a $100-million currency-stabilization loan, divided equally between the Treasury and the Reconstruction Finance Corporation. Appearing before the Senate Banking and Currency Committee in December, Hull scored Japanese aggression and made clear that sound currency was necessary to keep Chinese troops fighting and as "a symbol of the authority of the National Government."

The loan passed easily and was well received publicly, but Morgenthau thought that turning over so much money to the Kuomintang was "just like throwing it away." He wanted to dole out his half at $5 million monthly. When, in April 1941, the Chinese pressed for $50 million at once, he retorted, "They can go jump in the Yangtze." Roosevelt agreed with this position but told Morgenthau "it is a question of face saving" and persuaded him to give the Chinese their money at once, provided they pledged not to use it faster than $5 million monthly.

The question of military supplies was also difficult. Since 1937, Chiang's air adviser had been the retired U.S. Army Air Corps Captain Claire Chennault, who regarded Madame Chiang as "a princess" and claimed that long-range bombers manned by American pilots could destroy Japanese bases in China and carry the war to Tokyo. In December 1940, the Chinese asked for 500 planes: 200 long-range bombers and 300 fighters. Roosevelt thought that this signified their willingness to fight and reportedly said "Wonderful! This is what I have been talking about for four years." He told his Cabinet to work out the details, but Morgenthau thought that asking for 500 planes was "like asking for 500 stars," and Secretary of War Stimson derided the whole idea as "half baked." More politely, but no less firmly, Marshall said that the idea was impractical because neither planes nor pilots were available.

The British were opposed, fearing savage retaliation by Japan and recognizing that aid for China would come out of their allotment, but they were persuaded early in 1941 to give up 100 P-40 fighter planes. In April, Roosevelt, by executive order, allowed American pilots to enlist as mercenaries in the Chinese Air Force, receiving salaries of up to $750 monthly and $500 bounties for each Japanese plane shot down. Roosevelt sought to solve his money and supply problem by including China under Lend-Lease, placing responsibility for the flow of aid in the hands of White House Assistant Lauchlin Currie. The President appointed Owen Lattimore, newspaperman, businessman, and scholar, whom Admiral Harry Yarnell called "the greatest authority in America on China and Manchuria," as political adviser to Chiang.

The Chinese were less appreciative than might have been expected. They complained that the aid was insufficient, and that the Americans and British seemed more concerned over Japanese advances in Southeast Asia than aggression in China. They let it be known that they suspected that the Western powers were sustaining them only to divert Japanese attention from Western holdings in Asia. Lattimore soon felt that the Chinese should have been complaining less about lack of planes and artillery and focusing more on a strategy of guerrilla warfare. However, he said, "they don't have the confidence" for this and were too concerned with building the political machinery necessary to run China after the Western powers liberated them from the Japanese. Colonel George Sliney, artillery expert for the American Military Mission established in China in October 1941, complained that the Chinese were demanding so many supplies, not to fight the Japanese, but "to make the Central Government safe against insurrection" after other powers had defeated Japan. As head of the Military Mission, General John Magruder countered that if the Japanese were permitted to cut off the supplies to the Nationalists in Chungking, the army might collapse and "for the first time in this long war a real collapse of resistance would be possible," which might cause every other Asian nation to lose faith in democracy and precipitate an "unparalleled catastrophe."

By December 1941, the American dilemma over China was revealed. The Kuomintang, corrupt and with no inclination to change, seemed unwilling to defend its country against the Japanese, except insofar as mobilizing against them served as a pretext for war against the Communists. American officials had been unable to halt Japanese expansion in China by negotiation or rousing world opinion, nor had they been able to rouse the Kuomintang to reform or to a spirited defense of the country. Yet they felt compelled to supply more money and arms to the Kuomintang, partly because each allocation was intended to insure the investment the previous one represented, and partly because the administration feared the foreign and domestic political and economic consequences—as much imagined as real—of being responsible for the exclusion of the United States from China, as well as for the defeat, or "loss," of that country and the alleged effect that loss would have on the political and economic structure of the rest of Asia.

While officials thus worked out aid programs for China, at the start of 1941 their eyes were even more anxiously cast upon Japan's so-called Southward Advance. In January, the Japanese were pressing the Dutch East Indies for an unconditional flow of war matériel, the right to explore for oil and mineral deposits, and more residence and fishing privileges. At the same time, the government in Tokyo determined to force its mediation on Thailand and French Indochina, who were fighting over border provinces in the Mekong River region. In return, the Japanese were asking not only financial compensation but air and naval bases in Indochina near Saigon and at Camranh Bay and in Thailand near the Malay border. American diplomats in the region reported that the Japanese were underwriting the Thai air war in return for tin ore, rubber, and rice, and that their purpose was to drive the French from Indochina, taking Tonkin and Cochin China, leaving Laos and Cambodia to the Thais, and then using their bases in Thailand to challenge the British in Burma, in the Indian Ocean, and at Singapore.

By early February, Ambassador Grew was so depressed by Japan's demands and parading of forces, which were matched in part by the movement of Australian troops into Malaya and British requests for an American oil embargo against Japan and fleet movement to Singapore, that he concluded that the outlook had "never been darker." He later cabled Washington that Japan's Southward Advance had to be halted, that, while increased naval concentration entailed risks of war that should not be undertaken without readiness to fight, "those risks are less in degree than the future dangers which would inevitably confront us if we were to allow the Japanese advance to proceed indefinitely unchecked." But while the moment for "decisive action" was approaching, Grew recommended none.

Nor were officials in Washington ready to act. On January 6, Stanley Hornbeck, militantly unsympathetic to the Japanese, reminded the British that it was they who had always told the Americans "to go lightly" with oil embargoes lest they produce unfortunate repercussions in the Far East. The State Department soon persuaded the Standard Vacuum Oil Company to accept Japanese oil orders but to find reasons to delay deliveries. They also took all American tankers off the Japan route and restricted the use of storage, supply, and refining equipment.

The State Department showed a cautious attitude toward the Thai–French Indochina conflict, which the Japanese settled on March 11 by forcing the French to cede the rice-rich province of Battambang to Thailand and to pledge that Indochina would never be used by any other power for purposes hostile to Japan. The Japanese dropped their demand for bases and took a milder position in negotiations with the Dutch, who continued to resist their demands.

No one could account with certainty for the softer Japanese line, but Grew ascribed it to increasing doubt about a rapid German victory over England and recognition of a stronger American position that combined with their desire to avoid direct conflict with the United States. This did not mean that "Japan's long run policies have been scrapped or that the South Seas are less alluring than before," but that the Tokyo government had concluded that external and internal conditions counseled against action, and that "the wisest course is hesitation."

The Roosevelt administration had concluded that the Japanese did not want, or were not prepared for, war, and that the United States was not ready to make commitments to both the Atlantic and the Pacific theaters, a view that, Admiral Stark wrote in February, both he and the President shared. Equally significant, at this time public and private persons in both the United States and Japan were coming forward with proposals for negotiations between the twó countries.

Direct American-Japanese talks in 1941 were the brainchild of various persons, referred to within the State Department as the "John Doe Associates." These included Bishop James Walsh and Father James Drought of the Catholic Foreign Mission Society at Maryknoll, New York; Colonel Hideo Iwakuro, special adviser from the War Ministry to Japanese Ambassador Admiral Kichisaburo Nomura (who had just been persuaded to accept the Washington post because of his World War I acquaintance with then Assistant Secretary of the Navy Roosevelt); and Tadao Paul Wikawa, a Christian, English-speaking Japanese banker with an American wife. In late 1940, Bishop Walsh and Father Drought had talked with numerous officials in Japan, including Foreign Minister Matsuoka, and concluded that they wanted to improve relations. Working through Catholic Postmaster General Frank C. Walker, Drought and Walsh secured an interview with Roosevelt and Hull in January 1941 and put forward several proposals, including one that the President and Premier Konoye meet in Tokyo or Honolulu to reach a final agreement. For the next two months, they sent similar memoranda to the White House. Roosevelt was amenable to informal negotiations, and in his first meeting with Nomura on February 14, he emphasized that talks with Hull might be useful. The Secretary and ambassador met on March 8 for the first of about fifty meetings that they would hold before December, but they made no progress. Hull

lectured on public anxiety over the Axis Alliance and on the virtues of
the American liberal trading system over the "semi-barbarism" of the
military assault and rule some nations foisted on others, while Nomura
recounted how Japan had been discriminated against economically and
stressed that his country sought peace with China and America's friendship.

Father Drought pulled together a host of proposals into an "Agreement in Principle," which was reviewed and redrafted by Colonel Iwakuro—with Drought writing down the English equivalent of Wikawa's
oral translations of Iwakuro's changes, all of which were to Japan's
benefit. Anxious to get the negotiations under way, and convinced that
a Roosevelt-Konoye meeting could resolve ultimate differences, Drought
excitedly forwarded this new Draft Understanding to Hull on April 9.
The lengthy proposal stated that the Japanese would not be obligated
under the Tripartite Pact unless a signatory were "aggressively attacked," and that the United States would maintain its attitude toward
the European war solely on the basis of "protective defense" and "national security." In the Southwest Pacific, Japan would use only peaceful
means to secure oil, rubber, tin, and nickel, with the United States
helping Japan to gain these resources from the region and restoring
normal trade. Regarding the most significant issue, the Sino-Japanese
war, the United States would request the Kuomintang to negotiate a
peace agreement that would preserve China's independence and lead
to withdrawal of Japanese troops, although some would remain for
"joint defense against communistic activities and economic cooperation."
Chiang's government would have to coalesce with the Japanese-
backed regime of Wang Ching-wei in Nanking and recognize Manchukuo. The Open Door idea would be resumed, but interpretations and
application would have to be worked out. If the Chinese refused these
terms, the United States would cut off assistance. An American-
Japanese conference in Honolulu, opened by Roosevelt and Konoye,
would draft "instruments to effectuate" this agreement.

State Department officials felt that the Draft Understanding only provided for Japan to halt its Southward Advance in return for an unlimited
supply of war matériel, and that the United States would be virtually
guaranteeing either that China would make peace on terms that granted
Manchukuo to Japan, together with strong influence over the new coalition government in China, or that Japan could resume its war against
China without concern about third-party involvement. The Japanese
would be free to aid Germany if the United States decided to enter the
European war. Underlying these objections was Hornbeck's conviction
that negotiations would not help Japanese moderates wrest control from
the extremists, and that the Japanese would base their decision on

whether to move south solely on their estimate of the "physical situation" in both Europe and Asia. Hornbeck preferred "to deter Japan firmly but judiciously," with the hope that, if the British were sustained in Europe and the Japanese knew that an assault on British or Dutch holdings in the Pacific would lead to "a lengthy and probably disastrous war" (which would include America), they might turn from the Axis and toward a reasonable solution in China.

Hull agreed in the main, but nonetheless, on April 14, he got Nomura to agree that the Draft Understanding would be considered preliminary, with both sides free to put forth revisions or counterproposals. On April 16, Hull also presented Nomura with Four Points that were intended to establish the basis for talks. These included respect for every nation's sovereignty and territorial integrity, noninterference in other nations' internal affairs, support for the principle of equality of commercial opportunity, and nondisturbance of the *status quo* in the Pacific, except by peaceful means. Hull insisted that Japan endorse these principles and provide assurances that it would "abandon its present doctrine of military conquest" even before discussing the Draft Understanding. This he did despite the fact that most Great Powers had at one time subscribed to such principles and then violated them. Nomura posited Japan's position in Asia against America's "special relations" with Latin America and suggested that commercial equality might be discussed in conjunction with Sino-Japanese peace talks. Hull conceded that the *status quo* point would not be applied to Manchukuo until after a general settlement. Whatever the position of both men, and the points agreed on or not, Nomura was anxious for peace, but he was an amateur diplomat and only complicated prospects for understanding by not sending Hull's Four Points to Tokyo for a month and then giving the impression that he had shelved the issue. Not until September were the Japanese aware that they were important to Hull, and that they constituted a stumbling block to agreement. The Draft Understanding had reached Tokyo on April 17, but even here Nomura misled his superiors by describing it as an American offering rather than a joint American-Japanese (written by Iwakuro) preliminary basis for negotiations.

In the meantime, the Japanese Government, anxious to avoid a wider war in Asia but desiring to isolate the Chinese and secure diplomatic support for Japan's Greater East Asia sphere, in March 1941 dispatched Foreign Minister Matsuoka to Moscow. He failed to get agreement to a broad nonaggression pact that would have had the Russians recognize Japan's control of North China and Inner Mongolia, guarantee oil from northern Sakhalin, and cut off aid to the Kuomintang in return for Japan's recognizing Soviet control of Outer Mongolia and Sinkiang province. Matsuoka went to Berlin, where Hitler was silent about his plan to attack the Russians (so that the Japanese could not use this information to negotiate with them or the Americans). Seeking to use Japan as a Pacific dagger in order to intimidate the United States and Great Britain in the Atlantic, Hitler urged an assault on Singapore and pledged German support if Japan went to war with England, the United States, or the Soviet Union. Matsuoka returned to Moscow and on April 13 secured a limited pact pledging peaceful relations, neutrality in the event of third-party assaults, and respect for the territorial integrity of the Soviet Mongolian People's Republic and Manchukuo.

For the Japanese, this Russo-Japanese Neutrality Pact served conflicting purposes. Matsuoka's prestige was enhanced, and he believed that he could end the China Incident without negotiating with the United States. The Japanese Army's need or desire to secure its northern flank by attacking Russia was now abated, while the navy, hesitant to battle the Americans, could secure supplies in Thailand and Indochina and press for oil in the Dutch East Indies. Men of moderate viewpoint, such as Konoye, Interior Minister Baron Hiranuma, and their associates in business or imperial circles, thought that the Neutrality Pact would facilitate talks with the United States, and that these would ease the way to solution of the China conflict. They secured Hirohito's approval of the pact. On April 16, a Liaison Conference decided to use only political and economic pressure to advance Japan's cause in Southeast Asia, resorting to force only if Anglo-American-Dutch "encirclement" threatened the empire. The following day, the Drought-Iwakuro Draft Understanding arrived from Washington, and the Japanese Government was anxious to negotiate.

The fly in the diplomatic ointment was Matsuoka, who preferred to negotiate with the United States only through the threat of the Axis Alliance. He delayed approval of the Draft Understanding through textual objections, feigned illness, threats of resignation, and the ruse of an American-Japanese neutrality pact, which overture Hull discreetly turned aside on May 7. Finally, Matsuoka revised the Draft Understanding to state that Japan's purpose in the Axis Alliance was "defensive"—to keep current nonbelligerents out of the European war—and that the American attitude toward the war should be "directed by no such aggressive measures as to assist any one nation against another." The revised draft further provided that the United States would resume normal trade relations with Japan and request Chiang to negotiate peace on the basis of prior acceptance of Japan's November 1938 declaration of leadership of the New Order in Asia and Joint Declaration with Manchukuo and China (signed by Wang Ching-wei's regime in Nanking). Also provided for were recognition of the independence of Manchukuo and withdrawal of Japanese troops from China according to a bilateral agreement. If Chiang refused these terms for negotiations, the United States would end aid. Matsuoka dropped the previous pledge that Japan would use only peaceful means in the Southwest Pacific, and the stipulation for a Roosevelt-Konoye meeting was deleted—that is, postponed until the effect of an agreement could be assessed. These were the terms Nomura presented to Hull on May 12, 1941.

Even more than the Drought-Iwakuro Draft Understanding, this new draft was weighted in Japan's favor, especially with regard to opening negotiations with China, lack of a disclaimer on the use of force in the Southwest Pacific, and Japan's freedom of action under the Tripartite Pact and her ostensible challenge to American "aggressive" aid to Great Britain. Matsuoka told Ambassador Grew on May 14 and May 19 that, if the United States convoyed ships to England and this led to war with Germany, Japan would regard the United States as the aggressor and war would probably ensue. Understandably, Hull disliked the Japanese terms and felt matters were proceeding "hellward," although the administration was willing to iron out the differences.

The reasons for accommodation were twofold. Throughout the spring of 1941, American energies were devoted to organizing Lend-Lease, taking over defense of Greenland and Iceland, and keeping watch on the battle of the Atlantic, which included moving a quarter of the Pacific Fleet to that region and inaugurating the extended patrol system. Above all, Roosevelt did not want to antagonize Japan. When, on June 23—the day after the German assault on Russia—Ickes suggested an oil embargo, Roosevelt objected that this might "tip the delicate scales" and cause Japan to attack Russia or the Dutch East Indies. A week later, the President elaborated to Ickes that, while Japan might strike at Russia or the South Seas or "sit on the fence and be more friendly with us," control in the Atlantic depended upon peace in the Pacific: "I simply have not got enough Navy to go round—and every little episode in the Pacific means fewer ships in the Atlantic."

There was sentiment for détente with Japan for long-run purposes in the Pacific. When, in May, the State Department asked Grew to assess the Hull-Nomura talks and prospects for accord, the ambassador, in a turnabout from his coercive attitude in the "Green Light" telegram of September 1940 and the months thereafter, insisted that a majority of the Japanese Cabinet and imperial advisers wished to avoid conflict with the United States and were seeking an honorable release from their Tripartite Pact obligations. Grew sent numerous records of talks with confidants who insisted that Japan's intelligentsia and business leaders were far more attuned to the American political and economic systems than to their German counterparts. While Grew warned that the Japanese would maintain a highhanded diplomatic attitude toward the Dutch East Indies, they would avoid an attack that might imperil their position in South China or lead to a wider Pacific war. Roosevelt was disposed toward taking a patient and long-run view. When, on June 4, Morgenthau suggested that the cautious Hull be elevated to the Supreme Court, with Stimson becoming Secretary of State, the President retorted that he was not certain Stimson had been right regarding Manchuria in 1931, and that perhaps Hull's tactics would have been better.

The disinclination to antagonize Japan and the hope that a patient position might undercut Matsuoka and the pro-Axis element in Japan, open the way to a China settlement, and avoid a wider Pacific war led the State Department to undertake countless tedious reviews and redraftings (each followed by Hull-Nomura discussions) of Matsuoka's proposal of May 12, 1941. This was the document that the Japanese regarded as their answer to the "American plan" of April 16 (the Drought-Iwakuro Draft Understanding), and which the Americans regarded as an initial Japanese offer to establish the basis for negotiations. Under the circumstances, then, Washington and Tokyo officials tended to regard each other's counterproposals as a stiffening of position or an increase of demands.

Little progress was made during the next five weeks. The Japanese were prepared to limit their Tripartite Pact obligations to "defensive" moves only. They dropped references to aggressive American aid to Great Britain but reserved the right to act under the pact in event of an American-German war. The Japanese were willing to consider a staged withdrawal of troops from South China under a bilateral agreement with Chiang's regime, but they insisted on maintaining troops in other parts of China for "cooperative defense against communistic activities," matters of Sino-Japanese economic cooperation, and protection of Japanese interests. On June 21, Hull put forward an "unofficial, exploratory, and without comment" draft proposal asking that the bulk of Japanese troops in China be removed as soon as possible in accordance with a Sino-Japanese agreement, and that terms for the remaining troops be discussed later. Sino-Japanese economic cooperation was acceptable but not Japanese imperialism, and Manchukuo was left for "amicable negotiation." Hull attached an oral statement that was a characteristically doctrinaire reiteration of American principles and a challenge to Japan's sincerity in negotiation. He objected to recent public statements by influential, official persons that supported, and sought to exploit for Japan's advantage, Germany's "policies of conquest." He insisted that Japan's intention of retaining troops in Inner Mongolia and North China ran counter to America's "liberal policies," a polite way of saying that the troops were intended to maintain Japan's political and economic hegemony in those regions. Or, as Hull asked in an annex, did the Japanese intend to divest themselves of their monopolistic Development Companies in North and Central China and remove restrictions on trade, currency, and the movement of foreign personnel there?

Hull's position, or questions, subscribed to by the President and most officials, reflected concern for his Four Points, American national interests, and immediate geopolitical considerations. Unfortunately, various concerns were not always differentiated or were too easily fused, and there was an assumption that American principles or interests were compatible with those of other nations. If there was concern for China's sovereignty and for the principle of noninterference in other nations' internal affairs, there was equal concern for America's financial or trading position in China. If there was concern for the "rule of law" and peaceful change in international affairs, there was equal concern for the effect the Tripartite Pact would have, or was intended to have, on American freedom in regard to the conflicts in Europe and Asia.

The Japanese could not give Hull answers without carefully assessing their effect on Japan's domestic and foreign political and economic structure, given that nation's commitment of funds, troops, and national prestige in the China war. Not surprisingly, Nomura insisted on modifications before putting Hull's questions to his government, and Iwakuro and Wikawa said on July 2 that the Japanese could not, as Hull wanted, give evidence that their intentions would be in harmony with the spirit of an agreement with the United States until after reaching such an agreement. Japan could make no further diplomatic or field concessions without an accord with the United States. By this time, political and military events and decisions were again about to overtake diplomacy.

On June 10, 1941, the Dutch refused further economic concessions in the East Indies to the Japanese. Although the Japanese took no action, they determined to secure for themselves a supply of oil large enough to enable them to keep open every diplomatic or military option. Beginning on June 22, the Germans pressed the Japanese to attack Russia as well as Singapore. Matsuoka wanted to oblige, but the Cabinet and military preferred "watchful waiting." This led to the July 2 Imperial Conference decisions to (1) establish the Greater East Asia Co-Prosperity Sphere (including Southeast Asia and the East Indies), regardless of international developments; (2) settle the China Incident on a secure basis, which involved advancing into the southern regions and settling the Russian question; and (3) carry out this program "no matter what obstacles may be encountered."

The means to achieve these goals included movements into Indochina and Thailand to pressure Chiang's regime to "surrender"; negotiation with the United States and preparation for war against America and England; nonintervention in the German-Soviet war, unless imminent German victory provided the occasion for Japan to strike at Russia and secure for itself the fruits of victory; and fulfillment, at Japan's convenience, of its Tripartite Pact obligations if America entered the European war.

The Japanese Government hoped to assuage all sides contending for control of foreign policy, settle the China Incident, and obtain imperial self-sufficiency without war with the United States and England—unless necessary. The military were not ready to fight Russia and believed that the Southward Advance would increase its preparedness and budget allocation and not precipitate war with the United States. Konoye could resume negotiation with the United States. On July 12, the Japanese demanded that the Vichy French assent to their occupation of Indochina or face military seizure. Only Matsuoka wanted to attack Russia and not negotiate with the United States, and he sought to precipitate a crisis that would vindicate him then or later. Without Cabinet approval, he instructed Nomura on July 14 to demand retraction of Hull's "offensive" oral statement of June 21, which, surprisingly, the State Department did, with appropriate face-saving reservations. But Matsuoka had overreached himself at home, and Konoye and the military eliminated him by having the entire Cabinet resign on July 16 and reconstituting it with Konoye as Premier and Admiral Teijiro Toyoda, a relative moderate and friend of Nomura, as Foreign Minister. At the same time, the Japanese forced an agreement on Vichy, and on July 24 they began to move a force of 50,000 into southern Indochina, including Saigon and the nearby air bases and Camranh Bay.

American officials watched Japanese developments with cautious concern. They correctly surmised that Japanese behavior toward the German-Soviet war would be opportunistic, and this constituted reason to aid the Soviet Union and the Kuomintang in order to keep the Japanese bogged down in south China. Through MAGIC (the intercepting and deciphering of Japan's diplomatic codes that had begun in mid-1940), American officials knew the gist of the July 2 imperial decisions—although not the untransmitted means for carrying them out—but were inclined to negotiate, as indicated by retraction of Hull's oral statement. Japan's Cabinet shake-up of July 16 was seen as loosening ties with Germany, and when, on July 18, Morgenthau asked Roosevelt about economic retaliation or oil sanctions if the Japanese occupied Indochina, the President again retorted that this would only drive them to more drastic moves, a view the navy seconded. Only at Ickes' urging and partly because gasoline rationing was about to begin on the East

Coast, did Roosevelt agree to a reduction of the octane level of gasoline exported to Japan.

Western attitudes did stiffen on the eve of Japan's occupation of Indochina, which threatened the British at Singapore and the Dutch East Indies. Hull raged about Hitlerian methods in Asia but counseled only verbal protests. On July 24, Roosevelt tried to warn the Japanese that it might provoke an American oil embargo, but simultaneously he suggested that Indochina might be neutralized, with the Japanese obtaining foodstuffs and resources peacefully. When the occupation began, Roosevelt on July 26 froze Japanese assets in America and embargoed high-octane (military) gasoline, bringing trade to a grinding halt. Philippine forces were mustered into the United States Army under General Douglas MacArthur, while the British and Dutch froze Japan's assets and abrogated their trade agreements.

Ickes believed that Roosevelt did not want to strangle the Japanese but to "slip the noose around their necks" and "give it a jerk every now and then." The President probably hoped to "jerk" them back to a more peaceful behavior or perhaps entice them toward a *quid pro quo,* or away from war, by proposing to neutralize Indochina. The Japanese viewed economic and oil sanctions as proof of the Western effort to encircle them and deprive them of their empire, and they sidestepped the neutralization scheme by saying that their occupation was peaceful and for self-defense.

Konoye began to search for the means to an accord with the United States. Through Nomura on August 6, he proposed that Japan would put no more troops in the Southwest Pacific and would withdraw those in Indochina after settlement of the China Incident. In return, the United States would suspend its military build-up in the Southwest Pacific and help Japan gain resources from there and the East Indies. The United States would also resume trade, recognize Japan's special status in Indochina, and use its good offices to get Sino-Japanese peace talks under way. Weeks later, Nomura added that the Japanese could not conceive of fighting the United States for Germany's sake, and that they regarded the Tripartite Pact as merely nominal, although they could not nullify it.

The concessions were minor. The Japanese did not state terms for peace with China and would withdraw troops from Indochina in return for the United States's supplying, or underwriting, Japan's claim to needed trade, resources (including war matériel), and implied economic hegemony over much of Asia. America, meanwhile, might deal with its Atlantic problem free from fear of a Japanese attack.

These terms appear to have been less important to Konoye than his proposal now to meet with Roosevelt to reach a general settlement. To obtain approval for this meeting, Konoye held extensive discussions with the Cabinet, the military, and Lord Privy Seal Marquis Kido, who had frequent contact with the Emperor. The discussions revealed that Japan had about an eighteen-month supply of oil, which, in light of the Western embargo, meant that the problem of access to supplies had to be resolved within that time. Since it would take at least a year to secure control of Singapore and the East Indies and restore the wells the Dutch would undoubtedly blow up, the Japanese felt they had to choose the means by which they would resolve their Pacific course, and the nation's fate, very soon. Marquis Kido preferred a ten-year austerity program, but the military would not agree to this equivocal course. They would assent to a conference with two critical conditions. Konoye had to insist upon the Greater East Asia Co-Prosperity Sphere, and if the conference failed, as War Minister Tojo wrote to him, "you shall be prepared to assume leadership in the war against America." Upon instruction, Nomura on August 8 gingerly approached Hull about a Roosevelt-Konoye meeting and then put the idea to Roosevelt on August 17, while Foreign Minister Toyoda enlisted Grew's support.

The conference proposal aroused far less enthusiasm in Washington than the Japanese had anticipated. Whereas Konoye thought he was now consenting to the "American plan" of April (the Drought-Iwakuro Draft Understanding), the State Department thought he was renewing an offer made by the Japanese and "deleted" by them in their May 12 proposals. With Roosevelt just having returned from the Atlantic Conference, the prospect of his meeting with the head of a state hostile to England and Russia, "allied" to the German enemy, and at war with China posed diplomatic complications and raised the public issue of the specter of appeasement and a Far Eastern Munich.

More important, Hull believed that the Japanese had to choose between advancing further south or turning to a peaceful course. He insisted that they always offered "false and fraudulent avowals of peace . . . until they get ready to go forward." Nothing would stop them except force—which he did not favor—but he believed it best to "maneuver the situation until the military matter in Europe is brought to a conclusion." Stimson was of like mind, and together they concluded that the conference proposal was "merely a blind to try to keep us from taking definite action" while the Japanese moved on Indochina and Thailand.

The strongest urging for the conference came from Grew. As ambassador to Tokyo for a decade, he had to be disposed toward negotiations lest war ensue and his mission end in failure, and he saw the "unprecedented" invitation as a dividend of his get-tough policy of September 1940 and a sign that the extremists were not yet predominant.

From mid-August to October 1941, he insisted that the meeting would bring incalculable good, and he urged constructive conciliation—as opposed to appeasement—which would uphold American principles and induce the Chinese to surrender some sovereignty and qualify the Open Door. Grew did not recommend either specific Chinese concessions or acceptance of Japan's negotiating position, and he insisted that the United States could not demand clear-cut or concise assurances that were alien to the Japanese mind. His solution was to rely on Konoye's good will.

Roosevelt took a middle-ground position. He did not reply when Nomura on August 17 proposed the conference to him; he merely presented the State Department's post–Atlantic Conference, watered-down warning about further southward movement by Japan. In a second interview on August 28, Roosevelt expressed interest in meeting Konoye —for convenience, in Juneau, Alaska, rather than Hawaii—but he noted that the Premier's invitation offered no guarantee against Japanese advances during the talks, and he brushed aside Japan's fears about Russia or oil shortages.

The result was the inevitable compromise—two statements by Roosevelt for Konoye on September 3, one expressing interest in a meeting, the other insisting that clear agreement on Hull's Four Points was a condition for negotiations. The Americans also said that they would have to be in close touch with the Chinese, and that they had serious reservations about Japan's Tripartite Pact obligations, retention of troops in North China and Inner Mongolia, and discriminatory trade policies there.

Konoye was desperate to meet by late September. He was disappointed with Roosevelt's reply and the delay it implied in terms of achieving agreement on the conditions for a meeting. On September 6, he reiterated the Japanese terms, adding that they would remove their troops from China "as soon as possible" after concluding a treaty. He asked that the United States do nothing to obstruct a treaty. Konoye assured Grew at a secret meeting that Hull's Four Points were splendid as a basis for rehabilitating American-Japanese relations, and he pleaded for the conference to reconcile differences. In deliberations independent of diplomacy, the Japanese military, at a Liaison Conference on September 3, agreed that, if by October there were no prospects of their demands' being met, they would open hostilities against the United States, Great Britain, and the Netherlands. The Cabinet voted its approval next day, as did an Imperial Conference on September 6, although the Emperor, in an unprecedented action, broke his silence to speak in poetry about his despair at current "winds and waves of strife." At this the military pledged that war would be a last resort only.

The State Department was unmoved. Konoye's concession appeared to be relieving the United States of responsibility for the final terms, or outcome, of Sino-Japanese negotiations by not requesting America's good offices to get them started. Hull insisted that Japan's terms for peace with China affected all nations with interests in the Pacific, and an American-Japanese conference was unthinkable before knowing these terms. Nor would the United States pledge not to obstruct a Sino-Japanese agreement by cutting off aid to China. The initiative returned to Japan to propose acceptable peace terms with China before meeting with the United States.

Konoye reiterated the Japanese position on September 25 and asked for American good offices to achieve a settlement with China that would include recognition of Manchukuo, fusion of Chiang's government in Chungking with Wang's in Nanking, Sino-Japanese economic collaboration, and stationing of troops in China to ensure against "communistic and other subversive activities." These were nearly the terms the Japanese had been pressing since March; they were highly advantageous to them, if reasonable by their standards and not disproportionate to their decade or more investment of men, money, and national prestige in China.

Hull clung to his stock objections to Japanese troops in China, trade and resource preferences, and a nominal commitment to the Tripartite Pact and even argued that these terms constituted a narrowed Japanese position since they had originally sought a conference, and an agreement, on the basis of his Four Points without reservations. Roosevelt agreed, and Stimson added that the Japanese were "rattled and scared" by economic sanctions and the dispatch of bombers to the Philippines, and that a conference would lead to concessions "highly dangerous to our vitally important relations with China."

Suspicions about Japanese purposes were heightened by reports of military encroachments and violation of foreign rights in Indochina, which allowed Hornbeck to argue that either the Japanese Government could not control its military or it was "sanctioning and ordering a new step in the national program of conquest." Military Intelligence (G-2) reported that neither economic concessions nor a heads-of-state meeting would be worthwhile without a Japanese pledge both to quit the Tripartite Pact and not to attack Siberia, which was unlikely. The proper American course, then, was "power diplomacy."

The Americans told Konoye on October 2 that a conference was possible only after the Japanese had clarified their position on the Tripartite Pact and trade discrimination, and—the crux of it all—after they had given a "clear-cut manifestation" of their intent to withdraw troops from Indochina and China. If the document was ambiguous for diplomacy's sake, its meaning was not. To satisfy the American position,

Japan would have to endorse Hull's Four Points, quit the Tripartite Pact, agree to equality of commercial opportunity in Asia, and, above all, begin to withdraw from China.

Konoye understood this, although he made a final desperate effort to bridge the Japanese-American gap by throwing out to both the State Department and a conference of his own ministers on October 12 an "in principle" troop withdrawal from China, with the Chinese accepting reduced Japanese forces for peacekeeping. The Americans remained rigid and skeptical, while the Japanese Army refused the procedure as jeopardizing their position in Manchukuo and Korea.

The conference idea was dead, and Konoye, having reached the limit of his mandate, resigned on October 15. Until the present day, men have debated whether Roosevelt ought to have met with Konoye and perhaps thereby averted a war in the Pacific. Konoye was sincere, almost heroic, in his effort to reach an accord, even while he presided over, and was captive of, the imperial conferences that committed Japan to war if diplomacy failed. Possibly a summit conference would have generated a "spirit of Juneau," assuaged the governments and people of both nations, and provided at least a temporary reprieve from war. Whether Konoye could have carried his government, or controlled the military and gotten them first to agree to terms and then to honor them, was arguable, and at that he feared the likelihood of assassination.

The failure to agree to a summit conference was, of course, intertwined with, and symptomatic of, the failure to break the American-Japanese diplomatic impasse. The negotiations that had arisen within the context of the efforts of the John Doe Associates were fraught with confusion over who proposed what and when, and they were impinged upon by domestic political and international alliance complications. If the American public took a hardline view toward Japan and regarded China as a friend in need, Japanese extremists fired their public with visions of imperial destiny and animosity toward any nation that stood in the way. If the Japanese could not renounce the Axis Alliance—conceived as power diplomacy to intimidate opponents of their Asian policies—the United States could not appear to engage in any settlement that might leave the British feeling that they might have to go it alone in a second war in the Far East. Nor could they become involved in any arrangement that might undermine Russian resistance in Europe or the resistance of the Chinese, which kept the Japanese bogged down.

If the Japanese believed that their lack of resources forced an immediate choice between accord with the United States or war, Roosevelt took a more cavalier, or advantageous, view of time. As he wrote to both Churchill and King George VI on October 15, he was convinced that the Japanese would not undertake a Pacific war until the Russians were beaten, which meant at least two months of respite, and equally important in his eyes, public opinion and war production were improving daily—both of which, in his view, strengthened his hand in European or Asian undertakings. In addition, a summit meeting or negotiations that failed might precipitate a crisis for which the United States was not prepared.

The barrier to American-Japanese understanding was the way in which each nation viewed its traditions and causes. If Konoye represented a moderate element seeking accord, clearly the moderates, no less than the civilian extremists or the army, could not envision any settlement that did not grant recognition of Manchukuo and political and economic hegemony over Inner Mongolia and North China, preferences in Indochina, and dominance over the Western Pacific. Even the navy, which traditionally shied away from war with the United States, demanded a Southward Advance at the risk of war to ensure oil and other supplies. To an extent that the Japanese themselves did not perceive, in 1941 the disagreement between moderates and extremists, or civilians and military, was as much over tactics as goals. The moderates opted for a more subtle or flexible approach but were equally, and firmly, wedded to the Greater East Asia Co-Prosperity Sphere.

American officials, with almost astonishing rigidity and without regard for Far Eastern realities, accepted and defended precepts of American diplomacy from John Hay's Open Door policy in 1899–1900, through Woodrow Wilson's opposition to Japan's Twenty-one Demands upon China, to Stimson's nonrecognition policy of 1931–33. Occasionally, Roosevelt and some State Department people were prepared to make concessions or gloss violations of the faith, but to recognize such a breach in a formal document was almost unthinkable. And back of that was the fear that one breach might undermine the moral or legal precepts that they believed were the foundation of American diplomacy and world order. While American statesmen were deeply concerned about trade and investment in China and the whole Far East and had battled British imperial practices and interests as much as those of the Japanese, by 1941 national and economic interests were so shrouded in universal, legal, and moral precepts that they could hardly tell which was which, or likely assumed that they were indivisible, if not identical. It is clear that, while American diplomats did not take all that seriously the military aspects of the Axis Alliance, they did view it as an aggressive alliance designed to blackmail other powers, and in that sense they saw it, and the wars in Europe and Asia, as part of a program of global conquest or lawlessness, regardless of whether Japan and Germany actually coordinated their policies.

Finally, American diplomats lacked faith in the Japanese. They did not think that the Japanese wanted a summit meeting solely to forestall American action, but they doubted that they would honor a negotiated settlement or feared that their military might run amok during a conference, with the Tokyo government again saying it was unable to reverse a *fait accompli*. Either development would have been politically damaging to the Roosevelt administration at home and abroad, and even Konoye acknowledged as legitimate the distrust that militated against acceptance of his proposal. While it is fair to argue that American diplomats ought to have taken a chance at a summit meeting, and exchanged a Pacific *modus vivendi* for a free hand in Europe, this required not only a diplomatic-military reassessment but a sharp psychological break with traditions and modes of thinking past and present—perhaps even a re-evaluation of America's needs and responsibilities in Asia. Tragically, neither in the United States nor in Japan were many minds open to readjustments.

Negotiation continued after October 15, although it was virtually inevitable that it would prove useless. War Minister Hideki Tojo succeeded Konoye as Prime Minister. Although Tojo had been Chief of Staff of the Kwantung (Manchurian) Army during 1936–37 and was closely identified with Japan's involvement in China, foreign response to his accession to power was calm. As Grew noted, Tojo would be able to command both the army and the government (as Konoye had not), and he would be able to make the military responsible for, and adhere to, government policies. Both American and British military intelligence concluded that, for the time being, the Japanese would not move south, except perhaps into Thailand, and that they were more likely to strike at Vladivostok or the Soviet Maritime provinces. When Tojo formed his Cabinet, the Emperor commanded a full reappraisal of Japan's situation. This "clean slate" message meant that Tojo was not bound by the Imperial Conference decision of September 6 to go to war in October if negotiations with the United States were failing. Tojo and the Japanese did not view his coming to power as expressly to make war but to act decisively where Konoye had not.

Cabinet and military officials met in nearly continuous Liaison Conference sessions between October 23 and November 2. With the military insistent on a clear-cut policy, they decided to make two proposals to the United States. If these failed, war would follow. The Emperor was apprised, and on November 5 the Imperial Conference ratified the program. Japan's Plan A was a comprehensive long-range agreement consisting of one new point and three familiar ones. New was the offer of economic equality for all powers in China, if this nondiscriminatory policy was adopted throughout the world. Familiar were the proposals to withdraw forces from Indochina and China (an unspecified number were to be retained for twenty-five years in North China, Inner Mongolia, and on the Island of Hainan) and to interpret the Tripartite Pact defensively if the United States would give assurances that it would not take advantage of this interpretation in defining its attitude toward the European war. Implicit was the assumption that the United States would urge the Chinese toward a settlement and cut off aid if they proved intransigent. If Plan A was rejected, the Japanese would propose Plan B—a short-term *modus vivendi* calling for the end of mutual economic sanctions and suspension of American aid to China while Sino-Japanese peace talks began. If this was rejected, a decision for war would be placed before the Emperor on November 25, a date later postponed to November 29. To show their earnestness about negotiation, the Japanese announced on November 4 that they were sending Saburo Kurusu, a skilled diplomat and former ambassador to Germany, to assist Nomura. At the same time, Admiral Osami Nagano, Chief of Naval Operations, who had opposed both the Tripartite Pact and war with the United States, accepted Admiral Isoroku Yamamoto's plan to attack the American fleet at Pearl Harbor if Japan opted for war. In case this option were decided upon, on November 5 operational orders were issued for an assault on American, British, and Dutch territories, and on November 7 the date was set for December 8 (Japanese time), 1941.

At just the moment the Japanese were preparing another long-term proposal, the Roosevelt administration was concluding, on the basis of the March-October negotiations, that there was no chance to achieve such an accord. Such a conclusion meant avoiding, not precipitating, war. On November 5, the Joint Board of the Army and Navy, in a summary report, told Roosevelt that Germany was the primary and most dangerous enemy, and that any Pacific war would greatly weaken the struggle in the Atlantic. General Marshall and Admiral Stark insisted that war had to be avoided with Japan unless it attacked American, British, or Dutch territory or moved into Thailand West of 100° East, from where it would menace the British in Burma and the Indian Ocean. They insisted that no American forces be sent to assist the Chinese (supplies, however, would be continued) and no ultimatum be delivered to Japan. The next day, Roosevelt suggested a six month Sino-Japanese military truce or standstill, but Stimson doubted that the Chinese would be amenable. On November 7, the Cabinet, accepting Hull's view that the military had to remain alert for an attack "anywhere by Japan at any time," decided that negotiations would continue to allow a build-up of defensive forces in the Far East. At the same time, the administration would try to prepare the public to support a declaration of war if the Japanese attacked only British or Dutch territory.

When Nomura broached Plan A, Hull put him off with comments about how Japan might help lead the world toward peaceful solutions by removing troops from China. Roosevelt was equally evasive on November 10, and on November 15 Hull insisted that no agreement was possible unless the Tripartite Pact was abandoned or a dead letter, and the United States could not agree to a policy of world commercial non-discrimination because this involved realms in which other nations were sovereign. Two days later, Hull told the newly arrived Ambassador Kurusu that Japan was trying to dominate the Pacific "entirely, politically, economically, socially and otherwise." Plan A was talked to death, with the Japanese complaining to, or warning, Grew that they were shocked by the American failure to grasp the urgent need for an immediate accord.

Now, on November 17, Treasury Secretary Morgenthau put forward a proposal, drafted by his aide Harry Dexter White, whose purpose was stated in the title: An Approach to the Problem of Eliminating Tension with Japan and Insuring the Defeat of Germany. White proposed that the United States withdraw the bulk of its forces from the Pacific, place Indochina under a five-power commission (including America and Japan), with commercial equality for all, and sign with Japan both a twenty-year nonaggression pact and a trade agreement, giving as many concessions as possible, including a $2-billion credit at just 2 per cent annual interest. White also proposed that the Japanese withdraw all forces from China (to the 1931 level), Indochina, Thailand, and Manchuria (except for police purposes); recognize only Chiang Kai-shek's regime; sell three-fourths of its war-matériel production to the United States; and sign a nonaggression pact with the British, Chinese, Dutch East Indies, and Philippines.

White was proposing radical American economic concessions to appease the Japanese, while demanding that they abandon a generation of striving and commitment to their empire. Although some historians have viewed the White proposal as more generous to Japan than Hull's position, there is no reason to think that the Japanese woud have been the least interested. It is difficult to regard the contemporary comment by Maxwell Hamilton, chief of the Far Eastern Division, that White's plan was "the most constructive one I've seen yet," as anything other than a reflection of the desire to achieve any accord possible. Desire for even a temporary arrangement was running high, and on November 17 Roosevelt himself jotted down the basis for a six-month accord, which included resumption of economic relations ("some oil and rice now—more later"); no further Japanese troop reinforcements in Indochina or Manchuria or Southern Asia; no invocation of the Tripartite Pact, even if the United States entered the European war; and an agreement that the

United States would "introduce" the Chinese to the Japanese for peace talks but not take any part in them.

Reviews of the Roosevelt-White proposals showed that the military felt that a *modus vivendi* with Japan based on economic concessions would achieve time to reinforce the Philippines and concentrate on the Atlantic war, but Admiral Stark strongly opposed reduction of Far Eastern forces. State Department officials wanted to limit the *modus vivendi* to three months, and to restrict economic concessions to a mutual unfreezing of assets, with the British and French encouraged to follow suit. There would be no further military advance in Asia, and while the Japanese could retain their troops in Manchuria and China, they would have to withdraw from southern Indochina and keep only 25,000 in the north, which would eliminate the threat to the British and Dutch and ease pressure on the Chinese in Chungking.

While the State Department was preparing this *modus vivendi,* the Japanese on November 20 put forward Plan B, which similarly proposed a mutual halt of troop reinforcements and resumption of commercial relations; but, they stipulated, they would withdraw from Indochina only after a peace agreement with China, while the United States meanwhile would have to provide oil and end aid to China. Although Plan B would have left Japan in position to mount a final offensive against China, and despite even the MAGIC intercept of November 22 of the Foreign Ministry message to Nomura that the new deadline for negotiations was postponed to November 29, after which "things are automatically going to happen," American diplomats decided to make the revised Roosevelt-White proposals the basis for a reply to Plan B. In the meantime, they canvassed foreign views. On November 24, Roosevelt sent Churchill his *modus vivendi,* calling it a "fair proposition," but, he said, he did not have much hope that it would be accepted, and that "we must all be prepared for real trouble, possibly soon."

On the morning of November 25, Hull and Stimson discussed the *modus vivendi,* which Stimson felt safeguarded American interests by insisting that the Japanese halt all aggressive acts and evacuate the bulk of their forces from threatening positions, in return for American trade, commercial credits, and oil for civilian purposes. Stimson, however, did not think the Japanese would agree. Shortly thereafter, the two men joined Roosevelt, Knox, Marshall, and Stark for a War Council meeting, where anticipation and pessimism ran high. Roosevelt, as Stimson noted in his diary, commented that "we were likely to be attacked perhaps (as soon as) next Monday [December 1], for the Japanese are notorious for making an attack without warning." Thus, "the question was how we should maneuver them into the position of firing the first shot without allowing too much danger to ourselves. It was a difficult proposition."

Stimson's diary entry has led some critics to conclude that the administration sought to provoke the Japanese to war, perhaps with the fleet at Pearl Harbor as a lure, while administration defenders have argued that the diary entry was hurried or elliptic and thus misleading. The context of the November 25 meeting affords the best explanation. Clearly, the administration was seeking to avoid, even if only temporarily, a Pacific war in order to continue to reinforce the Philippines and to concentrate on the Atlantic. That was the purpose of the *modus vivendi*. The Americans were on guard against an assault on the Philippines or Hawaii but believed that the Japanese were far more likely to attack Thailand, the British in Burma and Singapore, and the Dutch East Indies, where major assaults came on December 7. What the Roosevelt administration feared was an attack on *only* British or Dutch territory, which would leave it constitutionally (and militarily) unable to respond. Hence the earlier November 7 Cabinet decision to rouse the public to regard an attack on British or Dutch territory as an attack on American territory, and now a November 25 War Council decision, as recorded by Stimson, to draft a message warning the Japanese that, if they crossed a certain line—that is, if they entered the Isthmus of Kra, breaking into the Indian Ocean toward Burma—and "if the British fought, we would have to fight." What Roosevelt had probably meant by his "we" was an editorial "our side," which included the British and Dutch; what he expected was a Japanese attack in Southeast Asia only; and what he wanted was to take a position, so that, if Japan also attacked American territory, this would not hurt too much, but that, regardless of where Japan attacked, the United States would consider it an act of war.

Hull left the War Council meeting intending to offer the Japanese a *modus vivendi*. Immediately he ran into objections. The Dutch were acquiescent but thought that the oil allotment had to be cut back. Chinese Ambassador Hu Shih virulently opposed Japan's retaining even 25,000 troops in northern Indochina, and cables from Chiang Kai-shek and American political adviser Owen Lattimore were adamant that a *modus vivendi* with the Japanese would undermine China's ability to resist and destroy America's prestige there, as the British had learned after they closed the Burma Road in 1940. Churchill now replied to Roosevelt's inquiry that he was proposing a "very thin diet" for the Chinese, and that, "if they collapse, our joint dangers would enormously increase." The British, Ambassador Lord Halifax explained, felt that the United States at least ought to "pitch its demands high and offering price low" and insist that Japan remove *all* army, air, and naval forces from Indochina.

Hull tried to argue that the purpose of the *modus vivendi* was to reduce the pressure on the Chinese, but he was clearly shaken by the cross-current of objections, tired of the months of tedious negotiations, and perhaps never wholly hopeful of, nor disposed to, real agreement. He was further dismayed by Stimson's report that G-2 had sighted some thirty to fifty Japanese troop transports off Formosa moving south (an expeditionary force that would attack Malaya), while five other divisions were moving from North China toward Shanghai. Hull decided to abandon the *modus vivendi* and substitute a "comprehensive basic proposal," as he told Roosevelt, who agreed next morning. Why the President did so is uncertain, but evidently he was swayed when, just before Hull arrived, Stimson telephoned to discuss the Japanese transport movements, a report of which he had sent to Roosevelt the previous evening, but which the President had not yet seen. Roosevelt, according to Stimson, then "fairly blew up—jumped up into the air so to speak . . . and said that changed the whole situation because it was an evidence of bad faith on the part of the Japanese that while they were negotiating for an entire truce, an entire withdrawal, they should be sending this expedition down there to Indochina."

Hull presented his Ten Point Note of November 26, which offered the Japanese concessions such as having their assets unfrozen, a trade agreement, and stabilization of the dollar-yen rate. In return, the Japanese were required to withdraw all forces from Indochina and *all* of China, including Manchuria; recognize only Chiang's government; sign a multilateral nonaggression pact covering the Pacific, and abandon the Tripartite Pact. Strictly speaking, this was not an ultimatum, for the United States neither proposed deadlines for troop withdrawals nor threatened action. Even Ambassador Grew, upon learning of the proposal on November 29, concluded that it was "a broad-gauge, objective, and statesmanlike document," which would allow Japan to obtain without further fighting its requisite "strategic, economic, finanical, and social security"—unless Japan wanted a "political and economic stranglehold on East Asia" and was determined to fight everyone.

The Ten Point Note, however, which Roosevelt told Stimson was a "magnificent statement" of American principles, could also be seen as a maximal, or uncompromising, reiteration of the American position, which looked toward a return to the pre-1931 *status quo*. The Japanese certainly would not accept the proposal at once, and the type of long-term negotiations required, such as had been in process since February, were now ending. Washington diplomats knew this, although they did not know or think that the Japanese would necessarily go to war immediately. They thought it likely that the Japanese would deliberately refrain from attacking American territory. Even such a "hardliner" as Stanley Hornbeck insisted to Hull on November 27 that the odds were

5–1 against the United States's being at war by December 15, 3–1 against war by January 15, and only 1–1 against war by March 1. Washington officials nonetheless decided on November 27 to send "war warnings" to their Pacific forces, but they neglected to tell the military chiefs in Washington that they were sending the Japanese the Ten Point Note only—not the *modus vivendi,* too—which might have reduced slightly the military's sense of urgency about impending events.

Admiral Stark, on November 24, already had informed Admiral Husband E. Kimmel, commander of the Pacific Fleet at Pearl Harbor, and Admiral Thomas C. Hart, commander of the Asiatic Fleet, that successful negotiations were "very doubtful" and to be alert for "a surprise aggressive movement in any direction," including Guam and the Philippines. Stark reiterated on November 27 that negotiations had "ceased," that this dispatch was a "war warning," and that an "aggressive movement" in "a few days" was likely against the Philippines, Thailand, the Kra Isthmus, or Borneo. Similarly, Stimson and Marshall informed General MacArthur in the Philippines, and General Walter Short, commander in Hawaii, that negotiations were virtually over and to take appropriate measures. If hostilities came, Japan had to "commit the first overt act," the military was told; it was instructed not to jeopardize American defense but "not, repeat not, to alarm the civil population or disclose intent." The message seemed perfectly clear to Stimson, who was close to the negotiations and assumed that "sentinels" never relax their guard for a second. But Short later called this cable a misleading "do/don't" message, an apt description of the message's ambiguous language, perhaps, but not a sufficient explanation of Short's, or the military's, unpreparedness in Hawaii and elsewhere. This same message was repeated to Admirals Hart and Kimmel on November 28, while the War Council concluded that the Japanese could not be allowed to move uncontested around southern Indochina or penetrate the Gulf of Siam or the Kra Isthmus and decided that Roosevelt should address Congress and appeal to the Emperor.

Meanwhile, Ambassadors Nomura and Kurusu had received Hull's Ten Point Note; they were disappointed but did not take it as an ultimatum. They broached an American-Japanese mid-Pacific conference (without heads of state), while urging their own government to make a counterproposal. But the Cabinet in Tokyo decided on November 29 that war was inevitable, and it brushed aside pleas to continue negotiations, or only to break relations, from the Elder Statesmen (the former Prime Ministers), including Prince Konoye and Admiral Yonai. The next day, a Liaison Conference unanimously confirmed the war decision, allowing only, at the Emperor's request, for a final note to the United States formally breaking both negotiations and diplomatic relations. The

Imperial Conference, with the Emperor remaining silent, ratified the decision on December 1, and the following day imperial headquarters instructed the fleet, which had left the Kuriles on November 25, to "Climb Mount Niitaka"—the signal to attack Pearl Harbor.

The Japanese had been pressing the Germans for assurances in event of hostilities, and by November 29 Ribbentrop had asserted that "Germany would of course join the war immediately" and sign a no-separate-peace pact. "The Fuehrer is determined on that point." After the war, Ribbentrop insisted that Ambassador Hiroshi Oshima had misinterpreted him. Regardless, throughout the autumn the Germans had been encouraging the Japanese to take a threatening diplomatic line with the United States and to attack the British, and during December 2–5 the Germans and Japanese negotiated a full military assistance and no-separate-peace treaty for Tripartite Pact members, which required only signing by the time events made this unnecessary.

During the first week of December, American officials in Washington remained almost mesmerized by the enveloping crisis and divided over what to do. There were reports of an enormous Japanese troop build-up in Indochina, and MAGIC intercepted Foreign Minister Shigenori Togo's order to embassies on December 1 to destroy all diplomatic codes and his message to Oshima the next day that war might come "quicker than anyone dreams."

On November 30, Churchill urged Roosevelt to warn the Japanese that further aggression would force the issue to be placed before Congress. Stimson, prepared to fight at once and supported by Hopkins, wanted a message sent to Congress about the community of American, British, and Dutch interests in the Pacific, while Knox wanted to emphasize the similarities between German and Japanese aggression. On December 1, Hull persuaded Roosevelt that a congressional message would create domestic divisions and inflame the Japanese, as would an appeal to the Emperor over the government's head. Welles was left to have an inconclusive talk with Nomura and Kurusu the next day about Japan's build-up in Indochina beyond the limits of the treaty with Vichy.

The British began to press for assurances in the event that Japan attacked only their holdings. Roosevelt remained evasive, but on December 1 he told Halifax that if Japan attacked "we should obviously all be together." Two days later, he pledged "armed support," even if the Japanese attacked only Thailand, and he approved Britain's plan for preclusive action if they threatened the Kra Isthmus. The only reservation was that the support might not be forthcoming for a few days, suggesting that Roosevelt intended to ask for a declaration of war from Congress if Japan attacked British or Dutch property or Thailand.

The State Department continued to debate the proposed congressional message when, on December 4–5, MAGIC intercepts revealed that embassy officials in Washington were under orders to leave in a few days, and that all codes had been destroyed. A break in relations was imminent, as was a clash somewhere in the Pacific, especially with reports of the movement of a major Japanese fleet and transports around southern Indochina. On December 6, General MacArthur in the Philippines and Admiral Hart of the Asiatic Fleet reported that they were prepared.

Roosevelt turned to an appeal to the Emperor. The State Department draft proposed a ninety-day truce and Sino-Japanese talks, perhaps in the Philippines. For reasons unknown, Roosevelt chose to warn that the build-up of Japanese forces in Indochina and Southeast Asia was a "keg of dynamite." He proposed Japan's military withdrawal from Indochina in return for assurances against attack there by the Americans, British, Chinese, and Dutch. The message was dispatched at 9:00 P.M. for Grew to deliver to the Emperor. Roosevelt deliberately chose a code the Japanese could intercept, and he informed the press of the message but not its content. Most likely, the President was acting at this late hour as much "for the record" as out of expectation of results, and regardless, the Emperor could not intervene in national affairs without his government's request, an unlikely event.

Thirty minutes after dispatch of the message, a naval aide brought Roosevelt the first thirteen parts of an ultimately fourteen-part Japanese message that MAGIC had been intercepting throughout the day, the content of which had become known in the State Department by 7:30 P.M. This Japanese message, sent to Nomura and Kurusu for them to deliver to Hull at 1:00 P.M. on December 7, was a long refutation of Hull's Ten-Point Note. After reading the text, Roosevelt said "this means war." Where war would come was not known (Roosevelt's own cable to the Emperor reflected the universal preoccupation with Indochina and Southeast Asia), but the place was irrelevant in the sense that Roosevelt intended that the United States fight even if only the British and Dutch were attacked. Hopkins, the only other person present, said that with war imminent it was a pity the United States could not strike first, but Roosevelt replied, "No. We can't do that. We are a democracy and a peaceful people." And with his voice rising, he added, "But we have a good record." The President tried to reach Admiral Stark, but learning that he was at the theater, preferred not to interrupt and spread alarm. They spoke later that night, but there is no record of their words.

By 10:00 A.M. on December 7, Roosevelt and his aides had learned the fourteenth point of the Japanese message: Diplomatic relations were being broken. This was not unexpected, and Hull, Stimson, and Knox continued to deliberate Roosevelt's proposed address to Congress until noon, with Stimson recording that Hull believed the Japanese were "planning some deviltry, and we are all wondering where the blow will strike." Meanwhile, Colonel Rufus Bratton, head of the Far Eastern desk in military intelligence, tried to reach General Marshall, who was out horseback riding as usual on this Sunday morning and did not return to his office until 11 A.M. As soon as the Chief of Staff read the fourteen-part message, he decided to warn all Pacific commands of the imminent break in relations (Admiral Stark, consulted by telephone, thought enough warnings had been sent). No one thought to use the "scrambler" telephone—which Marshall later insisted he would not have used (or used to call only the Philippines) because its poor security might have revealed that the Americans had broken Japan's diplomatic code. Marshall sent the message by what he presumed was navy wireless, the quickest means other than the scrambler. But navy wireless was busy, and the message inadvertently went by Western Union, with Pearl Harbor listed third in priority after Manila and Panama, and arrived hours after the disaster.

Shortly after noon, the Japanese Embassy, because of a confusion—there had been a big party the night before, and a ranking official typed the note, using the two-finger system and making all kinds of mistakes—asked that its emissaries' 1:00 P.M. appointment be delayed forty-five minutes. Hull agreed and then delayed receiving Nomura and Kurusu for another half-hour. For at 1:50 P.M., word had come to the Navy Department: "AIR RAID PEARL HARBOR. THIS IS NO DRILL." Secretary Knox exclaimed, "My God, this can't be true; they must mean the Philippines!" but Stark confirmed the report. Knox immediately called Roosevelt, who telephoned to Hull and Stimson that Japan had struck. Stimson asked whether that meant Southeast Asia, and the President replied, "Southeast Asia, hell. Pearl Harbor." Hull listened silently to Nomura and Kurusu, who were unaware of the attack in the Pacific, and then acidly denounced Japan's diplomacy and dismissed the ambassadors.

For several decades afterward, many people wondered or speculated how or why the Japanese were able to spring their undetected attack on the American fleet at Pearl Harbor. Exhaustive research has shown as conclusively as possible that there was no conspiracy within the Roosevelt administration to enter the European war through the Pacific "backdoor" by inviting or provoking a Japanese assault while withholding critical information from the military at their outposts. There were, however, diplomatic and military miscalculations. The Americans and the British assumed the Japanese probably would not want to fight them both at once, which is why the British sought an American guarantee in case the Japanese attacked only British territory, and why Roosevelt intended to ask Congress for a war declaration if this happened. The Americans believed that the fleet at Pearl Harbor was a deterrent, and the Japanese Naval General Staff agreed. Their commander in chief, Admiral Yamamoto, who planned the attack, insisted that all other military operations depended on eliminating the American Fleet, and he prevailed over his colleagues almost by force of personality. Then, American naval authorities could not believe that the Japanese would flaunt tradition and commit, as this venture required, all six of their major aircraft carriers to one attack. Nor did the Americans foresee the Japanese capacity (which they achieved only by November) to use torpedoes in the shallow Pearl Harbor anchorage.

The American B-17 bombers at Clark Air Field in the Philippines were caught on the ground by Japanese planes nine hours after word had reached General MacArthur and his aides of the Pearl Harbor attack. This happened partly because the Americans believed that their planes were beyond the round-trip flying (fuel) range of the Japanese planes based in Formosa 550 miles away, and partly because no one had anticipated that the Japanese would increase their range by readjusting their planes' fuel mixture and engine RPM's. And then, of course, the British at Singapore braced for an assault by sea, while the Japanese opted for the seemingly impossible task of hacking their way through the Malay jungle to capture Singapore from its unprotected rear. In all these developments, Western miscalculation, and perhaps conceit, or arrogance, with regard to their opponents' capacities, combined with brilliant and daring Japanese tactics to open the way to Japanese success.

Admittedly, there were many "signals" in the autumn of 1941 that indicated the possibility of an attack on Pearl Harbor. Grew had advised Washington of such a rumor as early as January 1941. No signals ever designated an attack on Pearl Harbor at some specific date or time and throughout the year countless signals (always clearer in retrospect) were competing with one another—that is, indicating the possibility of attack in any number of regions, from Russia to southern Indochina. The administration had warned all outposts to be prepared, and military officials at Pearl Harbor had gone on alert three times: in June 1940, when France fell; in July 1941, after the oil embargo; and in October 1941, when Tojo replaced Konoye. But it was feared that to do this continuously was too embarrassing and costly and might precipitate an incident. Moreover, the military at Pearl Harbor were concerned primarily about sabotage because they considered an air attack unlikely, and because the most likely hostile development was an attack in Southeast Asia.

And there, perhaps, is the ultimate irony. Both the administration in

Washington and the military in Hawaii were right in presuming where Japan was most likely to strike. The brunt of the Japanese assault on December 7, 1941, fell on British Malaya, Thailand, Singapore, and Hong Kong, as well as Midway, Wake and the Philippines. But to this list the Japanese had added Pearl Harbor. In short, the Japanese, by adding to their objectives the American Pacific Fleet, went far beyond what tradition deemed logical or feasible, and they succeeded—brilliantly.

Throughout December 7, administration officials discussed the President's intended address to Congress. Most preferred to include a review of American-Japanese negotiations and a denunciation of Germany for urging Japan into war. Only Stimson wanted to declare war against Germany as well as Japan. Roosevelt finally decided on his own brief message. Then, perhaps with an eye to history and drama, he requested that Mrs. Woodrow Wilson accompany his wife, when, shortly after noon the next day, he informed a Joint Session of Congress that on December 7, "a date which will live in infamy," the Japanese had launched their "unprovoked and dastardly attack." Within hours, the House voted to declare war on Japan by 388–1, and the Senate did so unanimously. The British and commonwealth governments, having held back at Roosevelt's request, now declared war on Japan, too.

There remained the war in Europe, the primary issue. The administration waited in expectation that its dilemma would be resolved for it. Indeed, the Japanese were pressing for a German declaration of war "at once" upon the United States, and on December 8 Ribbentrop replied that German ships would attack American ships everywhere, which extended the already undeclared Atlantic war. The ultimate decision, however, was Hitler's.

The Germans had been kept as much in the dark about, and were as much surprised by, the Pearl Harbor attack as anyone (similarly, the Germans had not given their "allies" notice of their attack on the Soviet Union in June), and they were not formally obligated under the Tripartite Pact because Japan had struck first. Nor did Hitler have any military or operational plans to deal with the United States, and there is only conjecture, no hard evidence, that he ever intended to attack anywhere in the New World, although it is not unlikely that triumph in Europe might have led him to raise his sights. Moreover, at precisely this time German armies were bogging down in the winter snow outside Moscow.

Perhaps Hitler was led by the belief that Japan's action was a fateful one that a man of history, as he saw himself, could not ignore. The Japanese would dominate the Pacific, and the crippled Americans could not hope to intervene in Europe for two or three years, by which time the British or Russians would have surrendered and Germany's hammer-lock on the Continent would be unbreakable. Perhaps Hitler was moved by his contempt for American society and his denigration of its military and industrial capacity. Perhaps the issue was national pride, or, as Hitler now remarked to his interpreter, "A great power like Germany declares war itself and does not wait for war to be declared on it."

Whatever the reasons, the Führer addressed a cheering Reichstag on December 11, 1941. He accused Roosevelt of being "mad, just as Wilson was," and he assailed him for inciting war and violating international law by attacking German ships. He contrasted his humble origins and suffering during and after the Frst World War with Roosevelt's aristocratic and privileged heritage. He attacked the President for surrounding himself with "the full diabolical meanness of Jewry" and blamed this influence and the New Deal for wasting the nation's resources and making war on Germany. But now, Hitler said, divine providence had entrusted him to take the lead in "this historic struggle which for the next five hundred to a thousand years will be described as decisive not only for the history of Germany but for the whole of Europe and indeed for the world." Mussolini and Italy immediately followed in Hitler's steps.

The same day, President Roosevelt informed Congress that "the long-known and the long-expected has thus taken place," and he asked for appropriate action. At 3:00 P.M. on the afternoon of December 11, 1941, the Congress of the United States passed a joint resolution of war against Germany and Italy. East and West had now joined in the Second World War.

Bibliographical Essay

The sources available for study of U.S. foreign policy and world politics between the world wars constantly increase in number as governments and individuals open their records to historians who investigate old and new problems from varied perspectives. This bibliography is neither definitive nor inclusive of all works read, and citation of studies in scholarly journals and foreign languages has been minimized. References are to the most generally significant materials and to those most influential in shaping this study.

GOVERNMENT RECORDS, 1917–41

The most important collections are the voluminous records of the U.S. Department of State in the National Archives, Washington, D.C., and the records of the British Cabinet and Foreign Office in the Public Record Office, London, England. Highly valuable are the State Department's multivolume publication for each calendar year, *Papers Relating to the Foreign Relations of the United States,* which also includes special supplements on *The Paris Peace Conference* (13 vols.), *Japan, 1931–1941* (2 vols.), and *The Soviet Union, 1933–1939,* and the ongoing series publications *Documents on British Foreign Policy, 1918–1939; Documents on German Foreign Policy, 1918–1945;* and *Documents Diplomatiques Français, 1932–1939.*

THE ERA OF THE FIRST WORLD WAR, 1917–20

For a sampling of early revisionist accounts of American entry into the First World War that criticize the Wilson administration's neutrality policies and pro-Allied sentiment and economic entanglements, see C. Hartley Grattan, *Why We Fought* (New York, 1929); Walter Millis, *Road to War: America, 1914–1917* (Boston, 1935); Edwin M. Borchard and William P. Lage, *Neutrality for the United States* (New Haven, Conn., 1937); and the scathing Charles C. Tansill, *America Goes to War* (Boston, 1938).

Superseding these works, and more comprehensive, is Arthur Link's multivolume biography of Woodrow Wilson, which includes *The Struggle for Neutrality, 1914–1915; Confusion and Crises, 1915–1916;* and *Campaigns for Progressivism and Peace, 1916–1917* (Princeton, N.J., 1960, 1964, 1965). Equally valuable are Ernest R. May, *The World War and American Isolation, 1914–1917* (Cambridge, Mass., 1959), a study that assesses most carefully the influence of German and American domestic politics on foreign policy; Daniel M. Smith, *Robert Lansing and American Neutrality, 1914–1917* (Berkeley, Calif., 1958); and Charles Seymour, *The Intimate Papers of Colonel House*, 4 vols. (Boston, 1926–28). Briefer analyses include Ross Gregory, *The Origins of American Intervention in the First World War* (New York, 1971); Arthur Link, *Woodrow Wilson and the Progressive Era, 1910–1917* (New York, 1954), and *Wilson the Diplomatist: A Look at His Major Foreign Policies* (Baltimore, 1957); and Daniel M. Smith, *The Great Departure: The United States and World War I, 1914–1920* (New York, 1965). The consensus of these works is that Wilson and his aides were moved to war primarily because they saw Germany's unrestricted submarine warfare and seeming intransigence over a negotiated settlement as an unacceptable challenge to America's inextricably intertwined national interest, national honor, and Great Power status. Also valuable for this era and later ones is Norman A. Graebner, *An Uncertain Tradition: American Secretaries of State in the Twentieth Century* (New York, 1961). Two signal works on German diplomacy and war aims are Hans W. Gatzke, *Germany's Drive to the West: A Study of Germany's Western War Aims During the First World War* (Baltimore, 1950); and Fritz Fischer, *Germany's Aims in the First World War* (New York, 1961).

N. Gordon Levin, *Woodrow Wilson and World Politics: America's Response to War and Revolution* (New York, 1968), is a turgid but stimulating book that argues that the Wilson administration's decision for war, and its subsequent policies concerning intervention in the Russian Civil War, the Paris Peace negotiations, and the fight over the League of Nations stemmed from its effort to achieve American pre-eminence within a liberal-capitalist world order safe from both traditional imperialism and revolutionary socialism. A similar but more comprehensive world-political analysis is provided in Arno J. Mayer, *Wilson vs. Lenin: Political Origins of the New Diplomacy, 1917–1918* (New Haven, Conn., 1959), and *Politics and Diplomacy of Peacemaking: Containment and Counterrevolution at Versailles, 1918–1919* (New York, 1967). George F. Kennan, *Russia and the West Under Lenin and Stalin* (Boston, 1960), emphasizes military security and the desire to rescue the Czech legion as the basis for American intervention in Russia; while Betty Miller Unterberger, *America's Siberian Expedition, 1918–1920* (Durham, N.C., 1956), underscores the desire to restrain Japan.

Inter-allied cooperation and conflict are examined in David F. Trask, *The United States in the Supreme War Council: American War Aims and Inter-Allied Strategy, 1917–1918* (Middletown, Conn., 1961), and Seth P. Tillman, *Anglo-American Relations at the Paris Peace Conference of 1919* (Princeton, N.J., 1961). Thomas A. Bailey, *Woodrow Wilson and the Lost Peace* (New York, 1944), criticizes Wilson as a rigid idealist, though moderating force, in the making of the Treaty of Versailles. John Maynard Keynes, *Economic Consequences of the Peace* (New York, 1920), excoriates everyone for allegedly attempting to set the European economic and political clock back a hundred years; Étienne Mantoux, *The Carthaginian Peace: Or the Economic Consequences of Mr. Keynes* (New York, 1944), is a virtual line-by-line rebuttal. Other helpful studies are Paul P. Abrahams, "American Bankers and the Economic Tactics of Peace: 1919," *Journal of American History* (hereafter *JAH*), LVI (December 1963); George Curry, "Woodrow Wilson, Jan Smuts, and the Versailles Settlement," *American Historical Review* (hereafter *AHR*), LXVI (July 1960); and Benjamin D. Rhodes, "Reassessing 'Uncle Shylock': The United States and the French War Debt, 1917–1929," *JAH*, LV (March 1969). Problems in the Pacific are discussed in two surveys: A. Whitney Griswold, *The Far Eastern Policy of the United States* (New York, 1938); and William L. Neumann, *America Encounters Japan: From Perry to MacArthur* (Baltimore, 1963). More detailed on the era are Roy Watson Curry, *Woodrow Wilson and Far Eastern Policy, 1913–1921* (New York, 1957); and Russell H. Fifield, *Woodrow Wilson and the Far East: The Diplomacy of the Shantung Question* (New York, 1952).

Controversy over ratification of the Treaty of Versailles is analyzed in Thomas A. Bailey, *Woodrow Wilson and the Great Betrayal* (New York, 1945); Ralph A. Stone, *The Irreconcilables: The Fight Against the League of Nations* (Lexington, Ky., 1970); and Wesley M. Bagby, "Woodrow Wilson, A Third Term, and the Solemn Referendum," *AHR*, LX (April 1955), and *The Road to Normalcy: The Presidential Campaign and the Election of 1920* (Baltimore, 1962). Daniel M. Smith, *Aftermath of War: Bainbridge Colby and Wilsonian Diplomacy, 1920–1921* (Philadelphia, 1970), stresses the policies of this era as the precursor of Republican diplomacy in the 1920's.

AMERICA AND EUROPE, 1921–33

For background and mood of the era, see Selig Adler, *The Isolationist Impulse: Its Twentieth Century Reaction* (New York, 1951), and "The War-Guilt Question and American Disillusionment, 1918–1928," *Journal of Modern History*, XXIII (March 1951); and Dexter Perkins, "The Department of State and American Public Opinion," in Gordon A. Craig and Felix Gilbert, eds., *The Diplomats: 1919–1939* (Princeton, N.J., 1953), which also contains excellent essays on numerous European and Asian diplomats of the interwar period. Reparations, war debts, and financing German rehabilitation are dealt with in Harold G. Moulton, *The Reparation Plan* (New York, 1924); Harold G. Moulton and Leo Pasvolsky, *World War Debt Settlements* (New York, 1926); Herbert Feis, *The Diplomacy of the Dollar: First Phase, 1919–1932* (Baltimore, 1950); and William A. Williams, "The Legend of Isolationism in the 1920's," *Science and Society*, XVIII (Winter 1954). Carl P. Parrini, *Heir to Empire: United States Economic Diplomacy, 1916–1923* (Pittsburgh, 1969), emphasizes the continuity of Open Door diplomacy; while Merlo J. Pusey, *Charles Evans Hughes*, 2 vols. (New York, 1951), is a useful but uncritical account of diplomacy in the Harding era.

The American desire to avoid foreign political entanglements—and to act unilaterally—is explained in David D. Burks, "The United States and the Geneva Protocol of 1924: 'A New Holy Alliance'?" *AHR,* LXIV (July 1959). Robert H. Ferrell, *Peace in Their Time: The Origins of the Kellogg-Briand Pact* (New Haven, Conn., 1952), shows how the Americans converted a French effort at a bilateral pact into a meaningless world one; while Robert James Maddox, "William E. Borah and the Crusade to Outlaw War," *The Historian,* XXIX (February 1967), shows how the senator used the issue for obstructive, political purposes. Helpful, too, are Donald R. McCoy, *Calvin Coolidge: The Quiet President* (New York, 1967); L. Ethan Ellis, *Frank B. Kellogg and American Foreign Relations, 1925–1929* (New Brunswick, N.J., 1961); and Robert H. Ferrell, *American Diplomacy in the Great Depression: Hoover-Stimson Foreign Policy, 1929–1933* (New York, 1962), vol. XI in *The American Secretaries of State and Their Diplomacy* series (Ferrell and Samuel Flagg Bemis, eds.). Works of special interest that focus on the American aspect of European diplomacy include Robert Gottwald, *Die deutsch-amerikanischen Beziehungen in der Ära Stresemann* (Berlin-Dahlem, 1965), which explains Germany's effort to use the balance of American power in its behalf; and Edward W. Bennett, *Germany and the Diplomacy of the Financial Crisis, 1931* (Cambridge, Mass., 1962), and Wolfgang J. Helbich, *Die Reparationen in der Ära Brüning: Zur Bedeutung des Young-Plans für die deutsche Politik, 1930 bis 1932* (Berlin-Dahlem, 1962), which are sympathetic to Germany's plight but critical of its aggressive diplomacy.

AMERICA AND THE FAR EAST, 1921–33

The best single analysis of the whole era from the Washington Conference to the Manchurian crisis is Akira Iriye, *After Imperialism: The Search for Order in the Far East, 1921–1931* (Cambridge, Mass., 1965). The conflict between foreign policy and naval concerns is analyzed in Gerald E. Wheeler, *Prelude to Pearl Harbor: The United States Navy and the Far East, 1921–1931* (Columbia, Mo., 1963), and "Isolated Japan: Anglo-American Cooperation, 1927–1936," *Pacific Historical Review,* XXX (May 1961); and Raymond G. O'Connor, *Perilous Equilibrium: The United States and the London Naval Conference of 1930* (Lawrence, Kans., 1962). The conceptions that American statesmen had about the American role in China and the Far East, as well as an account of their diplomatic activities, can be ascertained from the survey by Warren I. Cohen, *America's Response to China: An Interpretive History of Sino-American Relations* (New York, 1971); the careful study by Dorothy Borg, *American Policy and the Chinese Revolution, 1925–1928* (New York, 1947); Russell D. Buhite, *Nelson T. Johnson and American Policy Toward China, 1925–1941* (East Lansing, Mich., 1968); and Barbara Tuchman, *Stilwell and the American Experience in China, 1911–45* (New York, 1971), all of which suggest that many of the problems that plagued Sino-American relations in the later 1930's and 1940's were incipient in this period.

For an evaluation of American-Japanese conflicts, see the survey by

William L. Neumann, *America Encounters Japan: From Perry to Mac-Arthur* (Baltimore, 1963); the fair but critical studies by Richard Current, *Secretary Stimson: A Study in Statecraft* (New Brunswick, N.J., 1954), and "The Stimson Doctrine and the Hoover Doctrine," *AHR,* LIX (April 1954); and Armin Rappaport, *Henry L. Stimson and Japan* (Chicago, 1963). Elting Morison, *Turmoil and Tradition: A Study of the Life and Times of Henry L. Stimson* (Boston, 1960), is equally incisive and captures the sense of the man and his era beautifully.

M. G. Fry, "The North Atlantic Triangle and the Abrogation of the Anglo-Japanese Alliance," *Journal of Modern History,* XXXIX (March 1967), and *Illusion of Security: North Atlantic Diplomacy, 1918–1922* (Toronto, 1972), afford excellent insights into the debates between those British or Dominion leaders who favored an alliance with Japan and those who looked toward the United States. Most revealing about British values and attitudes toward Asian nations and problems, and the dilemma resulting from a lack of power to implement imperial ambitions and responsibilities, are William Roger Louis, *British Strategy in the Far East, 1919–1939* (New York, 1971), and Christopher Thorne, "The Shanghai Crisis of 1932: The Basis of British Policy," *AHR,* LXXV (October 1970), and *The Limits of Foreign Policy: The West, the League and the Far Eastern Crisis of 1931–1933* (New York, 1973).

Japanese diplomacy and politics are shrewdly assessed in Sadao Asada, "Japan's 'Special Interests' and the Washington Conference, 1921–22," *AHR,* LXVII (October 1961), James B. Crowley, *Japan's Quest for Autonomy: National Security and Foreign Policy, 1930–1938* (Princeton, N.J., 1966), Sadaka Ogata, *Defiance in Manchuria: The Making of Japanese Foreign Policy, 1931–1932* (Berkeley, Calif., 1964), and Takehiko Yoshihashi, *Conspiracy at Mukden: The Rise of the Japanese Military* (New Haven, Conn., 1963).

AMERICA AND EUROPE, 1933–41

Full-length studies of key policy-making officials of the Roosevelt administration include James MacGregor Burns, *Roosevelt: The Lion and the Fox* (New York, 1956), and *The Soldier of Freedom* (New York, 1970); Robert E. Sherwood, *Roosevelt and Hopkins: An Intimate History* (New York, 1948); John Morton Blum, *From the Morgenthau Diaries: Years of Crisis, 1928–1938* (Boston, 1959), and *Years of Urgency, 1938–1941* (Boston, 1965); and Julius W. Pratt, *Cordell Hull,* 2 vols. (New York, 1964), vols. XII and XIII in *The American Secretaries of State and Their Diplomacy* series. Although these statesmen—notably Hull and Morgenthau—often disagreed sharply about policy, they are presented in these fair but critical volumes as executive officers seeking to meet the demands of national security while trying to arouse a reluctant public to the danger on the international horizon. Helpful, too, is the brief but incisive work by Robert A. Divine, *Roosevelt and World War II* (Baltimore, 1969), as well as Willard Range's study *Franklin D. Roosevelt's World Order* (Athens, Ga., 1959) and the thorough two-volume biography of the man who was chief of staff during

1939–41 by Forest C. Pogue, *George C. Marshall: Education of a General, 1880–1939* (New York, 1963), and *Ordeal and Hope, 1939–1942* (New York, 1966).

Studies of influential congressmen and diplomats include Wayne S. Cole, *Senator Gerald P. Nye and American Foreign Relations* (Minneapolis, 1962); Beatrice Farnsworth, *William C. Bullitt and the Soviet Union* (Bloomington, Ind., 1967); Fred L. Israel, *Nevada's Key Pittman* (Lincoln, Neb., 1963); Marian McKenna, *Borah* (Ann Arbor, Mich., 1961); and Arnold A. Offner, "William E. Dodd: Romantic Historian and Diplomatic Cassandra," *The Historian*, XXIV (August 1962). Highly useful compilations of letters, diaries, and memoirs (the last must be measured carefully against diplomatic records) include Edgar B. Nixon, ed., *Franklin D. Roosevelt and Foreign Affairs (1933–1937)*, 3 vols. (Cambridge, Mass., 1969); Elliott Roosevelt, ed., *FDR.: His Personal Letters, 1928–1945*, 2 vols. (New York, 1950), and *As He Saw It* (New York, 1946); Orville H. Bullitt, ed., *For the President Personal and Secret: Correspondence Between Franklin D. Roosevelt and William C. Bullitt* (Boston, 1972); *The Memoirs of Cordell Hull*, 2 vols. (New York, 1948); Sumner Welles, *The Time for Decision* (New York, 1944) and *Seven Decisions That Shaped History* (New York, 1950); and Herbert Feis, *1933: Characters in Crisis* (Boston, 1966). Nancy Harvison Hooker, ed., *The Moffat Papers: Selections from the Diplomatic Journals of Jay Pierrepont Moffat, 1919–1943* (Cambridge, Mass., 1956); Fred L. Israel, ed., *The War Diary of Breckinridge Long: Selections from the Years 1939–1944* (Lincoln, Neb., 1966); *The Secret Diary of Harold L. Ickes*, 3 vols. (New York, 1953–55); Claude Bowers, *My Mission to Spain: Watching the Rehearsal for World War II* (New York, 1954); William E. Dodd, Jr., and Martha Dodd, eds., *Ambassador Dodd's Diary, 1933–1938* (New York, 1941); and Hugh R. Wilson, *Diplomat Between Wars* (New York, 1941), *A Career Diplomat, The Third Chapter: The Third Reich* (New York, 1960), and *Disarmament and the Cold War in the Thirties* (New York, 1963).

For a sampling of over-all evaluations of the foreign policy of the Roosevelt administration, some early "revisionist" accounts would include Charles A. Beard, *American Foreign Policy in the Making, 1932–1940* (New Haven, Conn., 1946), and *President Roosevelt and the Coming of the War, 1941* (New Haven, Conn., 1948); Harry Elmer Barnes, ed., *Perpetual War for Perpetual Peace: A Critical Examination of the Foreign Policy of Franklin Delano Roosevelt and Its Aftermath* (Caldwell, Idaho, 1953); and Charles Callan Tansill, *Backdoor to War: The Roosevelt Foreign Policy, 1933–1941* (Chicago, 1952). More favorably disposed, but nevertheless critically minded, traditional works include Robert A. Divine, *The Reluctant Belligerent: American Entry into World War II* (New York, 1965); Donald F. Drummond, *The Passing of American Neutrality, 1937–1941* (Ann Arbor, Mich., 1955); and the monumental *The Challenge to Isolation, 1937–1940* (New York, 1952), and *The Undeclared War, 1940–1941* (New York, 1953), by William L. Langer and S. Everett Gleason. Lloyd C. Gardner, *Economic Aspects of New Deal Diplomacy* (Madison, Wis.,

1964), emphasizes the influence of Open Door economics on diplomacy.

A thorough analysis of American relations with Germany and the question of European security is Arnold A. Offner, *American Appeasement: United States Foreign Policy and Germany, 1933–1938* (Cambridge, Mass., 1969). Robert A. Divine, *The Illusion of Neutrality* (Chicago, 1962); John E. Wiltz, *In Search of Peace: The Senate Munitions Inquiry, 1934–36* (Baton Rouge, La., 1963); and Manfred Jonas, *Isolationism in America, 1935–1941* (Ithaca, N.Y., 1966), treat their subjects comprehensively. For analyses of specific events or crises, see Brice Harris, Jr., *The United States and the Italo-Ethiopian Crisis* (Stanford, Calif., 1964); Henderson Braddick, "A New Look at American Policy During the Italo-Ethiopian Crisis, 1935–1936," *Journal of Modern History,* XXIV (March 1962); Robert A. Friedlander, "New Light on the Anglo-American Reaction to the Ethiopian War, 1935–1936," *Mid-America,* XLV (April 1963); F. Jay Taylor, *The United States and the Spanish Civil War* (New York, 1956); Allen Guttmann, *The Wound in the Heart: America and the Spanish Civil War* (New York, 1962), which examines the intellectual ramifications; and Richard P. Traina, *American Diplomacy and the Spanish Civil War* (Bloomington, Ind., 1968), which deflates Ambassador Bowers and is sympathetic to the administration's diplomatic dilemma. A variety of views on American involvement in the Munich Conference are taken in John McVickar Haight, Jr., "France, the United States, and the Munich Conference," *Journal of Modern History,* XXXII (December 1960); M. Baturin, "The United States and Munich," *International Affairs* (Moscow) V (April 1959); and William V. Wallace, "Roosevelt and British Appeasement in 1938," *Bulletin of the British Association for American Studies,* no. 5 (December 1962).

Important studies that deal with America's increasing involvement in the European war during 1939–41 include especially those listed above by Langer and Gleason; Philip Goodhart, *Fifty Ships That Saved the World: The Foundations of the Anglo-American Alliance* (Garden City, N.Y., 1965); Andrew I. Schwartz, *America and the Russo-Finnish War* (Washington, D.C., 1960); Robert Sobel, *The Origins of Interventionism: The United States and the Russo-Finnish War* (New York, 1960); Warren F. Kimball, *"The Most Unsordid Act": Lend-Lease, 1939–1941* (Baltimore, 1969); Raymond H. Dawson, *The Decision to Aid Russia, 1941: Foreign Policy and Domestic Politics* (Chapel Hill, N.C., 1959); Mark Lincoln Chadwin, *The Hawks of World War II* (Chapel Hill N.C., 1968); and T. R. Fehrenbach, *FDR's Undeclared War, 1939 to 1941* (New York, 1967). Two articles by Warren Kimball, " 'Beggar My Neighbor': America and the British Interim Finance Crisis, 1940–1941," *The Journal of Economic History,* XXIX (December, 1969), and "Lend-Lease and the Open Door: The Temptation of British Opulence, 1937–1942," *Political Science Quarterly,* LXXXVI (June 1972), show that American officials exacted a high price for the aid they afforded the British.

On the roots of the war in Europe, A. J. P. Taylor, *The Origins of the Second World War* (London, 1961), is the most provocative study, which, while overstating the extent to which Hitler was a traditional, if ruthless, German statesman given chiefly to improvising, has spurred a vigorous reassessment of international politics in the 1930's. Other helpful analyses include Keith Eubank, *The Origins of World War II* (New York, 1969); Arthur H. Furnia, *The Diplomacy of Appeasement: Anglo-French Relations and the Prelude to World War II, 1931–1938* (Washington, D.C., 1960); Laurence Lafore, *The End of Glory: An Interpretation of the Origins of World War II* (Philadelphia, 1970); William J. Newman, *The Balance of Power in the Interwar Years, 1919–1939* (New York, 1969); Raymond Sontag, *A Broken World, 1919–1939* (New York, 1971); and John W. Wheeler-Bennett, *Munich: Prologue to Tragedy* (London, 1948).

Indispensable analyses of Hitler and German foreign policy include Alan Bullock, *Hitler: A Study in Tyranny*, rev. ed. (New York, 1962); Gerhard Meinck, *Hitler und die deutsche Aufrüstung, 1933–1937* (Wiesbaden, 1959); E. M. Robertson, *Hitler's Pre-War Policy and Military Plans* (London, 1963); William L. Shirer, *The Rise and Fall of the Third Reich: A History of Nazi Germany* (New York, 1960); and Gerhard L. Weinberg, *The Foreign Policy of Hitler's Germany: Diplomatic Revolution in Europe, 1933–1937* (Chicago, 1970), a meticulous study. German relations with its totalitarian allies are analyzed in Frank William Iklé, *German-Japanese Relations, 1936–1940* (New York, 1956); Ernest L. Presseisen, *Germany and Japan: A Study in Totalitarian Diplomacy, 1933–1941* (The Hague, 1958); Theo Sommer, *Deutschland und Japan zwischen den Mächten, 1935–1940: Von Antikominternpakt zum Dreimächtepakt* (Tübingen, 1962); D. C. Watt, "The Rome-Berlin Axis, 1936–1940: Myth and Reality," *Review of Politics*, XXII (October, 1960); and Elizabeth Wiskeman, *The Rome-Berlin Axis: A Study of the Relations Between Hitler and Mussolini*, rev. ed. (London, 1966).

On America as a factor in Hitler's mind and German diplomacy, see the penetrating work by James V. Compton, *The Swastika and the Eagle: Hitler, the United States, and the Origins of World War II* (Boston, 1967); Saul Friedlander, *Prelude to Downfall: Hitler and the United States, 1939–1941* (New York, 1967); Alton B. Frye, *Nazi Germany and the Western Hemisphere, 1933–1941* (New Haven, Conn., 1967); H. L. Trefousse, *Germany and American Neutrality, 1939–1941* (New York, 1951); and Gerhard L. Weinberg, "Hitler's Image of the United States," *AHR*, LXIX (July 1964). The German Führer's most extended comments on the United States are recorded in Gerhard L. Weinberg, ed., *Hitler's zweites Buch: Ein Dokument aus dem Jahr 1928* (Stuttgart, 1961), translated as *Hitler's Secret Book* (New York, 1961); H. R. Trevor-Roper, ed., *Hitler's Secret Conversations, 1941–1944* (New York, 1944); and François Genoud, ed., *The Testament of Adolf Hitler: The Hitler-Bormann Documents, February–April 1945* (London, 1961).

Sharp critiques of British appeasement are Ian Colvin, *None So Blind: A British Diplomatic View of the Origins of World War II* (New York, 1965), and *The Chamberlain Cabinet* (New York, 1970); Margaret George, *The Warped Vision: British Foreign Policy, 1933–1938* (Pittsburgh, 1968); and

Martin Gilbert and Richard Gott, *The Appeasers* (Boston, 1968); while F. S. Northedge, *The Troubled Giant: Britain Among the Powers, 1916–1939* (New York, 1966), emphasizes the constraints on an overextended nation. Two favorably disposed but fair biographies that contain references from valuable (and still unavailable) source materials are Keith Feiling, *The Life of Neville Chamberlain* (New York, 1964), and Iain Macleod, *Neville Chamberlain* (New York, 1961). Equally valuable, and helpful especially on Anglo-American relations, are *The Memoirs of Anthony Eden, Earl of Avon: Facing the Dictators* (Boston, 1961); David Dilks, ed., *The Diaries of Sir Alexander Cadogan, 1938–1945* (New York, 1972); John Harvey, ed., *The Diplomatic Diaries of Oliver Harvey, 1937–1940* (London, 1970); and D. C. Watt, *Personalities and Policies: Studies in the Formulation of British Foreign Policy in the Twentieth Century* (Notre Dame, Ind., 1965).

AMERICA AND THE FAR EAST, 1933–41

Most thorough and judicious is Dorothy Borg, *The United States and the Far Eastern Crisis of 1933–1938: From the Manchurian Incident Through the Initial Stage of the Undeclared Sino-Japanese War* (Cambridge, Mass., 1964), which should be supplemented with the works cited on the 1920's by Buhite on Nelson Johnson and Tuchman on Joseph Stillwell. For close analysis of American relations with Japan, see Waldo H. Heinrichs, Jr., *American Ambassador: Joseph C. Grew and the Development of the United States Diplomatic Tradition* (Boston, 1966), and the diary-memoirs by Joseph C. Grew, *Ten Years in Japan* (New York, 1944) and *Turbulent Era: A Diplomatic Record of Forty Years, 1904–1945*, 2 vols. (Boston, 1952).

Three views of Roosevelt's muddled effort in 1937 are afforded in Dorothy Borg, "Notes on Roosevelt's 'Quarantine' Speech," *Political Science Quarterly*, LXXII (September 1957); John McVickar Haight, Jr., "Roosevelt and the Aftermath of the Quarantine Speech," *Review of Politics*, XXIV (April 1962); and Travis Beal Jacobs, "Roosevelt's Quarantine Speech," *The Historian*, XXIV (August 1962). Frederick C. Adams, "The Road to Pearl Harbor: A Reexamination of American Far Eastern Policy, July 1937–December 1938," *JAH*, LVIII (June 1971), assesses the implications of financial aid to China. Manny T. Koginos, *The Panay Incident: Prelude to War* (Lafayette, Ind., 1967), is thorough but overstates the case.

The fullest assessments of the intricate negotiations between the United States and Japan during 1940–41 are Herbert Feis, *The Road to Pearl Harbor: The Coming of the War Between the United States and Japan* (Princeton, N.J., 1950), which is critical but disposed to the American viewpoint; and Paul Schroeder, *The Axis Alliance and Japanese-American Relations, 1941* (Ithaca, N.Y., 1958), which argues that American diplomacy shifted from defensive to offensive tactics in the summer of 1941. Indispensable in helping to explain how the negotiations became so diplomatically and linguistically ensnarled are Robert J. C. Butow, "The Hull-Nomura Conversations: A Fundamental Misconception," *AHR*, LXV (July 1960), and "Back Door Diplomacy: The Proposal for a Konoye-Roosevelt

Meeting, 1941," *JAH,* LIX (June 1972). Richard N. Current, "How Stimson Meant to 'Maneuver' the Japanese," *Mississippi Valley Historical Review,* XL (June 1953), explains what the much-cited diary entry did and did not mean; while Raymond Esthus, "President Roosevelt's Commitment to Britain to Intervene in a Pacific War." *MVHR,* L (June 1963), shows the administration's intent to ask for a declaration of war from Congress if the Japanese attacked only British and Dutch territory. A brilliant explication of the military fiasco in the Pacific is Roberta Wohlstetter, *Pearl Harbor: Warning and Decision* (Stanford, Calif., 1962). For those still interested in the conspiratorial arguments, see the works cited earlier by Barnes, Beard, and Tansill, as well as George Morgenstern, *Pearl Harbor: The Story of the Secret War* (New York, 1947). For a full bibliographical and retrospective analysis of American diplomacy in the Pacific, consult Ernest R. May and James C. Thomson, eds., *American–East Asian Relations: A Survey* (Cambridge, Mass., 1972).

On Japanese diplomacy in the later 1930's, see Robert J. C. Butow, *Tojo and the Coming of the War* (Stanford, Calif., 1961), which is highly critical of Japanese expansion; F. C. Jones, *Japan's New Order in East Asia, 1937–1945* (London, 1954); and David J. Lu, *From the Marco Polo Bridge to Pearl Harbor: Japan's Entry into World War II* (Washington, D.C., 1961). Louis Morton, "Japan's Decision for War," in Kent Roberts Greenfield, ed., *Command Decisions* (New York, 1959), explains what the Japanese hoped to accomplish by their assault on American territory; while John Dean Potter, *Yamamoto: The Man Who Menaced America* (New York, 1965), is a popular biography of the man who planned the Pearl Harbor attack. David Bergamini, *Japan's Imperial Conspiracy* (New York, 1971), is a controversial work that seeks to implicate Emperor Hirohito more deeply in diplomatic-military decisions than previously believed.

Books dealing with Germany's relations with Japan and involvement in the Pacific tangle have been cited in the section on German foreign policy. The best evaluations of British Far Eastern policy amidst the dilemma of a two-front war and the ambivalence of Anglo-American relations are the study cited earlier by Louis, as well as Nicholas Clifford, *Retreat From China: British Policy in the Far East, 1937–1945* (Seattle, 1967), and Bradford A. Lee, *Britain and the Sino-Japanese War, 1937–1939: A Study in the Dilemmas of British Decline* (Stanford, Calif., 1973).

Index

Index